AF599584

# COME and BE SHOCKED

# COME and BE SHOCKED

## BALTIMORE Beyond JOHN WATERS AND *THE WIRE*

MARY RIZZO

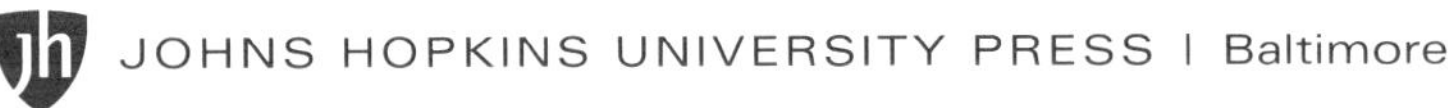
JOHNS HOPKINS UNIVERSITY PRESS | Baltimore

Printed in the United States of America on acid-free paper
9 8 7 6 5 4 3 2 1

Johns Hopkins University Press
2715 North Charles Street
Baltimore, Maryland 21218-4363
www.press.jhu.edu

Library of Congress Cataloging-in-Publication Data

Names: Rizzo, Mary, 1975– author.
Title: Come and be shocked : Baltimore beyond John Waters and The Wire / Mary Rizzo.
Description: Baltimore : Johns Hopkins University Press, 2020. | Includes bibliographical references and index.
Identifiers: LCCN 2019033883 | ISBN 9781421437910 (hardcover) | ISBN 9781421437927 (ebook)
Subjects: LCSH: Baltimore (Md.)—In popular culture. | Baltimore (Md.)—In literature. | Baltimore (Md.)—In motion pictures. | Baltimore (Md.)—Historiography
Classification: LCC F189.B14 R59 2020 | DDC 975.2/6—dc23
LC record available at https://lccn.loc.gov/2019033883

A catalog record for this book is available from the British Library.

Material from the introduction and chapter 4 also appears in Rizzo, Mary, "Image and Infrastructure: Making Baltimore a Tourist City" in *Baltimore Revisited: Stories of Inequality and Resistance in a U.S. City*, edited by P. Nicole King, Kate Drabinski, and Joshua Clark Davis; New Brunswick: Rutgers University Press, 2019; and are reprinted by permission of Rutgers.

*Special discounts are available for bulk purchases of this book. For more information, please contact Special Sales at specialsales@press.jhu.edu.*

Johns Hopkins University Press uses environmentally friendly book materials, including recycled text paper that is composed of at least 30 percent post-consumer waste, whenever possible.

**An eerie sight,**

**this black and white**

**Baltimore.**

—Laura Lippman, *Baltimore Blues*

# CONTENTS

# ILLUSTRATIONS

# ACKNOWLEDGMENTS

This book began under the hot lights of a TV camera. I'd never been interviewed for a spot on a reality TV show before. I wriggled on the stool, trying to hide my anxiety, even if the filming was taking place in a garage in Dundalk, Maryland. Charlene Osborne, 2009 winner of the Best Hon competition at Baltimore's annual HonFest, had invited me to participate in the making of a pilot episode of a show about the adventures of a group of "Hons," or women who embody this Baltimore icon of white working-class femininity best defined by her beehive hairdo and sassy attitude. The pitch was a play on a popular reality show: The Real Hons of Baltimore. She thought I could offer a historical perspective. The producer had something else in mind. "Can I call you Charlene's psychiatrist?" he asked. Better to call me a historian, I told him. Since the show never got picked up, I figure psychiatrists play better on TV.

Sitting there, the threads of this project began to coalesce. That a producer thought that Hons and Baltimore might be a viable subject for reality TV suggested that Baltimore already had some meaning for the public and that culture had helped shape that meaning. As my research over the next few years revealed, well-known as well as forgotten writers, filmmakers, poets, musicians, and producers worked alongside, in partnership with, and against marketing companies, tourism officials, and a municipal infrastructure to tell the story of Baltimore. While the Hon's cat-eye glasses and towering hairdo were one representation of the city, it competed with others. Divine's mohawk. Omar's shotgun.

This book examines the battles over Baltimore's image from the 1950s into the early twenty-first century. Through its representation in culture, Baltimore became a paradigmatic postindustrial city, allowing us to ask questions about the fate of cities everywhere.

From that day on, this project took shape with the help of many kind, generous, and thoughtful people. They have each made this book better in innumerable ways. All the mistakes that remain are mine alone.

Merging cultural studies with urban history required numerous trips to archives. Aiden Faust, head of Special Collections and Archives at the University of Baltimore, proved indispensable in navigating the Baltimore Regional Studies Archives, even making unprocessed materials available. They're lucky to have him. I perused the papers of several mayors at the Baltimore City Archives, with the help of their talented staff. Thanks, also, to the Maryland Historical Society for naming me a Lord Baltimore Fellow and providing me with special research access to their collections. Many thanks to the archivists and librarians at the University of Maryland, College Park; Maryland State Archives; Tamiment Archives at New York University; Schomburg Center for Research in Black Culture; and the Urban Archives at Temple University. Finally, my deep gratitude to the New York Public Library, where, as a researcher, I was allowed access to the beautiful Shoichi Noma room and its collections. Plus, I got to sneak out at lunch and watch the ice skaters in Bryant Park, which made writing and research much more relaxed.

*Chicory* magazine, the subject of chapter 3, requires its own set of thanks. Rediscovering this magazine of art and poetry was one of the highlights of this process. To understand its historical significance as a work of black cultural production, I relied on three of its editors, whom I interviewed. Sam Cornish, sadly, passed away before publication of this book, but I remember our interview fondly. Melvin Brown and Everett Adam Jackson both sat for interviews and provided me with historical material and their memories. Wesley Wilson, chief of the State Library Resource Center at the Enoch Pratt Free Library in Baltimore, has supported this project and is making *Chicory* more widely known and accessible. Thanks to the

Pratt and Rutgers University–Newark, the entire magazine collection has been digitized and is available through the Digital Maryland State Repository. While not directly related to writing this book, the Whiting Foundation gave me a seed grant to explore the possibilities of using *Chicory* for public programming, which allowed me to convene a group of community partners in Baltimore. Thank you to Whiting's director, Daniel Reid, for his astute suggestions on that project. And thank you to the community stakeholders, whose generosity, creativity, and passion inspire me, and to my graduate assistant, Sydney Johnson, for her work on this project.

Many people helped me understand Baltimore. For their insights into Baltimore's cultural history of the 1970s, I'd like to thank Philip Arnoult, Ben Carney, Ted Durr, Barry Meiners, Helen Szablya, and John Wilson. Baltimore is blessed with a power trio of public historians, from whom I have had the great honor of learning. Linda Shopes, Denise Meringolo, and Nicole King, thank you for sharing your bright light with me. While I'm critical of HonFest, the women who take being Hons seriously are some of the loveliest people you can know. Thank you to Charlene, Heidi Moore Trasatti, Rita Moore, and Susan Hodges Grant.

Rutgers University has supported this project in many ways. Two university research grants made possible the bulk of my archival research. A sabbatical leave—my first ever!—allowed me to finish the manuscript. Thank you to Dean Jan Lewis for making that happen. You are missed. My colleagues in Rutgers University–Newark's Federated Department of History are truly the best. Several have been extremely generous with their time and advice. Ruth Feldstein, Mark Krasovic, Alison Lefkovitz, Kyle Riismandel, Beryl Satter, and Whit Strub immeasurably improved this work by reading drafts, listening to me ramble about my ideas, and sending me links to articles about anything and everything to do with Baltimore. Perhaps because they're gluttons for punishment, Kyle, Mark, and Whit were part of a writing group, along with Lee Ann Fullington and Lisa Gill, where I presented some of this work. Thank you for your insights. Christina Strasburger, history department administrator, not only makes arcane university processes run smoothly; she does so with more warmth, humor, and smarts than anyone I know. Eric Ortiz, an excellent graphic designer, helped me in a pinch with some of the images here. Thank you both. Finally, Abigail Perkiss and Becky Amato, both outstanding urban historians, have shared their scholarly advice and, even better, their time for breakfasts, dinners, and drinks with me.

I am extraordinarily lucky to publish this book with Johns Hopkins University Press. It's an honor to have this book come out from the same press that published some of the urban history books I most admire, from Jon Teaford's *Rough Road to Renaissance* to Sharon Zukin's *Loft Living*. My thanks go to Greg Britton, editorial director of Johns Hopkins University Press, who supported the project at its very start. Elizabeth Demers guided me through the early stages. Laura Davulis, who stepped in halfway through, has been the kind of editor writers dream of: communicative, sharp, and funny. Neither of my peer reviewers were Reviewer 2. Thank you to both of them for their thoughtful suggestions.

During the final stages of this process, my father, Joseph Rizzo, passed away from cancer at the achingly young age of sixty-six. He was more interested in physics than history, but I know that he would have kept a copy of this book on his desk. My mother and sister displayed extraordinary resilience as we weathered that storm together. I'm sorry that we had to go through that, but I'm glad that we had each other. I'm lucky to have so many longtime friends, who supported me through all of this. Thank you (now let's hang out).

The biggest, most effusive thanks are for Whitney Strub, my partner in crime for nearly a decade. Without him, this book wouldn't exist. I'm sorry that I couldn't fit Don Dohler in this version. I hope someday you'll forgive me. Whit's brilliant research and exquisite writing constantly push me to be a better scholar. His dumb jokes, silly dances, and love make it all worthwhile. For you.

# COME and BE

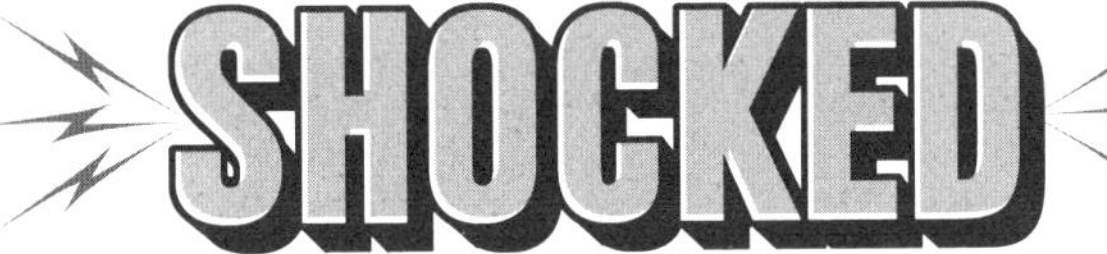

# INTRODUCTION

## Cities as Narratives

There are no songs entitled "Way Down upon the Patapsco" nor "The Baltimore Blues"; the city has inspired no outstanding novels; it is not planning a world's fair; it does not boast of the biggest, the newest, or the fastest anything. This does not indicate lack of city pride; it merely means that Baltimoreans are too sure of themselves and their city to feel the need of advertising its virtues.

—*Maryland: A Guide to the Old Line State,* 1940

Baltimore—The Greatest City in America

—Baltimore city slogan, 2000

Somewhere along the way, Baltimore lost its confidence about its identity. Following its heyday in the nineteenth century for its famously speedy clipper ships and its industrial economy of the early twentieth century, it seemed to falter. In the sixty years between the publication of the Works Progress Administration's guide to Maryland and the adoption of Baltimore's celebratory tagline, the city experienced the difficulties of many formerly industrial cities: loss of population due to suburbanization; industries, from canneries to steel factories, moving farther south or across oceans; and a shrinking tax base and public funding. But the shift points to more than just concerns about economic or demographic change. It suggests an existential problem. What defines Baltimore?

Starting in the 1970s, city leaders responded by aggressively marketing it as a city of arts and culture, one that hopefully would attract tourists and upwardly mobile residents. The hyperbolic 2000 slogan, from Mayor Martin O'Malley's administration, was one in a long list of urban branding campaigns that had begun in the 1970s under Mayor William Donald Schaefer. A coalition of political, business, and civic leaders orchestrated these campaigns to hide the problems of crime, unemployment, and poverty that many Baltimore residents experienced daily in order to create a story about Baltimore as a renaissance city, a place that is only getting better. Over the course of these six decades, this coalition promoted the idea that a city has a narrative—one that government should shape and control. At times, the story of the city seemed to become more important than its social reality. Throughout 2018, Mayor Catherine Pugh responded to the soaring homicide rate by saying that her administration was "working hard to write a new narrative."[1] Even when she resigned from office in 2019, following accusations that she illegally profited from a children's book she authored, she showed little concern about corruption or having created a leadership crisis. She apologized first "for the harm that I have caused to the image of Baltimore."[2] Activists and scholars critiqued this focus on image, recalling the words of geographer David Harvey: "If people could live on images alone Baltimore's populace would be rich indeed."[3]

What Baltimore city leaders have learned is that there is no one narrative of a city, even if there is an officially sanctioned one. Writers, filmmakers, poets, and public historians have produced their own stories about place that counter, critique, and, at times, support that of the city's civic and political elite. This book explores the contest over the meaning of Baltimore from the 1950s to the early twenty-first century through the lens of culture, a contest that has implications for postindustrial cities everywhere. Should culture promote positive representations of cities? Whose stories should be told and by whom? These questions were at the heart of a debate that raged between Mike Rowe, Baltimore native and the former host of the reality TV shows *Somebody's Gotta Do It* and *Dirty Jobs*, and writer and television producer David Simon in 2014. Rowe argued that Simon's TV dramas *Homicide* and *The Wire* "convinced millions of Americans that Baltimore is a fantastic place to buy drugs, find a whore, or get murdered. Better yet . . . all three at once." More than statistics or newspaper headlines, he believed these cultural representations determined how people, especially those who have never been there, see Baltimore.[4] What was needed, according to Rowe, were positive representations of regular working people, including those who have been crafting campaigns to make Baltimore a "destination city." Simon responded in a follow-up story by the *City Paper* and a post on his own blog. His work, which chronicles those Baltimore residents whose lives and neighborhoods have been devastated by political policies, had both an artistic and a civic purpose. It could even "help lead to redress and reconsideration of certain policies and priorities." He argued that the artist must tell stories that make the powerful uncomfortable, because "pretty, affirming stories" have a dire social cost for marginalized people with no megaphone of their own.[5]

Beyond the question of whether artists should be city boosters, snapping their suspenders to draw attention to the positive, or hard-eyed critics examining social hierarchies to condemn injustice, Baltimore's cultural history is also the story of Baltimore's shift to neoliberalism. Baltimore developed from a port city into an industrial and manufacturing center by the early twentieth century.[6] On the border of North and South, it combined the contradictions of the entire country. The largest free black population in the United States lived there before the Civil War, but its politicians pioneered legal residential segregation. It contained mill villages and decrepit tenement housing. But after World War II, suburbs siphoned off the middle class with federally guaranteed home mortgage loans, while redlining, discriminatory lending, and unethical practices like contract selling meant that the city's African American neighborhoods deteriorated. Shopping malls lured consumers out of downtown.

Baltimore's industrial foundation crumbled. Business leaders created the Greater Baltimore Committee, which worked with policy makers to draw middle-class people back downtown through large-scale infrastructure development. Beginning in the 1960s and gaining traction through the 1970s, these leaders connected infrastructure to image campaigns to create a tourism-centered service economy that prioritized neoliberal policies such as corporate investment over providing social services.

What does culture add to this story? Scholars agree that culture shapes how we see cities.[7] Literary scholar Carlo Rotella suggests that material places, which he calls "cities of fact[,] are everywhere shaped by acts of imagination: redevelopment plans, speeches, newspaper stories, conversations, movies, music, novels, and poems create cities of feeling that help guide people in their encounters with the city of fact. These texts affect material life."[8] For these scholars, the 1940s through the 1960s, the era of urban renewal and urban crisis, is the key moment when culture helps to explain the shifts cities—and the people who lived in them—experienced. Although this is a critical period in urban history, this chronology ignores the moment of postindustrialization, which historians have located in the 1970s, when cities shifted from industry to tourism, arts, and culture as major areas of municipal investment.[9] By focusing on the earlier period, they miss culture literally becoming a matter of public policy.

As both Harvey and sociologist Sharon Zukin have argued, culture is central to the shift to neoliberalism, defined as the ascendancy of the free market in all areas of life, the focus on individual rather than group rights, and the creation of entrepreneurial municipal governments.[10] It is impossible to explain the changes that have happened to cities since the 1970s, like gentrification, without understanding the role of culture. After the 1960s, when they became identified with urban uprisings as well as increasing crime rates, cities remade their image. They wooed real estate and corporate investment to attract wealthy people. Fiscal crises were understood as image crises.[11] Cities became fun. They were experiencing a renaissance.[12] Their ethnic neighborhoods were authentic or quaint. Artists lived and worked there. These arguments, made by writers, filmmakers, and artists as well as by municipal branding and tourism officials, attracted middle-class people who saw suburbs as dull and conformist.[13]

Culture also became an important economic and symbolic force in the war between cities, which competed against each other, and against suburbs, for investors and residents. Baltimore defined itself not only against nearby cities like Washington, DC, but also against other postindustrial cities like Pittsburgh or St. Louis that were engaged in their own rebranding efforts. Cities try to control and shape cultural images to their advantage, "underlining the convergence between economic structure and cultural project."[14] Alongside these structural changes, popular culture played a powerful role in defining these cities, as shown by the number that created their own film commissions to draw film and television shoots. These shoots offer both economic benefits and the opportunity to spread the image of the city worldwide. But popular culture also offers the possibility of resistance through critiquing these official stories and by giving visibility to marginalized communities. By placing the analysis of cultural texts within the historical changes affecting Baltimore and other cities since the 1950s, we see the rise of urban neoliberalism from a new angle.

By the 1980s, Baltimore had become a national leader in using tourism, arts, and culture to revitalize itself, cited in the national media, studied by urban planners, and touted in the media.[15] The Inner Harbor, in particular, made it "the envy of places like Cleveland and Philadelphia," both of which were competing for the middle-class traveler market.[16] By incorporating a narrative of urban renaissance through branding, marketing, and promotion while simultaneously building an infrastructure of hotels, convention centers, stadiums, and attractions for visitors, Baltimore became a tourist destination. Image and infrastructure worked in tandem. A promotional campaign could not bring visitors to a city with no amenities, but amenities needed to be married to a narrative of the city's uniqueness. Understanding who controls this narrative and who is included—or left out—is critical to seeing who has benefitted from the shift to a tourism economy.

Over the same period, Baltimore became the setting and topic of numerous cultural representations in movies, books, television, theater, and song. Surprisingly, though, Baltimore's impact on culture has been mostly ignored by scholars even though the city, through figures like John Waters, Anne Tyler, Barry Levinson, Laura Lippman, Charles S. Dutton, and David Simon, has become nationally recognizable. These representations have affected not only Baltimore itself but how we understand issues like urban governance (Simon), queerness (Waters), and race and ethnicity (Simon and Levinson). Several universities, for example, have offered courses on *The Wire* (2002–2008), an HBO drama about Baltimore's drug trade, as a window into deindustrialization, the criminal justice system, and education. Representations of Baltimore shape how we think about cities everywhere. By focusing on Baltimore starting in the 1950s, this book writes a prehistory of the contemporary moment where postindustrial cities vie with each other for tourists and upwardly mobile residents through branding. This book does not, however, tell the stories of famous artists who were born in Baltimore. Instead, it uses a diverse array of cultural texts—some well known, others forgotten—about Baltimore to understand how the image of the city has changed.

**Beyond Baltimore** | While a leader, Baltimore is not unique. Writers, filmmakers, and other artists have represented cities in culture for as long as there have been cities and culture. The intersection of economic, political, and cultural forces produces cities.[17] As cities changed, so did their representations. The dense and teeming cities of London and Paris spawned the complicated, sprawling stories of nineteenth-century novelists from Charles Dickens to Victor Hugo. New technology created new forms to represent cities. Film became *the* urban amusement, with urban audiences laughing at the antics of Charlie Chaplin as the Little Tramp in *The Immigrant* while "city symphony" films like *Manhatta* reveled in the busyness and industry of cities. Location filming became synonymous with urban films from film noir to blaxploitation. TV shows set in cities, from *Homicide: Life on the Street* to *Sex and the City* to *Broad City*, use real urban locations to ground their stories. There is no one message about cities in these representations. While American culture has long had an anti-urban bias that sees the city as a place of anonymity, danger, and questionable morality, many representations show the city as a place for adventure, self-invention, and freedom. Culture shapes how we build cities; the relationship between a city and its state, region, and nation; what individuals expect from that city; and what policies we create. As novelist James Joyce once explained, "I want to give a picture of Dublin so complete that if the city one day suddenly disappeared from the earth it could be reconstructed out of my book."[18] Examining these representations tells us about the relationship between people and place and how power shapes both.

Professional urbanists, from city planners to tourism officials, incorporate culture into their work as well. Urban planners, those seemingly rational technocrats who plot and map flows of traffic, and urban critics, who comment on urban development, express their visions through culture. Urban planner Kevin Lynch's influential *The Image of the City* argues that planners can learn about coherence and legibility from artists. A city path, for example, "might be organized as a melodic line, perceived and imaged as a form which is experienced over substantial time interval."[19] Sociologist William Whyte used film, dance, and music to understand the social life of small urban spaces in the book of the same name. The graph he made to see how people used the ledge in front of the Seagram's building in New York City reminded him of a player piano roll, so he asked a composer whether it could be played. "I hope one day it will be: A Day in the Life of the North Front Ledge at

Seagram's, Adagio."[20] Architecture critic Sigfried Giedion compared Robert Moses's highways to cubist paintings, abstract sculptures, and films.[21] Culture shapes cities at the most fundamental levels.

Cities often capitalize on their famous residents or on their appearance as the setting for a movie or book. Baltimore, where he died, and Philadelphia, where he lived, both claim nineteenth-century horror and mystery writer Edgar Allan Poe. Monroeville, Alabama, where writer Harper Lee grew up, welcomes thousands of fans of *To Kill a Mockingbird* even though it's set in fictional Maycomb. Similarly, the park where Australian film director Peter Weir's *Picnic at Hanging Rock* was filmed has become a pilgrimage site for fans wanting to figure out the eerie mystery of the film and the novel on which it was based.

Seeing such groundswell of interest, cities have publicized their associations with cultural texts. The industrial Philadelphia neighborhood that inspired a young David Lynch has been rebranded as "Eraserhood" in reference to the cult film *Eraserhead* that he based on his experiences there.[22] When HBO's *Boardwalk Empire* held a shoot at the Brooklyn Navy Yard, the former industrial site suddenly became a viable tourist spot. "There's no reason this couldn't be a stop on those red bus tours," Andrew Kimball, president and CEO of the Brooklyn Navy Yard Development Corporation asserted.[23] Efforts like Eraserhood or the Navy Yard take advantage of public interest in places they have seen represented in popular culture for economic development. Drawing people can lead to increased revenues for restaurants, hotels, museums, and other tourist attractions. When Baltimore filmmaker John Waters attended a Baltimore Chamber of Commerce dinner years ago, he had one suggestion: change the city's slogan to capitalize on what he saw as its most unique attribute, its eccentric people. His pitch? Come to Baltimore and Be Shocked. Several years later, the visitors bureau gave away bumper stickers with the slogan to fourteen hundred celebrities and media representatives attending the New York premiere of the musical *Hairspray*, based on Waters's film.[24] Waters, once called the "Prince of Puke," whose films were censored by the state of Maryland for depicting sex between a man, woman, and chicken, among other acts, had, by the end of the century, been incorporated into the tourist infrastructure.

**The Two Baltimores** | In 2015, an African American man from West Baltimore named Freddie Gray died while in Baltimore police custody. Residents and people around the country saw his death as one more example of police brutality and disregard for African American life in a recent lineage that included Michael Brown, Rekia Boyd, Eric Garner, and many others, growing out of decades of zero-tolerance policing. In the months following his death, journalists published numerous articles about the "two Baltimores." In general, they argued that the city was deeply divided between a poor, black population and a wealthier, white one.[25] This divide was also geographic. Baltimore has long been a hypersegregated city.[26] Because they were excluded from financial resources for decades by redlining, were allowed to deteriorate by political leaders, and were burdened by unpayable loans, called reverse redlining, in the lead-up to the fiscal crisis of 2008—black neighborhoods have higher rates of violent crime, drug use, poverty, and disease than white ones.

Unlike other large American cities with more diverse populations, Baltimore has primarily been divided between African Americans and whites. According to the census, 27 percent of the city's population is white, and 63 percent is black. Hispanic or Latino people make up less than 5 percent of the population, while Asian people are less than 3 percent.[27] This is much lower than in comparable cities. Philadelphia, for example, is 35 percent white, 44 percent black, 15 percent Hispanic or Latino, and 8 percent Asian.[28] Statistics show what many residents already know: to be born black in Baltimore determines, to a large degree, where people live, what they will likely earn, and how long they will live.

The social reality of the two Baltimores extends into culture. In 1977, singer-songwriter Randy Newman recorded "Baltimore" for his album *Little Criminals*, an album best known for the novelty hit

"Short People." "Baltimore" was serious. Over a plaintive piano melody, the song's narrator walks streets surrounded by prostitutes, the homeless, and addicts who can't understand what has happened to their city. For many members of the white working class, the permissive culture of the 1960s, the shift from integration to black nationalism, and urban uprisings that rocked cities in the 1960s explained urban decline and precipitated their political realignment.[29] The narrator dreams of fleeing to the country, returning to Baltimore only to be buried. While Newman claimed his song was about urban decay more widely, a Baltimore radio station collected letters from listeners complaining about how it represented the city. Hyman Pressman, the city comptroller, wrote a poem condemning it for not understanding "our great city's spirit."[30]

The next year, jazz chanteuse and pianist Nina Simone not only covered Newman's song but named an album after it. While Newman's version is a lament for the white working class, Simone's "Baltimore" takes the perspective of a black resident. Although Simone asserted that she had no role in choosing the songs on the album, by using the first person, the African American singer takes on the role of the narrator bemoaning the status of her city.[31] Simone's fame as a civil rights activist who uncompromisingly denounced white racism and violence in songs like "Mississippi Goddam" and who wore her hair in a natural style that resonated with Black Power, shifts the meaning of "Baltimore" and the representation of the city in it.[32] For Simone to carefully speak the line "ain't nothing here for free" must be read, from the perspective of a black woman, as an indictment of the unfinished business of the civil rights movement, in which freedom was a central organizing concept. Adding a reggae beat to the song creates a sonic connection to a larger African American diasporic culture. The same song, when sung by a white man and a black woman, had different meanings in a city literally divided between black and white.

Culture shapes and reflects racial consciousness. It can justify racial segregation. As historian Eric Avila has argued, film noir, Disneyland, and baseball helped define an "inclusive white identity among a heterogeneous suburban public," while cities came to be defined as African American.[33] Culture can also be a space for resistance. When Harlem Renaissance poet Countee Cullen was called a racial slur in Baltimore, he described it in his poem "Incident," forever associating the city with the trauma of his experience. And when civil rights activists in Baltimore fought segregation, their targets included movie theaters, an amusement park, and a segregated teen dance show on TV.

How are racial divides codified in the cultural representations of one city? Examining Baltimore suggests that cultural representations can be as segregated as real city streets. Since the 1950s but coalescing particularly since the 1980s, cultural texts about Baltimore have divided the city into two different geographies, which I call Charm City and Bodymore, an assessment that writer D. Watkins has similarly made.[34]

Charm City is defined by white working-class eccentricity. Like other industrial cities, many white ethnic working-class people lived in Baltimore. Because of its location, it also drew white people from Appalachia. Settling in neighborhoods like Highlandtown, Little Italy, and Hampden, they created their own social worlds with local customs that drew the attention of artists. As we will see, the portrayal of members of the white working class shifted over time. In the 1950s and 1960s, *The City of Anger* and *The Buddy Deane Show* showed them as innocent victims of integration. In the next decade, John Waters's characters dressed in exaggerated white ethnic working-class style and engaged in queer and deviant acts.

By the 1970s, Charm City began to cohere as the white working-class image of the city. Baltimore's best-known nickname was the result of a failed 1974 branding campaign created by the Baltimore Promotional Council. Visitors could collect various charms representing different aspects of the city to complete their bracelets. The word "charm" had a triple meaning, evoking Baltimore's southern hospitality, lingering ethnic and class-based cultural practices that seemed quaint to outsiders, and architecture from earlier eras.

"Charm" appealed to varying constituencies both in and out of the city. Welcoming to tourists, it identified a vague but evocative cultural, historical, and architectural uniqueness that differentiated Baltimore from colder or more modern cities.

But "charm" is also racialized, with white ethnic neighborhoods and cultural activities defining it, ignoring the majority African American population of the city. By the 1980s, representations of white working-class Baltimore emphasized a kind of "gentle lunacy."[35] With the popularity of nostalgic texts about Baltimore's midcentury past like *Hairspray* and *Diner*, Baltimore became increasingly associated with that period. By the end of the twentieth century, this became the center of an annual heritage festival, HonFest in the Hampden neighborhood. This event, which has grown in popularity to become a multiday affair and is examined in the final chapter, uses the image of the Baltimore Hon—a white working-class woman from the early 1960s with a tacky style and sassy personality—as the image of the neighborhood and, by extension, the city.[36]

If Charm City is fun, kitschy, and white, Bodymore is dangerous, deadly, and black. Bodymore encompasses the neighborhoods outside the limits of the Inner Harbor and other areas that are constructed for the comfort and leisure of tourists and affluent professionals. While news coverage inordinately focuses on urban crime, influencing public perception, popular culture can have similar effects, turning certain areas into "landscapes of fear."[37] In the episode "Bop Gun," from the TV show *Homicide: Life on the Street*, Robin Williams plays a father who brings his family to Baltimore from Iowa for a vacation. As they walk through South Baltimore, a group of black teens robs them. One shoots and kills Williams's wife in front of her terrified children and husband. As Kay, one of the homicide detectives, explains, it was not simply Mrs. Ellison who got shot, it was "a tourist" who "gets shot outside the stadium." Al, the unit's commander, notes that it's "not the kind of thing that keeps white folks coming to town." Culture reflects reality: Bodymore must be kept separate from Charm City. Artists assert that they are simply portraying the Baltimore they know, obscuring their role in perpetuating Baltimore's cultural segregation. Their choices cast long shadows on how visitors and residents understand the city and the resources allocated to different populations by politicians and civic leaders.

Recent depictions, like the first season of the popular podcast *Serial*, complicate this image. The series focuses on whether Adnan Syed, a young Muslim man, convicted of murdering Hae Min Lee, his Korean American girlfriend, in Baltimore, really committed the crime. While fans responded to the mystery, the show depicted the racial, ethnic, and religious diversity of contemporary Baltimore in new ways. Public historians and artists are bringing stories, like that of the Lumbee Indian community in Fells Point, to light, as well.[38] But, for much of its history, the division between black and white Baltimore concealed these other stories. From 1953's *City of Anger* to *The Wire* in the early twenty-first century, white artists have focused their attention on black poverty, destitution, and crime in Baltimore. While many of these artists were liberals hoping their work would improve people's lives, their depictions helped define the borders of Bodymore. Black cultural producers, from poets writing in *Chicory*, a neighborhood literary magazine, to actor, producer, and director Charles S. Dutton of the TV show *Roc* in the 1990s, also examine the terrain of Bodymore, offering their own perspectives and counternarratives. These two cities lie side by side, existing simultaneously. As this book shows, representations of segregated places replicate that segregation.

Charm City and Bodymore are ideas that have shaped the segregation, racism, urban renewal, and activism that historians of Baltimore have studied.[39] Understanding how a film or a TV show shapes and reflects society requires more than examining its depiction of a place. We must understand the political economy by asking, Who gets to produce culture? Who has access to funding? Whose work is circulated? How does the meaning of a text change as it circulates? Culture is a space of struggle over power, politics, and place. As cultural historian George Lipsitz argues, "Politics and culture maintain a paradoxical relationship in which only effective political action can win breathing room for a new culture, but only a revolution in culture can make people capable of political action. Culture can seem like a substitute for politics, a way of posing only imaginary solutions to real problems, but under other circumstances culture can become a rehearsal for politics, trying out values and beliefs permissible in art but forbidden in social life."[40] Historian Rhonda Y. Williams has shown how regular folks, like black women living in public housing in Baltimore, became activists who confronted people in power.[41] Equally important are the ways that other working-class black Baltimoreans wrote about their experiences with police brutality, urban renewal, and politics in the pages of the poetry magazine *Chicory*, created with funding from the War on Poverty. For these residents, poetry allowed them to discuss problems and imagine solutions. *Chicory* was political, from its creation by white liberals to its publication of poetry about black nationalism. Through a deep examination of the political economy of culture, this book looks at the relationships between social movements and federal and city policy, uncovering unexpected linkages between them.

Cultural representations are intended to work at different scales. Sometimes the city represents only itself. More often, though, the city is a stand-in for all cities of a certain type. *The Wire* is set in and about Baltimore, but it represents all postindustrial cities struggling with the loss of work. For tourism officials, the city must be represented as having unique qualities that can draw visitors. But the city cannot be too unique. Visitors need familiarity to feel comfortable. Harborplace, the shopping and dining destination on the Inner Harbor, is unique because it references Baltimore's industrial past but is familiar to everyone who has ever been in a mall.

Scale determines the meaning of the representation, leading us to ask, Who made this? Who consumes it? Overall, the scale of cultural representation can be categorized in one of two ways: defensive or expansive. Defensive representations are those that are focused on maintaining the social status quo. Like the white homeowner associations studied by historian Thomas Sugrue that kept black people out of their neighborhoods, culture plays a role in justifying segregation.[42] I broaden the idea of defensive representation to include those texts that portray the city as a unique entity whose problems are easily resolved. Expansive representations use the specific city to make larger claims about class, gender, race, sexuality, and politics. Depending on their audiences and how they circulate, the same text can be both defensive and expansive. Club music, for example, starts out with specific local meanings within Baltimore to become representative of urban blackness when it reaches audiences outside of the city.

There's more culture about Baltimore than can be discussed in depth in one book. Some likely suspects may not appear here or show up only briefly. Memoir is not a major topic. Journalist Ta-Nehisi Coates, who grew up in Baltimore and whose father Paul Coates was a member of the Baltimore Black Panther Party and founder of a black nationalist publishing company and bookstore, is one of Baltimore's more famous writers, having explored his youth there in *The Beautiful Struggle*. D. Watkins, who has written two nonfiction books, *The Beast Side* and *The Cook Up*, about growing up in Baltimore, is another important voice in and of the city. In the chapters that follow, however, we'll concentrate on works of fiction, especially those that are reflective of historical trends, like urban renewal.

White men dominate cultural production about Baltimore. Digging deep into the archives surfaced work by black women and men as well as white women about Baltimore beyond a few famous names. Interestingly, a woman, Sandy Hillman, has played a critical role in shaping Baltimore tourism and branding infrastructure since the 1970s, though she did so behind the scenes. That it was easier for me to find work by white men suggests the limitations experienced by artists of color and women in getting their work funded, made, and circulated. These realities led black writers of urban fiction from the 1980s to today to self-publish and sell their books out of their cars or on street corners, working around a publishing system that mostly ignored the African American urban market. Even for artists who secured mass-market backing for their work, it can be difficult for researchers to access it. In order to watch the 1990s TV show *Roc*, created by Charles S. Dutton, which aired on the Fox network, I had to purchase bootleg DVDs of the series on the gray market because it is not otherwise available.

**All the Pieces Matter** | Part I, "Renewal and Resistance," examines the period of urban crisis and urban renewal, focusing on how artists capitalized on municipal and federal policy to comment critically on it. At the same time, urban renewal relied on its own process of image-making that led to the development of municipal arts organizations. As urban renewal slowed owing to citizen activism against it, politicians like Mayor Schaefer saw tourism, arts, and culture as clean industries that could spur economic development.

In chapter 1 we'll consider the relationship of culture to the critique and maintenance of residential segregation. While William Manchester offered a liberal critique of blockbusting in his forgotten 1953 novel, *The City of Anger*, the popular teen dance series *The Buddy Deane Show* refused to integrate, even in the face of the rising tide of youth civil rights activism. In each case, white Baltimoreans are presented as victims of efforts at integration. "From Blight to Filth" is a look at urban renewal through the lens of the early films of John Waters. Urban renewal leaders used blight to take ownership of urban spaces, but Waters turned blight into filth, reveling in depicting criminality and radically queer identities. However, these early films marginalized African Americans. Waters turns white innocence into white queer deviance. The comedy *Amazing Grace*, starring Moms Mabley, criticizes urban renewal through an African American perspective.

The Enoch Pratt Free Library published *Chicory*, a grassroots poetry and art magazine from 1966 to 1983, which is the subject of chapter 3. Federal funding from the War on Poverty supported the magazine initially. While it offered a space for working-class black

Baltimoreans, including many young people, to express themselves with little editorial intervention about issues as varied as Black Power, urban renewal, police brutality, and black culture, it was part of a larger program of "human renewal" intended to use culture to help African Americans assimilate into white middle-class life. It offered a uniquely working-class African American perspective on the city.

The election of William Donald Schaefer as mayor of Baltimore represents a turning point. "Hollywood East" examines the way the Schaefer administration connected arts, branding, and culture to development projects to shift Baltimore to a postindustrial economy. He created a municipal infrastructure, including a film commission, that envisioned the arts as economic development—but only if they portrayed the city in controlled ways that emphasized middle-class, family fun.

Part II, "Good Mo(u)rning Baltimore," turns to cultural production in the wake of Baltimore's supposed renaissance. These chapters show the solidification of the racialized narratives of Baltimore as Charm City and Bodymore. "Accidental Tourists" covers seven films and novels about Baltimore made between 1985 and 1990. While very different, each centers on how changes in the city caused white people to feel alienated in the midst of a supposed era of renaissance. For a number of these cultural producers, alienation was best soothed by sinking into nostalgic images of the supposedly simpler Baltimore of the 1960s.

By the early 1990s, television became a site where artists pushed back against the image of Baltimore as a renaissance city by focusing on black working-class life in the sitcom *Roc* and murder, drug addiction, and crime in *Homicide: Life on the Street*, *The Corner*, and *The Wire*. Each show used African American history to promote a particular analysis of Baltimore's—and other cities'—problems. *The Wire*, the most successful of these shows, offered a scathing political critique, but, for many viewers, its depiction of quasi-mythological gangsters gave its depiction of Baltimore as Bodymore an unintended allure.

Finally, "Welcome to Baltimore, Hon," takes on debates over the heritage of Baltimore in the early twenty-first century through the circulation of Baltimore's homegrown style of dance music, called "Baltimore club," which was produced and consumed within the African American community, and the Baltimore Hon, an icon of white working-class Baltimore femininity promoted within a formerly blue-collar neighborhood called Hampden. The epilogue draws these threads together by turning to the new crop of artists who are making work about Baltimore and suggesting what cities and cultural producers can learn from this book. When in 2016, the *Baltimore Sun* asked, "Why is Baltimore so wired to 'The Wire'?" it acknowledged the powerful impact of this representation on the city.[43] What this book shows, however, is that popular culture shaped Baltimore in complicated ways long before *The Wire*.

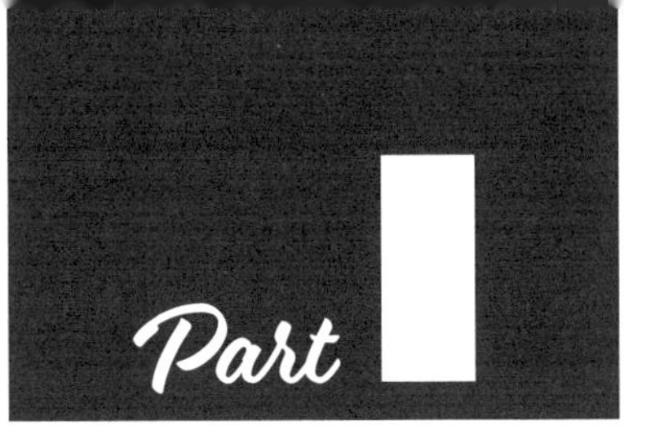


# RENEWAL and RESISTANCE

# THE CITY OF ANGER

## Blockbusting and Cultural Representations of White Innocence

Although Aubrey Bodine, famous photographer of Baltimore and its environs, symbolized mid-twentieth-century Baltimore with his images of spotless marble steps, mobility rather than stability defined a city undergoing deindustrialization, suburbanization, and the internal migrations of people searching for a decent home. Drawn by the wartime boom, African Americans, white ethnic immigrants, and white migrants from Appalachia moved into the cramped warrens of the city's downtown while restrictive covenants, anti-black violence, and de jure and de facto segregation kept both black and Jewish people locked in certain neighborhoods. By the mid-1940s, the need for housing was so great that supposedly impermeable racial boundaries broke. In 1944, a black family moved across Fulton Avenue on Baltimore's west side into a neighborhood that had let its restrictive covenant lapse. The white, mainly Catholic residents blamed Jewish realtors for creating a panic by telling residents that their housing values would fall once black people moved into the neighborhood.[1] They organized and even called on the mayor to issue a moratorium on real estate sales in response. When these tactics failed, they sold their houses, quickly resegregating these neighborhoods.

Real estate speculators and black-market lenders exploited fears about racial mixing and property values through blockbusting. White homeowners living in areas that bordered black neighborhoods saw their home values stagnate and ultimately drop as racial turnover appeared inevitable. Black people saw white neighborhoods and the possibility of home ownership as preferable to the often squalid neighborhoods they lived in. However, they had virtually no access to bank loans because of housing policy begun in the New Deal that formalized residential segregation and incentivized lenders (and sellers) to follow suit. Real estate speculators served as middlemen between white people wanting to sell and black people wanting to buy. They bought the first properties in a neighborhood at high prices and sold or rented those properties to black families. White people were panicked into selling at increasingly lower prices. Agents also profited by selling the homes at inflated prices through shady contracts to black buyers with no other options.[2] By the mid-1950s, this process of blockbusting had become the "most troublesome area of friction between races" in Baltimore.[3]

Both black and white Baltimoreans protested blockbusting. At its heart, the conflict revolved around competing definitions of rights. Black people sought the right to live where they could afford without impediment. They decried blockbusters for the profits they made from desperate people who often could not keep up with payments driven to exorbitant rates by the dual housing market. African American attorney Sampson Green, who served on the Maryland State Human Relations Commission, condemned "the whole exploitative operation of banks that redlined black areas of the city" and city and state politicians who were "insensitive to the problems of black families desiring to purchase homes, which made it possible for individual speculators to profit."[4] White people, however, condemned blockbusting because they saw it as a ceding of property that rightfully belonged to them to black people who, they believed, were unable to properly care for it. Powerful cultural, political, and legal forces told them "that racial minorities simply threatened white-owned property," and it was in their best interests to prevent them from getting access to it.[5]

Although scholars have examined blockbusting's role in the deterioration of central cities and the rise of conservative politics, little attention has been paid to its cultural dimensions, even though one of the greatest American plays of the twentieth century, *A Raisin in the Sun*, by Lorraine Hansberry, tells the story of a black family questioning whether to be the first to move into a white neighborhood.[6] Cultural texts, from radio shows like *Amos 'n' Andy* to images of "welfare queens" driving Cadillacs while living on public assistance, shaped white beliefs about their right to property by depicting the supposed profligacy and irresponsibility of black people. But, more than just depiction, culture was also a site, like a neighborhood, where battles over ownership and control played out through what I am calling "cultural blockbusting," where a dominant group evacuates cultural activities or spaces after a marginalized group begins to participate in them. This framework acknowledges that culture should be understood as a kind of property, an idea operationalized by, for example, world heritage programs that protect cultural activities the way they do historic buildings or places.[7] Examples of cultural blockbusting abound. After the integration of public pools, white people built private pools in their backyards, leaving the public pools to be patronized primarily by black people.[8] Men dominated cheerleading until women took their place during World War II. When they refused to stop cheering, men mostly left the sport.[9] Even in the internet age, this dynamic continues. White people left the early social networking platform Myspace, which was associated with people of color, for Facebook, seen as a safer space because its users were more likely to be white.[10] Seeing culture as property allows us to understand the virulent reactions of dominant groups to the integration of others into cultural spaces and practices.

In different ways, the two cultural texts we consider here produced and reflected white attitudes on blockbusting in Baltimore, each creating narratives of, in James Baldwin's words, white innocence that absolved white Baltimoreans for profiting from segregation or resisting integration.[11] Novelist and nonfiction writer William Manchester centered blockbusting in his lurid 1953 novel of a deteriorating Baltimore, *The City of Anger*. The first postwar novel about Baltimore tells the story of Charlie Bond, a working-class white man, who gets caught up in a scheme to prevent his neighborhood from being blockbusted, setting in motion a chain of events that ends with his daughter Dulcy's murder by an intellectually disabled black man, Sam Crawford. With its white working-class characters, grim tone, and focus on corrupt institutions, it is a precursor to works by Robert Ward, Laura Lippman, Rafael Alvarez, and, outside of the novel format, David Simon, especially in *The Wire*. Like Simon, Manchester, also a reporter for the *Baltimore Sun*, fictionalized real stories, like integration on Fulton Avenue, to expose the race, class, and gender inequalities that allow the wealthy and powerful to extract profits from the poor. But, Manchester's tepid liberal critiques of exploitative capitalism and racism aside, he ultimately reinforces white anxiety about protecting their property through his stereotypical depiction of Crawford as irresponsible, sexually voracious, and violent. Faced with a neighbor like Crawford, the novel suggests, white homeowners' fears are justified.

While *The City of Anger* characterized blockbusting as the eruption of tensions between black and white Baltimoreans, the sudden cancellation of *The Buddy Deane Show*, a popular local televised teen dance show, enacted it. From 1957 to 1964, *The Buddy Deane Show* represented Baltimore as wholesome, youthful, and segregated. It set aside one day each month for black teen dancers, but there was no mixing between the races on air. Filmed in the working-class white enclave of Woodbury, in an area known as Television Hill, its white teen dancers, mainly from working-class neighborhoods, used their on-air time to become local celebrities and representatives of proper white youth culture.[12] Like the families of Fulton Avenue, Buddy Deane, the host of the show; the teen dancers; their families; and many viewers saw the show as their property, a white neighborhood of the airwaves. However, in the early 1960s, at the height of the civil rights movement, activists cleverly appropriated its racist logic against the show to briefly integrate it.[13] Whites viewed this as a takeover that would result in the loss of its cultural and monetary value for the white host, dancers, and viewers, mirroring how white Baltimoreans saw blockbusting.

These works show the role of culture in reflecting and shaping ideas about race, geography, and property. Even though their politics differed—Manchester offered a liberal take on postwar housing discrimination while Deane was politically conservative—both texts ultimately absolve white Baltimoreans for profiting from segregation or resisting integration by asserting their rights to protect their real and cultural property. By depicting blockbusting, Manchester showed the seething racial and class conflicts over space in the divided city that led to significant percentages of white residents leaving for homogenously white suburbs. Although the *Buddy Deane Show* never explicitly addressed blockbusting, its segregation reflected the racial geography of the city, making it the staging ground for an explosive instance of cultural blockbusting at the height of the civil rights movement.

**The Newsman's Archive** | Like Baltimore, William Manchester bridged North and South. Although his mother was from Virginia, he was raised in Massachusetts, where his father's family lived. Born in 1922, he studied to be a journalist and served in the marines during World War II. When he returned from war, he earned a master's degree in journalism for a thesis about Baltimore's famed wit H. L. Mencken, who hired him to write his biography and got him a job as a reporter at the *Sun* in 1947. His biography of Mencken appeared in 1951, followed by *The City of Anger*. He left Baltimore for Wesleyan University, where he worked as an editor, adjunct professor, and writer-in-residence for decades, becoming nationally known for his nonfiction.

Manchester's voluminous personal papers document residential segregation, racism, and blockbusting. Segregation had long been a local priority. In 1910 Baltimore held the dubious distinction of being the first city in America to create a law that identified exactly where black people could live.[14] Copied by other cities, the Supreme Court struck down the Louisville, Kentucky, version as unconstitu-

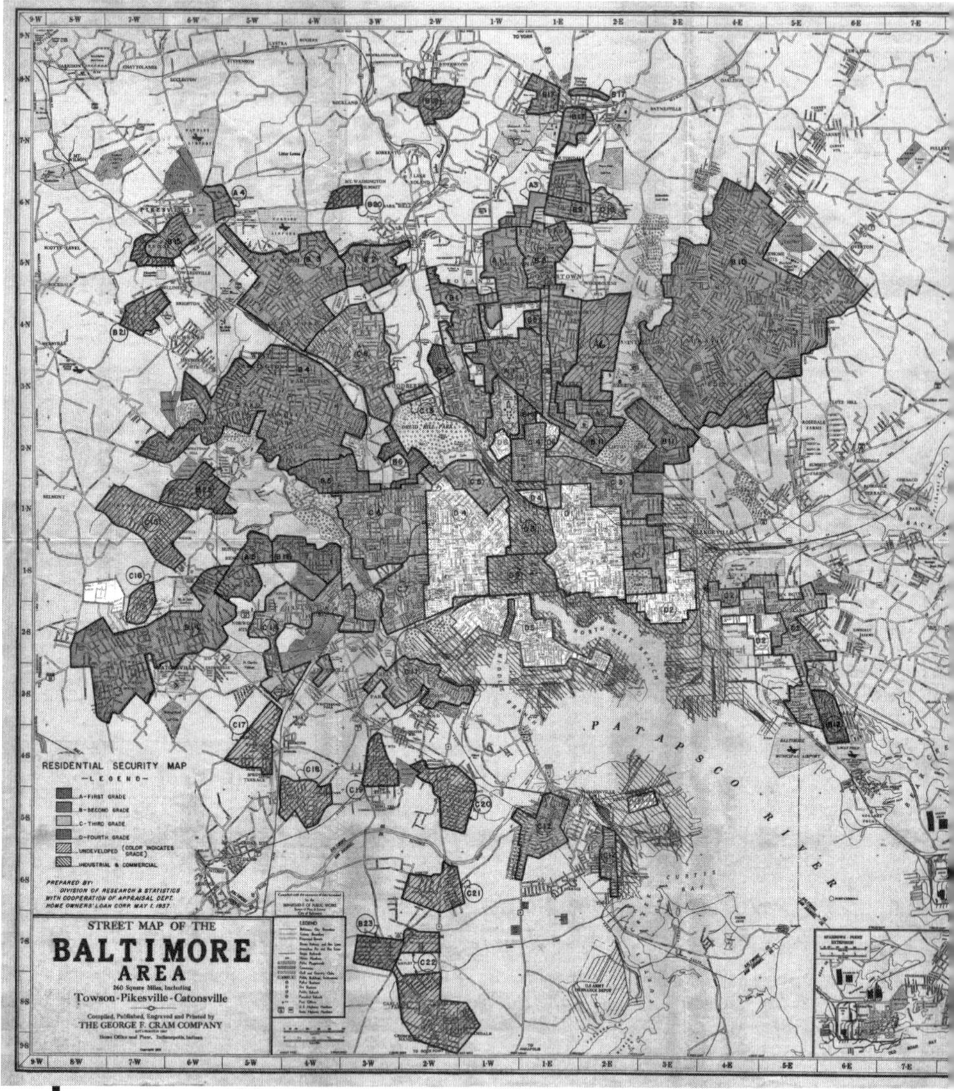


Redlining map of Baltimore. Federally insured bank loans could not be made to anyone purchasing property in the areas graded D, which appeared in red on the original map.

JScholarship, the digital repository of the Sheridan Libraries, Johns Hopkins University

tional in 1917. By the 1930s lenders were denying loans to people buying property in areas identified by the Home Owners' Loan Corporation as risky because they included black or foreign-born people, industrial or commercial activity, or shoddy housing. In this way, the practice of redlining replaced unconstitutional legal segregation with an equally racist economic and political segregation. Banks refused to lend to black people. Powerful groups like the National Association of Real Estate Boards and federal agencies agreed that neighborhoods should maintain their segregated quality. As historian Beryl Satter notes, "Since the presence of a single black family usually led to mortgage redlining, whites had a powerful economic incentive to keep such families out."[15]

Because of their vulnerable position, black Baltimoreans faced a stark choice: either live in decrepit conditions in crowded neighborhoods or work with unethical real estate speculators, known as blockbusters, to buy property on contract in other areas of the city. Manchester collected many stories about the effects of residential segregation and contract sales on black Baltimore. When Mrs. Hord, a black woman who bought a house without ever receiving a copy of the contract, deed, or title, missed two weeks of payment, she was taken to People's Court. She learned that if she had been renting the house, it would have cost $9 a week unfurnished. As the owner, she paid $41 per week and had no equity. When another woman, named Goldie, purchased a home, the agent paid the former owner to reimburse him for his down payment, scribbled a new name over the old contract, and told her that a notary was not necessary.[16]

Manchester researched the tactics used by blockbusters, like one who bought a house in each of thirteen blocks for more than market value only to then pay half of market value for additional houses in those same blocks as white people panicked and sold their houses. In the end, the blockbuster earned $150,000 from the deals.[17] In 1956, Manchester profiled Dan, a blockbuster and landlord, in the *Reporter*. Dan was a member of the "Forty Thieves," a group of real estate agents who banded together to buy properties when they realized that they were continually competing against each other at auctions. Dan began as a manager of apartment buildings in poor areas, charging tenants for repairs that were never made and increasing rents without telling the owners while pocketing the difference. He moved into blockbusting and contract sales later. When Baltimore began to enforce housing code violations under the Baltimore Plan, Dan realized that he would be responsible for expensive structural repairs. Instead of making repairs, he sold the buildings to the tenants with no money down on a contract basis. When he forwarded the violations to the new owners, it became clear that it was only a matter of time before they would default and Dan would be able to sell the property to someone else. For the city, Dan's business practices led to overcrowding, poverty, increased crime, and disease. For Manchester, Dan and his fellow speculators represented the "spreading rot in metropolitan areas" that needed to be rooted out through greater government oversight.[18]

Manchester fictionalized these real stories into a liberal critique of residential segregation and blockbusting mixed with sensationalistic violence and pop psychology. Author John Dos Passos wrote of *The City of Anger* that it "is the novel every police reporter has dreamed of writing."[19] The novel is structured around two pairs of men: Jarvis Cameron and Ben Erik, and Charlie Bond and Sam Crawford. Cameron and Erik are powerful, wealthy, and politically connected, though one comes from an established family and the other is a ward boss. Both are involved in illegal activities, especially the illegal lottery called "the numbers." In their war with each other, Cameron arranges a complicated and ultimately successful scheme to bankrupt Erik by publishing in a popular magazine that a specific number will win and then fixing it so it does. While we learn little about Erik's family, Cameron is shown as cold and angry toward his wife and children, which leads to his daughter's dissolution into alcoholism. The forces of law and order are represented by Bernard Zipski, an upstanding police commissioner. His subplot about revealing corruption in the police is minor but was enlarged in *The Takers*, a 1955 teleplay of the novel that eliminated the blockbusting plot entirely.

Bond and Crawford are connected through Cameron's side business as a funder of blockbusting and the numbers. Crawford obsessively plays the numbers, fervently hoping for a big payout that will allow him to buy a new house for his family, possibly in Bond's neighborhood. Bond works for Erik until he decides to start his own numbers business to replace the money he's put into efforts to stop the sale of a neighbor's home. The final, fixed play bankrupts him, and he is unable to pay Crawford his winnings, leading to Crawford's descent into madness and murder.

Manchester's novel draws from social realism, proletarian literature, and pulp fiction. While Manchester's favorite author, James T. Farrell, focuses solely on the small world of Studs Lonigan in his famous trilogy, in *The City of Anger* Manchester zooms across class and race lines in the tradition of authors from Victor Hugo to Richard Wright who used the city as a microcosm through which to understand social structures. Unlike other oppressed workers depicted in industrial novels, however, Bond has no community, whether through a union, religion, or friends.[20] Described in its second edition as a "political novel," Manchester hoped it would reveal how corruption and racism affected working people and the "right people" would learn from it and change real policies.[21] However, Manchester's book is hardly naturalistic or political. While he based characters on real people, he turned them into symbols of social problems. In doing so, he showed the limits of his liberalism. While he could see how racism forced black people into untenable living situations and how elite whites exploited working-class whites, he expressed this through simplistic psychological explanations, especially in the case of Crawford.

**Plotting White Innocence in *The City of Anger*** | Understanding that, in Baltimore, geography was destiny, Manchester approached his novel with a cartographic vision, even drawing maps of his fictionalized Baltimore to keep track of the characters' movements through the city. For example, Hoot Vogel, a homeless alcoholic, walked "on West Concord, . . . stepped lightly for two blocks, entered an alley, walked to the rear, and turned sharply into a dark and grimy passageway between buildings."[22] Although Manchester did not name his titular city as Baltimore, it is clear from the descriptions of space and from his personal papers that Baltimore is the referent. The city hugs the old waterfront and includes a racetrack that is much like Pimlico, which opened in Baltimore in 1870. When a journalist asked the chief of the Baltimore police department's vice squad if the novel's version of the numbers racket looked like what was happening in the city, he replied, "Look like it? . . . Man, this is it."[23] A legend for the hand-drawn maps also shows the process of fictionalization. Baltimore's real Edmondson Avenue becomes Gaylord while Gilmor Street becomes North Colvert. Never mentioned by name in the book, Aliceanna Street, the border of maritime Fells Point, is drawn onto the map of the novel's Sticktown, the refuge of hardened alcoholics and mariners.[24] The edge of the "black belt" is Fulton Avenue. If this map was laid over the security map on page 26, everything below Hope Street would be rated D, or industrial.

Like the real geography of Baltimore, the geography of *The City of Anger* is divided by race, class, and gender. Racial distinctions are more meaningful than political borders in this geography. "Where was the Seventh District?" Bond asks himself (156). That kind of place designation means nothing to him. It is a political boundary, not a lived one. His lived boundary is the edge between the black neighborhood and his white one. His comprehension of the relationship between white and black disenfranchisement is limited; as a striver toward a middle-class way of life, he sees class difference as predominant. When he tells his wife that a nearby house "had been split into cheap apartments" and is "swarming with indigent mountain people," she argues that "white slums were merely transitional. They never paid. A white man could live anywhere, and only floaters would rent there, but a black, any black, had to find what he could within the belt" (154).

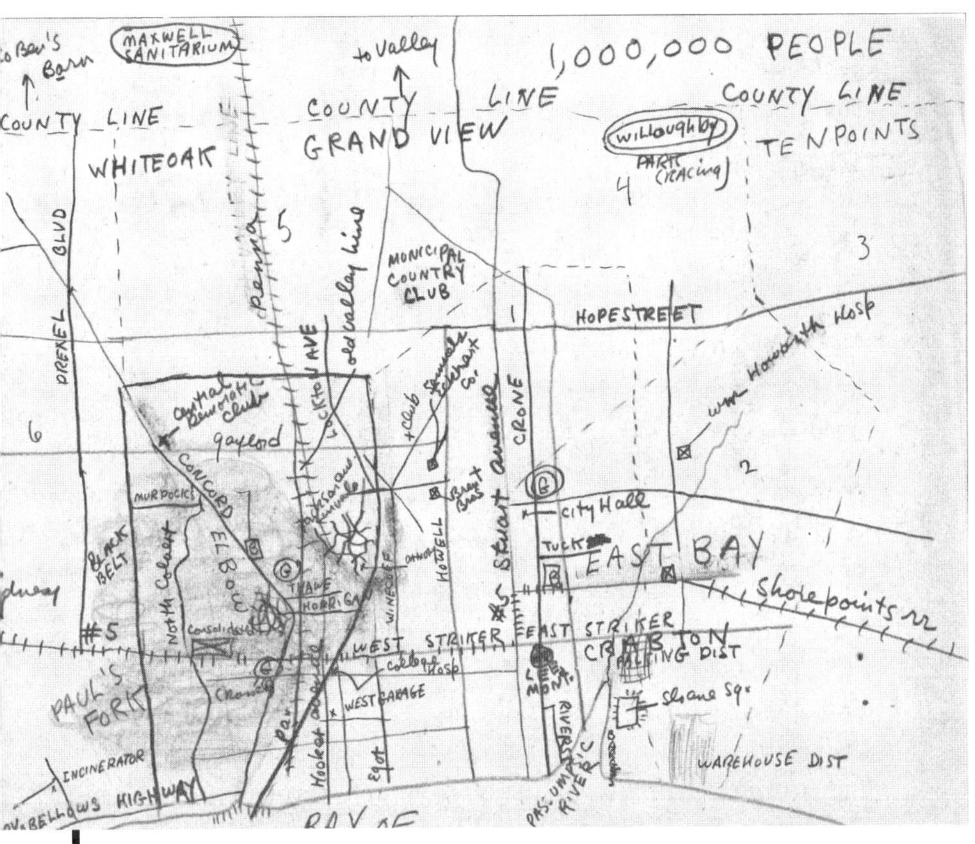


William Manchester's hand drawn map of the fictionalized Baltimore of *The City of Anger.* The Elbow, a black slum where Crawford lives, abuts white neighborhoods, like Bond's. Blockbusting is a looming threat.

Manchester Papers, Wesleyan University Library, Special Collections and Archives

Bond is not racist. Like many white people of this era, he couches his concerns about the neighborhood in terms of property values.[25] He is contrasted with Cameron, who spews racist epithets, and his formerly wealthy neighbor Lucy Carter. She reminisces that "when her father was alive there were no tramps on Linvale Place, nor anywhere else in the neighborhood. None would have dared come. And a Patecka, or a Redsedski, or a Nigra who tried to move east of Kendall Square, would have been horsewhipped" (158). She yearns for a WASP-dominated racial and ethnic purity from an earlier historic period. That Manchester locates racist ideas in elite or formerly elite characters suggests that he sees white working-class concerns about racial change as not driven by racism. In fact, Bond and Crawford interact several times because the numbers bring them together, though they are not friends. In the end, Bond, from his small territory, cannot see how forces put in motion by Jarvis Cameron have led to the loss of his savings and his job. After he learns that his only child has been murdered, he expresses his despair in spatial terms. "It was a terrible thing, not knowing how to get out" (465).

Bond and Crawford are linked throughout the novel. Crawford's "shoulders and Charlie's were crooked with the same hunch, and he was bareheaded as Charlie was. From behind," the two men, one white, one black, "looked oddly alike" (430). While Bond's troubles come from his class position, however, Crawford's world is circumscribed because of his race. The victim of repeated inequities, Crawford struggles to survive. When he is brought before a judge for a petty crime, he is sentenced harshly. He had been living with his wife and child in one room with seven people sharing a bathroom until an unscrupulous realtor sold him a house at the intersection of two dead-end streets in the Elbow, the worst slum. To pay for expensive repairs, they take in a boarder, pushing them into a smaller space within their own house, paralleling the larger struggle of blacks who were being forced into urban ghettos.

While Manchester explicitly acknowledges that racism limits Crawford's life, his actions are ultimately explained through simplistic Freudianism and Cold War–era theories of psychopathic sexuality.[26] He is described mentally as "a very large child" but "with the tempered muscles of a brute and a restless savagery in his heart and an old, childhood hatred burning deep within him" (238). Crawford is conceived when his mother is raped. His lack of a father is central to his psychological development in a trope that combines 1950s "momism" with stereotypes about black matriarchal families.[27] His mother perverts her desire for the absent father into molestation of her son. Other children learn about the sexual abuse and ruthlessly tease Crawford. The molestation and humiliation make him unable to control his sexual urges, the embodiment of the stereotypes of the coon and the black buck.[28] He attacks a black girl, fathers a child outside marriage, and is dishonorably discharged from the army for desertion before the novel begins. His mobility, however, is what makes him a threat to white people.

While Manchester negatively depicts Cameron and Carter as virulently racist, in making Crawford Dulcy's murderer, he gives credibility to white fears of black criminality. The novel stages the murder as the outcome of the blockbusting process. Once Bond cannot pay him his winnings, Crawford hides out in the house that has been sold to the blockbusting realtor, which is empty as workers divide it into apartments. He buys the knife he will use to kill Dulcy from a white store owner, who charges him twice the usual price, in a final, ironic commentary on the racist inequalities he has faced his whole life. Crawford finds Dulcy playing with a friend on Christmas Eve. He stabs her repeatedly, the prose turning into an unpunctuated series of images of red blood on fresh snow. The murder is the culmination "of all the loveless nights of his life rolled into one," from childhood trauma to housing discrimination (438).

Crawford's only recourse is motion: he runs. The police, with their surveillance abilities, emphasize the importance of geography as they check reports on Crawford's location against "the great master map of the city" (466). Instead, Crawford crosses the invisible boundaries that separate the neighborhoods for a last time in his futile attempts to find his way home: "West Concord lay just ahead. There. Behind the jut of fence. But it wasn't there. But it should have been. Well. There. Beyond that green police call box. Behind that brick privy. Around that corner. The Elbow would be there. It must be, had to be . . ." (473). Unaware of or ignoring the lines that dictated where he was supposed to be, Crawford, as the novel's most mobile character, is the one who most troubles the real city's racialized boundaries. His death reasserts them.

While Manchester shows how elites exploit the black and white working class through politics and corruption, his map is not large enough to encompass the real causes of racial conflict: federal government policies that created redlining and supported housing segregation. In the end, *The City of Anger* presents a nightmare scenario of blockbusting that centers white innocence and spectacularizes black violence. Bond, a working man without racial prejudice, is simply a victim of economic forces beyond his control, even when he is caught up in the effort to stop his neighborhood from being blockbusted. Crawford, although a victim of a racist society, is the embodiment of black male stereotypes: "Vile. Depraved. Perverted. Bestial. He was everything they said he was" (438). His murder of Dulcy is the culmination of white fears of racial integration—not only will Bond's house lose value; he has lost the future as represented by his daughter. Dulcy, a name that evokes sweetness, is a perfect symbol of innocence that justifies the continued segregation of white neighborhoods to protect property.

***The Buddy Deane Show* and Cultural Blockbusting** | In 1960, a new dance became popular across the nation. Called the "Madison," the line dance appealed with its simplicity. While more adept dancers could add steps, no energetic jitterbugging or complicated moves were required. Instead, dancers simply followed the directions of a caller who told them what to do next, which ranged from tracing an *M* on the floor to imitating Jackie Gleason's trademark "and away we go" shuffle. By 1964, even French New Wave film director Jean-Luc Godard had his titular group of friends dance it in *Band of Outsiders*.

The Madison symbolized the complicated cultural politics of race in Baltimore. Created by black Chicagoans, black Baltimoreans danced "the Madison in the aisles of a record store in the 500 block of North Gay street" and "on the sidewalk in front of the store, inventing new steps by the score."[29] Seeing its popularity, two black disk jockeys in Baltimore, Al Brown and Eddie Morrison, released separate records with songs and calls for the dance in 1960.

But it was being featured on the segregated *Buddy Deane Show* that ensured that white teens in Baltimore and, soon enough, the rest of the country, would be dipping and swaying in Madison time. With TV as their platform, they performed youthful white innocence for an adoring audience of peers. Debuting in 1957, just after *American Bandstand*, *The Buddy Deane Show* grew in popularity until it was the hottest show in its time slot. When the show featured the Madison—which Deane referred to as the "the big dance of the season . . . the biggest dance we've seen in a long, long time"—the group of white teens dressed in their knee-length skirts and skinny ties followed the directions of Al Brown, who remained a disembodied voice behind the white bodies that commanded all attention.[30] Even the cover of Brown's 1960 record *Madison Dance Party* with the Tunetoppers depicted a white family. When dancers were needed for an instructional video and a several-city tour to teach the dance, two white regulars on *The Buddy Deane Show*, Joan Darby and Jonas (Joe) Cash, were chosen.

More than simply taking credit for black cultural production, *The Buddy Deane Show* constructed an idealized image of the white Baltimore teen by marginalizing black youth. In contrast to heartthrobs like Elvis Presley, whose gyrating hips brought sex to mind, or the "white trash" mobs who attacked sit-in protestors, these white teens behaved with decorum.[31] By carefully controlling their appearance and behavior, the *Deane Show* made them symbols of Baltimore's homogenously white neighborhoods. Their youthful wholesomeness masked the racist foundation of the segregationist show.

The show maintained this image through its tight control of and rules for dancers. The teen dancers were managed by Arlene Kozak, Deane's assistant. She created the powerful Committee, a subset of dancers, to monitor the others. Regular dancers who were fan favorites needed character references to become members of the Committee. The show's rules ensured compliance with Cold War domestic containment culture, which promoted traditional gender roles. A girl, for example, could never dance with another girl on the show. Risqué dances, like the Bodie Green, were forbidden.[32] As in much mass culture of the era, youth were portrayed as monogamous couples or engaged in acceptable forms of physical intimacy: their slow dances were never too close or they danced the twist, which doesn't require touching. Black dancers followed the same rules, though they were never allowed to become members of the Committee. Integration of black and white teens would have upset one of the most rabidly enforced social mores of the time—the ban on interracial dating and sex.

Sex was not the only issue on the minds of concerned parents. "Seeing" was "absolutely central to the meaning of the 1950s," thanks, in part, to the ubiquity of television.[33] While television was still in its adolescence, ownership of TV sets grew quickly, making the potential audience for a show huge compared to nearly every other medium. Pointing a television camera at teen girls and boys in 1957 gave them an aura of celebrity and made them a point of emulation for viewers. As Baltimore teen John Waters remembered of *The Buddy Deane Show* dancers, "These were the first role models I knew. The first stars I could identify with. Arguably the first TV celebrities in Baltimore."[34] John Barton, who danced on the show during Special Guest Day, concurred, saying that the most important aspect of the show was how viewers identified with the dancers and musicians.[35] Viewers, and their parents, mimicked the dancers to learn the steps. By doing so, they were also learning how to be a teenager, a category of youth "invented" by postwar consumer culture. With their parents' affluence, teens had considerable spending power. Indeed, the idea of the teen was so linked to consumer spending that there were arguments over whether working-class teens even existed.[36] Advertisers and marketers convinced young people that they had an identity unique from their parents and younger siblings. By creating this category, they also made teens ask, What does a teenager look and act like? *The Buddy Deane Show* gave Baltimore youth one answer.

Deane, the Committee, and many of the viewers wanted to keep their show segregated and saw civil rights activists' attempts at integration as a kind of cultural blockbusting, a taking of "their" property. Local "television and housing formed overlapping and reinforcing sites of struggle over segregation" in the 1960s.[37] White people wanted to maintain their control over both culture and geography, and "blockbusting made urban whites increasingly sensitive" and unresponsive to black claims on either space.[38] In this era, blockbusting moved from being solely about housing to being more about white-controlled property in various forms, including culture. If whites resisted neighborhood integration because housing represented the bulk of their wealth, then *The Buddy Deane Show* offered a kind of psychic equity in which white youth were given a stage from which they could set a standard of teen identity that others would emulate. The show's image of the city as homogenously white, youthful, and nonthreatening was important to Baltimore's economic, social, and cultural redevelopment out of the decay depicted in *The City of Anger*.

To have black teens on the show or as members of the Committee would have undermined the logic of segregation by making black youth into role models for the audience—including white teens. The idea of white teens emulating black teens frightened white parents, especially because their children *were* fascinated with African American culture.[39] This fascination was lumped in with concerns over juvenile delinquency, antisocial behavior, and deviance. Baltimore psychologist Robert Linder coined the phrase that would come to define some white youth when he titled his book *Rebel without a Cause*. Parents, censors, and guardians of morality tried to stop these rebels from acting out and influencing others. Dress codes forbade young people from wearing blue jeans, associated with juvenile delinquents, in schools.[40] Comic books came under congressional fire for their violence and sexuality, which supposedly warped young minds. The schizophrenic result was "white teenagers dancing to soulful Negro artists—Sam Cooke, Jackie Wilson—and clean-teen white performers—Frankie Avalon, Fabian—whose talents often seemed limited to their haircuts."[41] White youth even learned dance steps from black students at their integrated high schools, but there would be no televisual integration.[42] But this would work for only a short while, especially in the face of a committed group of black civil rights activists.

**Ladies and Gentlemen, the Nicest Kids in Town!** | Three powerful African American families dominated civil rights in Baltimore. Carl Murphy ran the *Afro-American* newspaper chain and, with his brother, George, served on the board of the Urban League. Lillie Mae Jackson led one of the most powerful NAACP (National Association for the Advancement of Colored People) chapters in the nation from the mid-1930s until the 1970s. Her daughter, Juanita, founded the Young People's Forum and helped direct the Buy Where You Can Work Campaign in the 1930s. She married Clarence Mitchell Jr., who became the chief lobbyist for the NAACP. His brother, Parren Mitchell, was a director of Baltimore's Community Action Agency and a congressional representative.

Through the institutions controlled by these families and with the help of Baltimore's black churches, black Baltimore fought discrimination and inequality. In 1934, lawyer Thurgood Marshall won Donald G. Murray admission to the University of Maryland law school, which had no separate-but-equal counterpart in the city, setting a key precedent for the *Brown v. Board of Education* decision in 1954. The NAACP and the Colored Women's Democratic Club doubled the number of black registered voters in Baltimore between 1940 and 1952. In 1942, the NAACP, the *Afro*, and other groups marched to Annapolis to protest police brutality, including an incident in which a black servicemember lost an eye after a beating by police. They won the hiring of more black police officers and the creation of a new commission to study issues affecting African Americans. In 1952, thanks to efforts by the Urban League, the NAACP, and Americans for Democratic Action, the Baltimore Polytechnic Institute desegregated.

By the early 1950s, civil rights activists focused on direct action against segregated public establishments, a tactic that particularly appealed to students. A Baltimore chapter of the Congress of Racial Equality (CORE), an interracial organization that advocated Gandhian nonviolence, formed in 1953 and shone a light on segregated establishments. Morgan State College, a historically black institution, became a center for activism as students formed the Civic Interest Group (CIG) as the main campus organization for civil rights work. August Meier, a white professor at Morgan State, became one of CIG's faculty advisors. He helped students articulate their vision for the movement rather than simply following the lead of the NAACP. For Meier, CIG brought together students from different universities and high schools to create a heterogenous membership that could be effectively mobilized to eliminate "discrimination in places of public accommodation" through "nonviolent tactics of negotiations, sitting-in and peaceful picketing."[43]

While lunch counters and department stores were targets of activists—Baltimore department stores were especially hated for their vile practice of not allowing blacks to try on clothes before buying them—students at Morgan State focused attention on businesses close to campus, especially those located in the Northwood Shopping Center. When threatened with protests, every business except the Northwood Theater integrated. Protests, led by CORE, began against Northwood Theater in 1953 and continued with increasing frequency.[44]

In early 1962, CIG targeted Northwood Theater with its largest and most militant demonstrations. Black Morgan State students, paired with white Goucher College or Johns Hopkins University students, would attempt to buy tickets.[45] They purposely broke Maryland's trespass law to provoke the police into arresting them. More than four hundred activists were arrested over the course of six days of protest.[46] As the first mass arrests took place, there was no way to raise enough money to pay the punitive bail, so the students stayed in jail. Parents and administrators clamored for the jails to give students access to textbooks and extra milk, causing other inmates to hold a sit-down strike. This pressured the mayor, Philip Goodman, who was facing a primary challenge and could not risk the continued bad press, into forcing the owner of Northwood Theater to desegregate the facility immediately.[47] Celebrating students attended the first integrated showing of *In Search of the Castaways* on February 23, 1963.

As Lizabeth Cohen has argued, the civil rights movement was, in part, a way for African Americans to claim rights as consumers as well as citizens.[48] While civil rights activists fought for the right to consume goods like food at a lunch counter, they fought equally for the right to consume cultural products. As the closest movie theater to campus, Northwood's segregation impacted students' access to mass culture. As scholars have argued, film, television, and radio in the twentieth century helped to create a national culture, which became a common touchstone that created a sense of national identity, even though it did not stamp out local or folk cultures.[49] In the 1950s, more people bought television sets, but, with only a few networks on the air, the increasing number of viewers watched the same programs. Baltimore, for example, had three channels, and there were very few black faces on them; popular singer Nat King Cole's show was cancelled in 1957 for lack of national advertising sponsors.[50] Film, too, worked similarly. The studio system resulted in a large but controlled body of movies distributed. It would not be until the late 1960s and 1970s that black and independent filmmaking truly competed with its dominance. For young activists, access to the movies was meaningful in ways that their parents might not comprehend: "Adults who wondered about all the fuss over one single theater were told that it was the principle that counted."[51] Youth knew. Full citizenship included being able to go to the movies or see yourself on TV.

It was in this context that two student groups, CIG and BAYOU (Baltimore Area Youth Opportunities Unlimited), a local chapter of the Northern Student Movement, protested *Deane*'s segregationist policy.[52] Why would activists concerned with access to physical spaces like restaurants and movie theaters be interested in local television? With its huge popularity, *The Buddy Deane Show* existed as part of Baltimore's cultural geography. Activists understood that the show was a powerful fantasy image of the city as two neighborhoods, a white one and a separate but unequal black one represented by the segregated monthly Special Guest Day. It also fit with efforts to desegregate other spaces of leisure, like the Gwynn Oak Amusement Park. Led by clergy from various faiths, black and white protestors marched into the park on July 4, 1963, only to be quickly arrested. As activist and scholar Todd Gitlin remembered, a white segregationist attacked an interracial group with a chunk of concrete.[53] By the end of August, the park desegregated, but, in the middle of the dog days of summer, this place of joy was ironically a battleground between peaceful civil rights activists and recalcitrant whites.

Buoyed by the momentum of earlier local and national successes, young civil rights activists saw an opening provided by the hiring of Herb Cahan as general manager of WJZ-TV in 1962. Cahan, unlike Deane, supported integration. He even appeared on air to publicly proclaim his support of CIG's efforts to integrate Northwood and other civil rights activities. He hoped to integrate the *Deane Show*, but the powerful Deane and the Committee claimed that they would lose dancers and viewers. Tentative efforts at integration came through shows that included black children (removing the threat of interracial romance) and veterans.[54]

CIG mounted a protest on Thursday, June 28, 1962, outside the studio. Black R&B singer Ray Charles was scheduled to perform for a whites-only audience. A small group planned to picket outside using Charles's fame to bring attention to the inequity of young black fans not being allowed to hear him perform. They held signs riffing on the title of one of his most famous songs by linking it to a staunchly segregationist southern state: "Buddy Deane's got Georgia on his mind."[55] Little did they know that Charles had taped his performance and would not appear live on the show. Because they were unable to interrupt Charles's entrance into the studio, their picket did not have the public impact they hoped, but it did show the station that student activists were aware of the *Deane Show*'s segregation and that they were willing to protest that only a "few Negro groups [are] allowed . . . on rare occasions, which are few and far between."[56]

BAYOU regrouped and realized that it could use the ticket distribution system to stage its next protest, an on-air integration. Teens who wanted to dance on the show would write to request tickets. Because there were really two shows—a white one and a black one—the Committee had to figure out a way to identify the race of the person inquiring. Because Baltimore was deeply segregated, geography was one nearly foolproof method. As Bill Schaffer, a Committee member, explained, the Committee used the zip code of the requester to identify whether teens should be given a ticket to a regular show. If black teens mistakenly received tickets for a white day, they would simply be told to come back on Special Guest Day.[57]

Once civil rights activists understood this process, they subverted its racist impulses to use it for a dance-in. Marc Steiner, a civil rights activist in Baltimore and longtime radio DJ in the city, remembered how his integrated fraternity at City College, Bigotry or Brotherhood, tried to use the ticket system against the show: "We decided to write to get tickets. Each ticket was good for two people. So the white guys would ask black girls to be their dates and the white girls would ask black guys. The plan was to try to get into the show with interracial couples." The studio, however, refused to let them in. "We sat on the steps awhile and then they told us we would be arrested if we didn't get off the steps."[58]

When BAYOU made its successful integration attempt on August 12, 1963, it used the same strategy but did it on a Special Guest Day when, perhaps, there were fewer people controlling access to the studio. As Danny Schechter, who was involved in the Northern Student Movement and later became a television producer, described, local African American teens wrote to the show to get tickets for Special Guest Day. They invited white tutors from the Northern

Student Movement to accompany them. With chartered buses to take them from BAYOU's office at 622 North Aisquith Street to the studio five miles away on Television Hill, at the edge of Druid Hill Park in the primarily white, blue-collar neighborhood of Woodbury, the group planned an interracial dance-in on air.

According to Schechter, "The black students went into the studio first while the whites waited in the parking lot until the last minute. With two minutes to airtime, we rushed into the studio for the live show. The ticket taker was confused but let us in. The TV crew was equally perplexed. TV then was still black and white but those two colors weren't meant to be mixing in Bal'more, not then, not ever."[59] Because it was a live program, they had to continue filming. Viewers like Mary Curtis, a black fan, described the studio's response: "A white guy would grab a black girl and the screen would dissolve into squiggles and squares—like the producers were trying to hide what was really happening." Bill Henry, who also watched this very special episode, remembered the lights "got so dim the kids were silhouettes . . . but you could still tell it was white and black kids dancing together."[60] According to John Baker, a production department employee, the interracial couples "held hands and waited. After an awkward pause, Buddy introduced the next record."[61] Because all guest organizations were invited to speak on camera, Schechter and a black teenager "made political speeches, speaking out against segregation on the show, looking right into the stupid grin plastered on Buddy Dean's [*sic*] face. He was beside himself. Seething."[62]

The response was immediate. The Baltimore *Afro-American* covered the event, leaving one of the only contemporaneously written records. Schechter condemned the show for its segregation policy and demanded that four African American couples be added to the Committee. The studio refused to acknowledge that it had a policy against integration, instead playing up recent efforts like an integrated session sponsored by the YMCA (Young Men's Christian Association).[63] Schechter met with WJZ-TV executives and Spiro Agnew, then Baltimore County executive, who told him that the integrated dance had "set back race relations in Baltimore County by twenty years."[64] The station reported receiving numerous bomb threats.

By the fall of 1963, Cahan cancelled Deane's contract. *The Buddy Deane Show* aired for the last time on January 4, 1964, starting a public war of words. The station justified its decision by pointing to lower ratings, but integration was the real issue. Cahan even told Clarence Logan, the leader of CIG, "I can't resolve the problem with the parents. I have to get rid of the show."[65] Deane even argued that "integrated dancing is more delicate than schools or jobs."[66]

For Deane and his supporters, the show's cancellation made them innocent victims of cultural blockbusting. He described himself as "caught in the middle" between "Negro groups [that] were insisting he integrate the show and white extremists [that] were insisting otherwise."[67] Deane displaced segregationist beliefs onto these unidentified "white extremists," separate from both the activist "Negro groups" and the innocent white teen dancers and Deane himself. Like the white homeowners who blamed black people and activists for falling property values through blockbusting in the 1950s and 1960s, Deane ignored the profits he had earned over years from exploiting the segregated television marketplace. The white teen dancers lost their status as local icons and representatives of a fantasy Baltimore that erased black people, especially civil rights activists. In a telling decision, station management doubled security for the last show.[68] While no problems were reported, they clearly feared the kind of violence or vandalism by white youth that often accompanied black families moving into white neighborhoods.[69]

## Two Cultural Texts, Two Visions of Baltimore

*The City of Anger*, rooted in muckraking journalism, told a story of power, race, and corruption that its author hoped would reveal hidden truths about the city. *The Buddy Deane Show* depicted a seemingly well-controlled separate-but-equal city hiding racism behind an upbeat, Brylcreemed veneer. Taken together, they capture a period of resistance to racial integration in housing and culture. As they both show, concerns about territory, property, and mobility undergirded debates over blockbusting, civil rights, and television. Blockbusting became not simply a description of housing change but also a metaphor used by white people to describe their efforts to control their property, whether real or cultural.

Their differences mark two templates that most cultural representations of Baltimore would fall into in the following decades. *The City of Anger* attempted to intertwine the fates of black and white Baltimore residents but faltered because of its simplistic psychological explanations and stereotypes of black men. The sprawling novel, which mercilessly tightens the screws around its black victim/villain, Crawford, eventually forces him to murder. Geography prevents him from identifying who has caused his despair. The links between the wealthy Jarvis Cameron with his racetrack and country estate just outside the city and Crawford's dilapidated house in the heart of the slums, financial precarity, and spectacular loss playing the numbers are as invisible to him as electricity coursing through a wire. The racial geography of the city ensures it. While these circumstances pit Crawford and Bond against each other, representing conflicts between the white ethnic working class and African Americans, Manchester attributes their exploitation to local elites, rather than to broader forces represented by federal policy.

*The Buddy Deane Show*'s segregated cultural depiction mirrored the reality of many of Baltimore's neighborhoods—homogenously white, though precariously so. The imagined community of *The Buddy Deane Show* was an idealized one populated by well-dressed and well-behaved young white people who represented the future through their chaste heterosexual romances on the dance floor. The show was a kind of property that gave value and meaning to white youth. Special Guest Day could be tolerated by the whites who ran the show and the teens who danced on it because there was a clear separation between the two neighborhoods. But, as civil rights activism in Baltimore grew, the show became a target. For whites, this was a kind of cultural blockbusting where black people, with the help of people like Herb Cahan, encroached on a previously all-white space. Deane and the Committee, like many white homeowners, resisted integration by claiming that their property would lose value. When they lost, they refused to compromise but, instead, left their neighborhoods behind.

The afterlife of these texts differed as well. After writing *The City of Anger*, Manchester left journalism for a new career at Wesleyan University. While he published other novels, his fame came from his nonfiction, including *Portrait of a President*, about John F. Kennedy, and *The Death of a President*, about his assassination. *The City of Anger* was republished in 1967 and again in 1985. Its bleak portrait of Baltimore merged with similar images to justify urban renewal projects, to which we turn in the next chapter. Manchester died in 2004.

After his show's cancellation, Buddy Deane moved back to Arkansas and bought several radio stations. He died in 2003. The program was mostly forgotten except by a group of devoted former dancers and one especially fervent fan. In 1988, John Waters rewrote history in *Hairspray*, a movie about a show like Deane's in which the integrationists won. Because of the film and its remakes, *The Buddy Deane Show* has become a topic for scholars and journalists. The irony, of course, is that what the show really tells us about resistance to integration in Baltimore is obscured by the more popular fantasy, something we'll see happening in a later chapter.

Although these two cultural texts—*The City of Anger* and *The Buddy Deane Show*—are very different, it is in their endings, not their beginnings, that they parallel each other. The novel closes with a riot by poor African Americans caused unwittingly by the political maneuverings of Cameron and Erik, who had used them as their pawns. While Baltimore would not experience riots until 1968 and 2015, Manchester presciently predicted how the geographical, financial, and political isolation of black people in the city would lead to violent unrest, even in the face of local leaders who thought otherwise.[70] *The Buddy Deane Show* came to a close with a final, tearful episode. While the image of swaying young white bodies seems radically divorced from a riot, in the context of cultural blockbusting, it is not as different as it seems. When the whites who controlled *The Buddy Deane Show* were confronted with integration of their neighborhood of the airwaves, they didn't relocate or integrate. They simply burned the whole neighborhood to the ground.

# FROM BLIGHT TO FILTH

## John Waters in the Age of Urban Renewal

The ruin displayed in *The City of Anger* consumed civic and business leaders who struggled to counter Baltimore's poor public image, which made the city cultural shorthand for urban decay in the post–World War II period. In the Tony Award–winning Broadway musical *Kiss Me Kate*, protagonist Fred Graham asks the president of the United States, "Is it true you've declared Baltimore a disaster area?"—a joke with no connection to the plot but that earned a laugh in 1948. Alfred Hitchcock set the finale of his 1964 film *Marnie* on the sleazy Baltimore waterfront instead of England as in the original novel by Winston Graham. Marnie confronts the childhood sexual trauma that has haunted her against the backdrop of a garish rear projection of the harbor. Once more, Baltimore was the location for sexual deviance and violence.

Deviance and violence, however, appealed to the young John Waters, who would film all his movies in Baltimore. Waters wanted to shock audiences. With civil rights activity rising in Baltimore and around the nation and the sudden cancellation of *The Buddy Deane Show* in the face of integration, nothing was more controversial than interracial romance. Made for thirty dollars in 1964, his first film, *Hag in a Black Leather Jacket*, depicts the wedding ceremony of a black man to a white ballerina, whom he carries around in a garbage can, by a Ku Klux Klan member, on the roof of Waters's parents' suburban house. It even referenced *The Buddy Deane Show* by having Mary Vivian Pearce dance the forbidden Bodie Green.

Described by Waters as a "boring, arty short," the film has no moral or progressive politics.[1] It simply revels in the socially inappropriate. It is a swear word scrawled on a bathroom wall, a teenage sneer caught on 8-millimeter film. After *Hag* played in a Baltimore coffeehouse, recouping its initial investment, Waters left to study film at New York University but returned after being expelled for drug use. Dreaming of making movies, he moved from the suburbs to downtown Baltimore, where bohemian, white, and queer young people used an aging city undergoing rapid redevelopment in order to promote their countercultural vision.

Even though Waters made movies in Baltimore during a moment of intense urban change, his work is rarely considered within the context of urban history. He is generally situated within queer or underground filmmaking.[2] However, he leveraged the changes happening in the built environment as a result of urban redevelopment to present a uniquely queer vision that helped define Baltimore's image, albeit in way that marginalized black Baltimoreans. By the 1970s, no filmmaker would be more important in shaping how people saw Baltimore than Waters. As writer Larry Grobel mused, "Joyce had Dublin, Utrillo had Paris, Grosz had Berlin, and Waters has Baltimore."[3]

The relationship between film and urban renewal from the 1950s into the early 1970s is striking in Baltimore, where educational, underground, and Hollywood films shaped ideas about and critiqued urban renewal. Like civic and business leaders across the country, Baltimore officials in the 1950s and 1960s saw their utmost duty as remaking the city into a rational and modern space by eliminating blight.[4] They turned first to neighborhood conservation, or the systematic use of housing code enforcement to spur repairs, and then to urban renewal, a federally funded program of urban redevelopment, to dramatically remake the city.

Visual representations like film became critically important in defining blight to the public to justify these efforts.[5] *The Baltimore Plan*, a 1953 educational film commissioned by the Baltimore Redevelopment Commission, the precursor to the Baltimore Urban Renewal and Housing Agency (BURHA), defined blight as a menace through the figure of a white female social worker who ventures into a disorderly black neighborhood. Through code enforcement, the neighborhood becomes a clean and orderly place where residents conform to hegemonic gender roles. While the Baltimore Plan was superseded by urban renewal in the late 1950s, the film's nationwide tour spread images of Baltimore blight and redemption far and wide. As James Rouse, Baltimore developer, proponent of the Baltimore Plan, founder of the Greater Baltimore Committee, and urban renewal mastermind, stated, "By creating the image of a rational potential of a city, we generate the power to carry it forward."[6]

For young filmmaker John Waters, who began making movies in Baltimore in the 1960s, Baltimore's decrepitude and redevelopment were opportunities to portray the city as a space of deviance and alternative sexuality. Because housing costs were low in older, downtown locations like Fells Point, he and his friends could afford to live there. They contributed to a burgeoning queer art scene that marked these areas as ripe for later gentrification. Like civic and business leaders, Waters was obsessed with urban blight. Unlike them, he did not want to eradicate it. Instead, he participated in a process of what I call urban filthification as a response to both neighborhood conservation and urban renewal. Through his location filming and stories about criminality and deviance, he turned blight into filth—a space of antisociality generative of radically queer identities.[7]

Waters's early films, *Mondo Trasho* (1969), *Multiple Maniacs* (1970), *Pink Flamingos* (1972), and *Female Trouble* (1974), depicted blight to revel in the perversity and deviance found in blighted areas. Unlike the respectable social worker figure, these films center on Divine. Played by a cross-dressing Glenn Milstead, Divine was an obese, insane criminal character who participated in perverse acts from murder to incest to coprophagia. Her exaggerated look and behavior made her the visual and narrative center of these films. Two scenes of Divine strutting on public streets and Waters's guerilla filming tactics, though, show us how this queerness marginalized African Americans, who became onlookers to white queer identity. Finally, Waters's whiteness allowed him to film on the streets of Baltimore in locations that were already under urban renewal, which made them zones of desolation that were only lightly monitored and perfect for his depictions of deviance.

*Amazing Grace* (1974), a film starring famed comedian Moms Mabley, serves as a counterpoint in using urban renewal as the catalyst for a plot about black politics in Baltimore. A Hollywood film made by Stan Lathan, an African American director who would later direct the Baltimore-set TV show *Roc*, *Amazing Grace* starred black actors and was meant for black audiences. Unlike either the Baltimore Plan or Waters's films, it argues that blight is always defined for political purposes to disenfranchise African Americans. One of the first black films about Baltimore, it depicts Baltimore as a paradigmatically black city, one with a vibrant, politicized black community fighting back against urban renewal. Taken together, these texts reveal the role of film in promoting, using, and critiquing urban renewal in Baltimore. While on the surface Waters's early films and *Amazing Grace* critique urban renewal, the former has more in common with *The Baltimore Plan* film. Like the architects of the plan, Waters's carefully constructed narratives about the city benefitted white people, queer performers in the place of developers, but marginalized people of color in the process.

**From Neighborhood Conservation to Urban Renewal** | Officials measured Baltimore's decline in several ways. Grossly substandard buildings housed the poorest, mostly African American, residents. In the worst areas, they lived without indoor plumbing above waterlogged basements next to rat-infested alleys. Baltimore was the nation's seventh-largest city but was first for the percentage of its homes without indoor or flush toilets.[8] The growing suburbs, predominantly white thanks to federal lending policies, siphoned off white and middle-class residents. This decentralization lowered the city's tax base. Downtown department stores suffered from competition with shopping malls that could promise white shoppers they would rarely encounter shoppers of color while also providing amenities like free parking. Business owners saw the assessed valuation of the central city decline by 34 percent from 1931 to 1945.[9]

A coalition of reformers, social workers, urban businesspeople, politicians, journalists, architects, and planners in Baltimore tried to address housing and declining economic activity. As in cities across the nation, they adopted an "ethic of city rebuilding" that unsettled the central city for decades.[10] Baltimore's city leadership and advocates for the poor experimented with neighborhood conservation, or the attempt to use code enforcement and repairs to improve housing conditions. This group, led by social worker Frances Morton, found supporters in Mayors Theodore McKeldin and Tommy D'Alesandro, mortgage banker James Rouse, and banker Guy Hollyday, and, nationally, in real estate and construction organizations. Unlike public housing advocates, they based their plan in the free market, maintaining segregation in Baltimore, rather than fighting it. By fixing up black neighborhoods, they could justify the continuation of redlining.

By the mid-1950s, while these efforts had become codified as part of the 1954 housing law, Baltimore had shifted to urban renewal to address both housing issues and downtown economic problems. Also supported by Mayor D'Alesandro, Rouse, and Hollyday, these efforts were led by the Greater Baltimore Committee (GBC), an association of business leaders, and the Baltimore Urban Renewal and Housing Authority. Urban renewal utilized public-private partnerships to purchase land, demolish buildings, displace residents and businesses, and then replace them with new houses and, especially in the downtown, corporate and civic buildings.[11]

The roots of neighborhood conservation date to the mid-1930s, when social worker Frances Morton's research revealed the terrible living conditions in a section of East Baltimore. The *Baltimore Sun* published her analysis in a muckraking exposé in 1936, bringing visibility to these issues. In 1941, Morton founded the Citizens' Planning and Housing Association, a civic group devoted to improving housing in the city. Her solution was for the city to enforce its existing housing code. She proposed systematic block-by-block housing inspection combined with community efforts to clean up these areas.

Called the Baltimore Plan, an area of East Baltimore near where she conducted her research became the test site for these ideas from 1951 to 1953. With D'Alesandro's support, inspectors from several agencies checked each house for health, fire, electrical, zoning, and building violations. These were compiled and sent to the owner with the threat of being taken to the newly created housing court, the nation's first. While well intentioned, the plan ignored the wiliness of slum landlords. As they realized that code enforcement would eat into their profits, many sold their buildings on a contract basis to their tenants, who would find themselves bankrupted when they couldn't afford the repairs.[12] Hollyday fundraised for the Fight Blight Fund to defray costs, but it affected few people.[13]

Ultimately the Baltimore Plan improved the pilot area somewhat but was not replicable on a large scale. However, it came to national significance thanks to the conflict between public housing advocates and free market supporters. For public housing advocates, slums could never be cleaned up. They needed to be demolished and the poor housed in government-run residences. Developers, too, promoted slum clearance but for less altruistic reasons, as they saw the potential profits in large-scale building projects. Neighborhood conservation and the Baltimore Plan appealed to the National Association of Real Estate Boards and the National Association of Homebuilders, two powerful lobbying groups who saw in this option an alternative to what they thought of as the creeping socialism of public housing. Conservation had the further advantage of maintaining segregated neighborhoods and bringing profits from home repairs. They were able to pressure President Dwight D. Eisenhower to include neighborhood conservation as part of the Housing Act of 1954, which also funded urban renewal.[14]

The failures of the Baltimore Plan were clear to local leaders. Rouse, Hollyday, and other city leaders shifted their support to urban renewal for both residential and commercial purposes. The Greater Baltimore Committee, founded in 1954, became the major player in the urban renewal that would dramatically reshape the city. Modeled after Pittsburgh's Allegheny Conference (and part of a wave of similar groups created in cities nationwide), the GBC included executives from businesses with entrenched interests in the economic vitality of downtown, like Albert D. Hutzler Jr., owner of Hutzler's department store. The GBC created a model of public-private partnership to remake large areas of the city to please private business owners. The GBC identified several priorities, including highway construction and an improved port. The urban renewal subcommittee, one of the most active and influential, saw "no action program more vital to the entire community than . . . slum clearance, the stabilization and strengthening in values of downtown Baltimore," and mass transportation.[15]

Beginning in the 1950s, several neighborhoods, including downtown and Harlem Park, were designated sites for redevelopment. Business and city leaders cheered as "grubby blocks of elderly office buildings became a place of plazas, fountains, arcades, and spanking new skyscrapers."[16] Ostensibly to get rid of outdated, dangerous housing, in reality African Americans and other people of color were often expelled from areas where they had long lived. In Baltimore between 1950 and 1964, twenty-five thousand people were displaced, 90 percent of them black.[17] Just a decade later, well over a thousand acres of land in downtown Baltimore and its surrounding areas were in some phase of the urban renewal process.[18] While historic preservationists and community activists argued for rehabilitating old buildings rather than tearing them down, projects like the building of a new post office in the Shot Tower Industrial Park area and the demolition of a section of Baltimore's infamous red-light district, the Block, to construct a new police headquarters continued unabated.[19]

**Defining Blight in the Baltimore Plan |** Blight was the overarching concept that justified both conservation and renewal. Homer Hoyt and Frederick Babcock, real estate economists, theorized that neighborhoods declined in patterns. Completely derelict areas were slums. But, before they became slums, they went through an in-between phase of blight. What defined blight? Almost anything. As legal scholar Wendell Pritchett explains, "Blight was a rhetorical device that enabled renewal advocates to reorganize property ownership by declaring certain real estate dangerous to the future of the city."[20] Blight was defined as everything from aging buildings, proximity to industrial areas, and the residence of immigrants and people of color. Left untreated, blight led to crime, disease, deviance, and, eventually, a slum. It could spread, as well. As a pamphlet by the Housing Authority of Baltimore made clear, the city was "living in the shadow of its slums." With the area of West Baltimore near Harlem Park shaded, it was clear where slums were located. A large box added ominously that "crime and disease are more prevalent in the blighted areas . . . and affect the entire city."[21]

Politicians and other renewal supporters paired images of blight with photos and drawings showing the progress possible if the blight was arrested through redevelopment. At a public meeting in 1953, W. A. C. Hughes, from the NAACP, claimed that a proposed redevelopment area in Baltimore was not a slum. Clark S. Hobbs, redevelopment commission chair, countered by brandishing photos of the block where Hughes lived and forcing him to admit that it showed several dilapidated properties.[22] In cities around the nation, housing and urban renewal authorities used brochures and films to teach the public how to identify blight and what it cost taxpayers. In *The Dol-*

*lars and Sense of Urban Renewal*, a pamphlet published by the Baltimore Urban Renewal and Housing Agency, the "alternative to urban renewal" was a photo of rowhouses with crumbling fences and trash-filled yards.[23] Another pamphlet differentiated appropriate living conditions from blighted ones. Garbage thrown in streets or alleys was a "no," because it attracted rats. Rags, paper, and other trash piled up in yards was a "no" because of the fire hazard posed. Each "no" included a photo of the offensive act and was followed by a "yes" statement explaining the alternative, also with a photo.[24] Such material educated people to spot blight in their own communities.

Film distributed images of blight alongside narratives of race, class, and gender. The Los Angeles City Housing Authority produced *And Ten Thousand More* in 1949, to show slum conditions and advocate for public housing.[25] The American Committee to Improve Our Neighborhoods (ACTION), which Rouse helped create, made the film *Man of ACTION* (1955), which placed responsibility for stopping blight on the shoulders of individual homeowners who needed to keep up with maintenance and repair to stave off the devil of decay.[26]

To extol their success in Waverly, redevelopment officials commissioned a film from the Encyclopaedia Britannica's film bureau, which specialized in educational films. Costing $20,000, its production was supported by the National Home Builders Association and the National Association of Real Estate Boards. Called *The Baltimore Plan*, the film premiered at the Valencia Theatre in Baltimore on February 5, 1953, at an event that included national media and industry leaders.[27] It toured nationwide to prove to communities that the Baltimore Plan's model of code enforcement and rehabilitation was "a way to transform blighted areas into gleaming safe communities."[28] A pamphlet with discussion questions accompanied the film to create public conversation about the issues it raised.[29]

Its primary purpose was to show the rehabilitation potential of a blighted African American neighborhood. The film does not blame black residents for the condition of their neighborhoods, but it also does not present them as capable of making changes without being led to do so by white authorities. Presented as documentary, *The Baltimore Plan* was a highly constructed narrative. The film, which ends with before-and-after shots of the area, takes place over an undetermined period but is presented as happening as we watch. The filmmakers even planned to include scenes from a real community meeting that took place on December 10, 1951, attended by Mayor D'Alesandro, but, when no members of the community showed up, the director left it on the cutting room floor.[30]

"Like all large American cities," a title card from *The Baltimore Plan* reads, "Baltimore, Maryland has extensive blighted areas—residential, commercial, and industrial 'slums.'" *The Baltimore Plan* depicted the "rational potential" of the city to eradicate its blighted areas, through a process of inspections and code enforcement, with community support intended to identify problem areas and clean them up before they slipped into complete disrepair. The film visualized the inhumane conditions of life in impoverished Baltimore as part of a narrative of urban redemption in which a female social worker is supplanted by male authorities who develop a plan to enlist community members and city inspectors to investigate neighborhoods for housing violations.

Before the film can describe the solution, it wallows in blight, using the unnamed white female social worker as our avatar. She enters the slums speaking in a first-person voice-over. We see a gas lamp being lit on a cobblestone street. An arabber passes with a wagon of produce to sell. A black woman leans out a window blowing bubbles with her gum. African American children play unsupervised in the street. The social worker narrates her reaction, which is meant to also be ours. Ironically, given what we have just seen, she notes, "It seemed like another world, deserted and unpeopled . . . It's as though I stepped into a strange city, a city from which all people had fled." She knocks on doors looking to speak to stay-at-home mothers, one of whom, she hopes, will be the neighborhood leader she is searching for. Her expectations of hegemonic middle-class femininity are misplaced (though a young black woman answers the

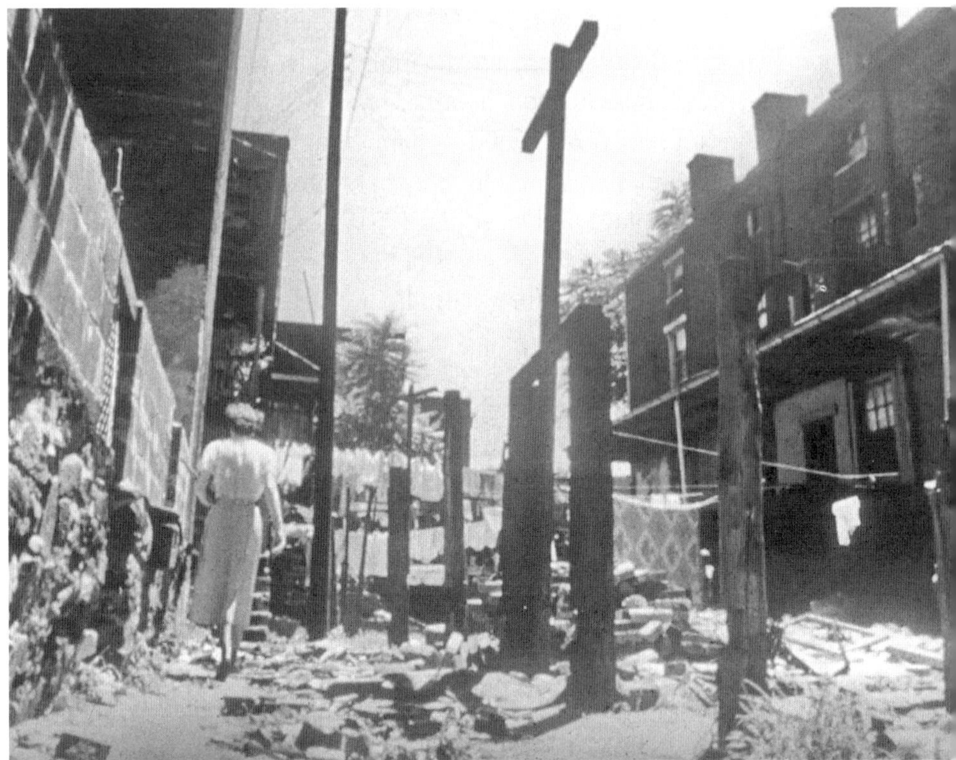

A white social worker walks through the blighted alleys of a decrepit Baltimore in *The Baltimore Plan*.

door just after she leaves). The film refuses to blame the poor for these conditions, unlike much of the social science discourse of the era, which blamed "certain racial and national groups" for "greater physical deterioration of property than groups higher in the social and economic scale."[31] She says, "Though it may seem a jungle in its ugliness and disorder, its real life is in the people who live here, the only place they have to live. People with the same kindliness and neighborliness as elsewhere."

These voice-over sentiments, though, are no match for the power of the visuals. The camera lingers repeatedly on images of decay, like a dirty outdoor toilet. A fly crawls over the body of a dead rat. Ramshackle alley fences conceal vicious dogs. Steps up to back doors are shaky and unsafe. Garbage covers sidewalks where weeds climb through cracked brick. The social worker's clean light-colored skirt and shirt contrast with this decay in long shots that show her framed by squalor. The discrepancy signals the argument being made in the film and by urban renewal leaders: this blight is out of place, shocking, and needs to be eradicated. It is only when this is seen by people from outside the slums that change can happen.

In a strange doubling, the voice-over explains Frances Morton's role in creating the plan without naming her. It describes how she had gone into these areas in previous decades and been "shocked by the housing conditions she saw." The director of public welfare, a commissioner of health, and a newspaper editor seized on her report to make change. Once the white female social worker has seen the problem, she can then pass it on to the predominantly white male authorities of the municipal bureaucracies. The media play a central role in distributing the images, incensing citizens who don't live in such squalor that these conditions exist. Once the bureaucrats and media have brought attention to the problem, then the community of residents is needed to actualize these plans. An older black woman who is a "neighborhood leader" is tapped to help the social worker with organizing the cleanup of the pilot area. But, for the most part, black people in these neighborhoods are mere onlookers. Their gaze at the decrepitude of their surroundings does not matter.

With the help of the housing court and the Fight Blight Fund, the neighborhood is revitalized. The final shots of the film show clean yards with new fences and flower gardens replacing rat-infested alleys. Children playing in the streets are now monitored by mothers, suggesting a renewed populace as well as environment. Blight, however, was often used to justify the displacement of even middle-class black residents. Even BURHA acknowledged in a 1959 report on Harlem Park, the first residential urban renewal project in Baltimore, that both in the outer area (which was rehabbed) and the inner area (which was cleared as slums) the residents had higher than average incomes compared to other black people in Baltimore.[32] The "pliable concept" of blight, used to displace unwanted people and create a new, orderly city, inspired the queer visions of John Waters.[33]

**Becoming John Waters |** Before the pencil mustache, Commes des Garçons suits, and cult fame, John Waters was a queer kid living in the Baltimore suburbs. He was born in 1946 to an upper-middle-class family in Lutherville, Maryland. His father was the president of a company that sold fire equipment, while his mother, a grad of the liberal Southern women's college Sweet Briar, took care of the house. Waters rebelled against his class and racial background through his lifelong obsessions with both working-class white and African American culture (especially music), as well as his fascination with crime. As a young man, he adopted a yippie political philosophy and a proto-punk attitude defined by an obsession with violence, aggressive self-presentation, and disinterest in middle-class morality.

An avid moviegoer, Waters particularly loved sexploitation, grindhouse movies, horror, and European art cinema. His influences ranged from experimental queer filmmaker Kenneth Anger to the campy American underground directors Mike and George Kuchar. His short time in film school in New York City introduced him to the queer cultural scene there. Weaving together these influences with his own inimitable sensibility, he followed up *Hag in a Black Leather Jacket* with *Roman Candles* (1966), a Warhol-inspired four-projector experimental film. In 1968, he moved into narrative filmmaking with *Eat Your Makeup* (1968), the story of a crazed woman who forces young models to work themselves to death.

Urban Baltimore, not its suburbs, became the location for all the films that followed. With low-cost housing available and several colleges in the area, especially the Maryland Institute College of Art (MICA), downtown Baltimore was a mecca for young radicals. Socialist feminists and lesbians congregated in the neighborhoods of Waverly and Charles Village, publishing the feminist periodical

*Woman: A Journal of Liberation*, starting cooperatives, and working with the local Black Panther Party. A short-lived Gay Liberation Front formed in 1969. The Metropolitan Church, led in Baltimore by a white man, Reverend Stan Harris, and a black woman, Reverend Lapaula Turner, welcomed gay parishioners and ran an STD clinic.[34] Waters even took the name of his 1977 film *Desperate Living* from a lesbian journal published in the city. But it was the bar scene that most affected him. As a teenager, Waters snuck into a "semilegal" gay club where he saw Pencil, "my first other-side-of-the-tracks drag freak" who lived "with his parents in East Baltimore, way out near the barn where the streetcars turned around."[35] His films were marked by characters modeled on Pencil who traversed wildly different spaces in the city.

New Left and Black Power politics were in the air as well. Black activists continued to fight for equal rights, becoming more militant and nationalistic. Anti-war protestors, including, most famously, Father Philip Berrigan, condemned the Vietnam War as an imperialist atrocity. Countercultural newspapers, like *Harry*, spread the word about events at anarchist bookshops, small theaters, and coffeehouses around the city. But Waters and his friends were not particularly politically active and disavowed the hippie counterculture. In the late 1960s, Waters "felt like a fish out of water. As the rest of my generation babbled about peace and love, I stood back, puzzled, and fantasized about the beginning of the 'hate generation.'"[36] Instead, they called themselves "freaks" or yippies. Abbie Hoffman and Jerry Rubin, turned off by the seriousness of the anti-war left, founded the Youth International Party in 1967, in time to disrupt the Democratic National Convention in Chicago in 1968. As a political party, the yippies were "nonexistent, but as impresarios of the new symbolic politics, Rubin and Hoffman were nonpareil."[37] Their hyperbolic rhetoric, street theater, and embrace of chaos resonated with Waters.

As gay activists proclaimed themselves "out of the closet" and sought public visibility, Waters used his films to create social spaces for people like drag queens who were marginalized even within the gay community. Knowing the right bars allowed him to connect with this social world. He remembered "another favorite strange bar . . . near the waterfront. The clientele is made up of hillbilly truck drivers who come to cruise the half-finished sex changes who hang out in between medical appointments at the nearby Johns Hopkins Hospital."[38] His lack of indignation or moral outrage at people who were often vilified defined his early movies. As he understood, by putting them on the screen—even in exaggerated versions—he was claiming cultural space for them at the same time that they were being removed from real spaces in Baltimore. Mount Vernon, for example, was once a popular neighborhood for male hustlers to pick up customers, but its historic architecture and proximity to downtown led to them inevitably being displaced to provide "the type of residential atmosphere to attract civic leadership and upper-income persons."[39]

Waters landed in this "semi-political socio-cultural stewpot" with his longtime friends Pat Moran, who appeared in several of his films and cast others; Glenn Milstead, who would become famous as the three-hundred-pound drag queen Divine; Mary Vivian Pearce, a Jean Harlow lookalike; and Mink Stole, infamous as the purveyor of the "rosary job" in *Multiple Maniacs*.[40] They soon connected with like-minded bohemians, including Vincent Peranio, Cookie Mueller, David Lochary, Susan Lowe, and George Figgs. Peranio created a quasi-commune in a bakery in Fells Point. They frequented Pete's Hotel, which can be seen in *Multiple Maniacs*, and met Edith Massey, an overweight barmaid of indeterminate age who once wanted to be a dancer and who spoke in a baby doll voice with a heavy Baltimore accent. This group became the core of the Dreamlanders, Waters's "parody of a movie studio."[41] Together, they created cinematic history. Not only was Waters one of the first people to film on the streets of Baltimore, with profound effects on the development of the city's cultural tourism apparatus, but his movies created an entire world populated by drag queens, drug addicts, queers, freaks, and criminals, much in the style of Jean Genet, one of Waters's heroes. The films are often based in familiar genres, like the monster movie or melodrama, but pushed to extremes.

While Waters was a singular genius in bringing his vision to the screen, he was not alone in making films in Baltimore, though there weren't many other filmmakers in the city. Chris Buchman, an optician, and Rex Schneider, an artist, made two films with Baltimore subjects. *Flower Mart* (1965) examined the annual Baltimore cultural event, while *Dantini the Magnificent* (1969) told the story of a local magician. They created a production company and produced an award-winning film on the Paris Peace Talks in 1969. Although the filmmaking community in the city was small, aesthetic differences mattered. Buchman and Schneider were aware of Waters's films but considered them "chic decadence."[42]

Waters drew on local resources, like colleges, which had developed a basic infrastructure for film, first by training and financing students and then by offering them opportunities to screen their work. Production equipment came from university film departments or local TV stations. Johns Hopkins University; MICA; University of Maryland, Baltimore County (UMBC); and the University of Baltimore offered filmmaking classes, and the University of Baltimore hosted the first Baltimore Film Festival in 1970. It featured experimental work by locals, like a silent adaptation of Ambrose Bierce's short story "The Occurrence at Owl Creek Bridge," by Joel Siskin, a Hopkins student. MICA student Henry Saxe used various chemicals to create undulating images moving randomly around the screen. Waters, the "old man of experimental film" in Baltimore at age twenty-two, screened *The Diane Linkletter Story*, a short inspired by the drug-induced suicide of Art Linkletter's daughter.[43] However, there were limitations to what could be done in the city. Facilities to process 16-millimeter film existed in Baltimore, but 35-millimeter had to be sent to New York. A "moonlighting local TV news cameraman with a single-system 16 mm film camera was the sole technician" on Waters's early films.[44] By the time of *Female Trouble*, though, Waters needed more technical skill. UMBC, thanks to ambitious film professors, owned state-of-the-art production equipment, which was loaned to Waters, who also got some technical advice as well. Even though Waters was still figuring out how to make films himself, being on his film crew became an important training opportunity. Steve Yeager, a production assistant on *Female Trouble*, went on to direct *On the Block* and produce *Divine Trash*. Waters's set designer and giant-lobster craftsman Vincent Peranio became a professional designer and art director for film and television. Pat Moran became a well-known casting director for shows like *Homicide* and *The Wire*. But, before these successes, they were simply a group of young bohemians chasing their dreams like an out-of-control monster down an abandoned Baltimore street.

**Filth, Beautiful Filth** | Although John Waters has been called the "Pope of Trash" and the "Prince of Puke," when he created his film production company in the late 1960s, he gave it the strangely romantic name Dreamland Studios. The name shows both his love of Baltimore—it was a dreamland—and how he constructed his own vision of it—it was *his* dream, after all. Like urban renewal leaders, Waters pointed his camera lens deliberately. Both constructed visions of blight. But Waters hated what neighborhood conservation and urban renewal did to the city. "Don't pay any attention to the guide books," he wrote condemning the municipal tourist apparatus that he would later become part of. "They'll tell you all about the 'New Baltimore,' the Inner Harbor, the Baltimore City Homesteading Program, and the City Fair; but this is not why I choose to stay in Baltimore. It's the unbelievable people" who represented an older, antimodern way of life threatened by the new.[45] Urban renewal's drive to modernize and rationalize meant the destruction of the decaying built environment and the displacement of the people Waters favored. In the films that made him a cult hero, he adopted the obsessions of urban renewal, while rejecting its goals. Instead of sleek modernity, his dreamland was populated by deviant outcasts.

By seeking out decaying areas of the city, Waters ironically followed the logic of *The Baltimore Plan*. He too carefully chose his locations, using visuals and voice-overs to make sure that viewers would feel disgust.[46] As he said in 1975, "Baltimore lends itself to the type of film I'm making. It's a sleazy city with a lot of sleazy people around."[47] Echoing the quasi-documentary quality of *The Baltimore Plan*, Waters downplayed his role in constructing Baltimore. He suggested that he was simply capturing Baltimore as it was, that he just pointed his camera at what was happening on the street. His actors were assumed to be real people playing themselves, but Waters never allowed improvisation. His control as director was absolute, but, because his characters were so strange, viewers ironically thought they had to be real. Even the local underground countercultural newspaper *Harry* accepted them as true. Its review of *Multiple Maniacs* conflated the fictional version of Baltimore with the real one. "Many fine old Baltimore monuments from the Fells Point area are depicted: Pete's Bar, glue-sniffing transvestites, rowhouses, a cop on the take. Existential realism, indeed."[48] Waters's films, like urban renewal films, were viewed as documentaries rather than constructed narratives, even by viewers who were deeply familiar with the areas being depicted.

Though the stated goal of urban renewal was to eradicate blight, Waters wanted something more like urban filthification. For Waters, filth defined a negative relationship to dominant social identities. Filth encompassed queer sexuality, criminality, and anti-bourgeois values. Like urban renewal leaders, he saw blighted areas of the city producing filth, but, unlike them, he depicted filth as generating identities—identities that were at least as viable as socially accepted roles like worker, citizen, activist, or heterosexual. His films, especially *Pink Flamingos* and *Female Trouble*, are defined by "their unforgiving embrace of the perverted, the obscene, the criminally insane, the monstrous and the pathologically unhygienic, without any attempt to bring such subjects or acts into cultural intelligibility or sanction."[49] Clearly a reaction to the countercultural politics, New Left, and gay liberation happening around him, Waters's films must also be seen in relationship to the urban renewal that was remaking Baltimore and cities around the nation.

*Pink Flamingos* elaborates on the politics of filth that Waters had been developing in his earlier films. This twisted version of the Hatfields and the McCoys follows two families: Babs Johnson (played by Divine), her mother, Edie, and son, Crackers, and Connie and Raymond Marble, as they battle for the title of "filthiest people alive." The Johnson family lives outside "the teeming metropolis known as downtown Baltimore," in the unincorporated town of Phoenix, Maryland.[50] Depicted as "white trash," their going into Baltimore to indulge in crime mirrors the anxiety that followed the migration of rural whites into the city during World War II. The city-dwelling Marbles are no paragons of propriety, however. Raymond scares women in parks by exposing himself (with a sausage tied to his penis) and then steals their purses. Their large house hides a grotesque secret. They have imprisoned young women who are impregnated by their servant Channing (played by Channing Wilroy, who had been a Committee member on *The Buddy Deane Show*). The babies are sold to lesbian couples. The Marbles begin the war with Babs when they send her human feces as a birthday present. Babs and Crackers then break into the Marbles' house. They lick the furniture, engage in incestuous sexual relations, tie Channing up, and release the women, who castrate him. Meanwhile, the Marbles burn down Babs's beloved trailer. Finally, Babs captures the Marbles and tries them in a kangaroo court, inviting the media to watch as she executes them. The film ends with the infamous scene of Divine, both as Johnson and herself, eating real dog feces off the sidewalk. One reviewer asked, "Is this part of the new world they have in mind?" acknowledging that Waters was creating a new world, much like the urban planners hard at work in city hall.[51] But whereas the city's goal was the creation of environments that encouraged socially approved behavior, Waters depicted queer family units cohered around filth.

This becomes more specifically connected to urban space in *Female Trouble*. This film follows the downward trajectory of Dawn

Davenport, played by Divine. She runs away from her suburban home to Baltimore, where she becomes a single mother to her daughter, Taffy, and works as a waitress, dancer, prostitute, and thief. She marries a hairdresser who works in a salon owned by Donald and Donna Dasher. Obsessed with crime, they convince Divine to model for them even after she is disfigured when her husband's Aunt Ida throws acid in her face. Insane and under the control of the Dashers, who encourage her to greater depths of criminal behavior, she shoots the audience that has come to see her perform. She's imprisoned. The film ends with her death by electric chair.

Filth is explicitly connected with urban decay. As Connie and Raymond Marble approach Divine's apartment in a rundown section of the city (actually Fells Point), we see them walking through an alley that looks like an outtake from *The Baltimore Plan*. There's garbage on the street, a trash bag, and a door falling off its hinges. Connie, played by Mary Vivian Pearce, is disgusted, saying, "God this neighborhood is hideous, I'm scared rats are going to bite my nylons." Her words echo the disgust expressed by Frances Morton and the social worker in *The Baltimore Plan* but with no sense of pity or desire to help. Raymond, played by David Lochary, finds beauty instead of repulsion. He replies, "Crime breeds in these neighborhoods, so it's really a perfect place for our crime. I rather like it . . . [Y]ou must get used to this lowlife world. Here lies beauty. Crime and beauty." Never seen as beautiful in a conventional sense, these neighborhoods appeal because of their "lowlife" qualities. While Raymond adopts the language of the reformer—"crime breeds in these neighborhoods"—he has no interest in stamping it out. Instead, it defines these spaces as productive—of crime, new social identities, and communities, but only for white people. There was an unacknowledged racial component to these discourses: while blight was generally depicted as affecting black people, filthification created spaces for white queerness to become publicly visible.

Countercultural youth, underground art lovers, and members of the LGBTQ community responded by buying tickets in droves.

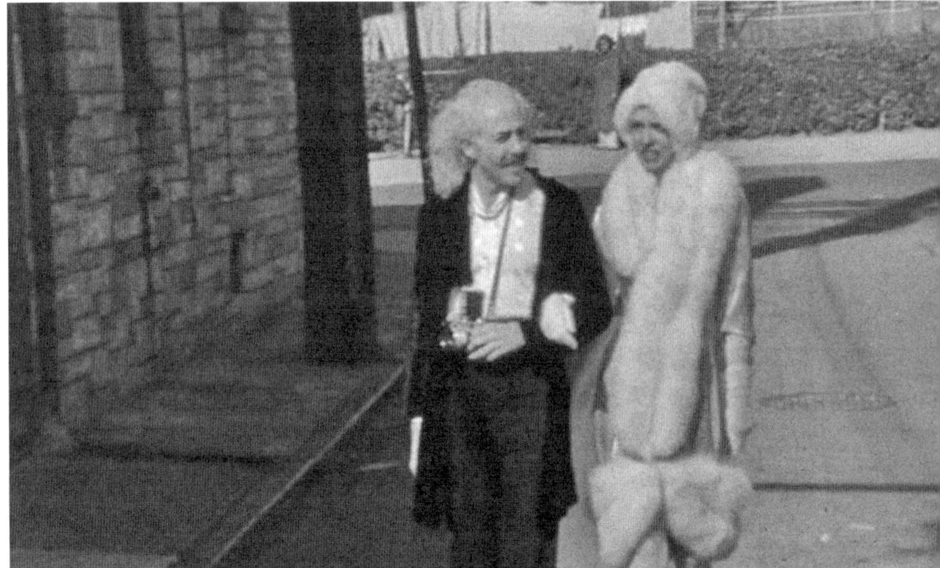

Raymond Marble summarizes his, and John Waters's, theory of urban filthification in this still from *Female Trouble* (1974). Blight should be maintained to nurture deviant identities.

R. H. Gardner, the theater and film critic for the *Baltimore Sun*, saw Waters's movies "as repelling in their tastelessness as they are (save for intermittent flashes of humor) unbearable in their dullness. Yet, wherever they are shown, lines, composed mostly of the blue-jeaned young, form around the block."[52] *Variety* agreed, predicting that *Female Trouble* would be "a probable sleeper in urban and college markets . . . Film purists, establishment critics, and ordinary folk will shudder."[53]

**Divine Liberation |** Even though Waters began making films in the age of gay liberation, his characters don't affirm simple sexual identities. As Richard Dyer has written, *Female Trouble* "is not in any obvious sense gay: most of the characters are heterosexual, or sometimes lesbian, and mostly concerned with self-advancement, filth, hairdos, killing, eating, and fucking."[54] Queerness, rather than gay identity, defines its point of view. But like the gay liberation movement, Waters's characters, especially Divine, are obsessed with public visibility.

By the early 1970s, the gay liberation movement urged gays and lesbians to proclaim their sexual identity publicly to friends, family, and neighbors. More than just an individual act, coming out was part of a larger strategy of visibility, summarized best in the gay liberation motto of "out of the closets and into the streets." As Martha Shelley proclaimed in the countercultural newspaper *Rat*, "Look out straights! Here comes the Gay Liberation Front springing up like warts all over the bland face of Amerika, causing shudders of indigestion in the delicately balanced bowels of the movement."[55] Going public affirmed an unapologetic gay identity defined through its difference from mainstream American values. It showed straight people how many gay people there were, helped create a sense of community, and became the basis for political organizing. As historians have shown, though, even within gay liberation, organizations debated who should represent the movement.[56] Drag queens were not welcome throughout the gay community, especially as the 1970s became dominated by the gay clone aesthetic of hard-bodied masculinity.[57] Trans women were disparaged in certain lesbian circles. Refusing to place himself in any political or social movement, Waters depicted transvestites, drug addicts, grotesque bodies, and sexual perverts in neutral if not positive terms, claiming public visibility for marginalized communities both within the LGBTQ community and outside it. Importantly, he did so by filming on the streets of Baltimore, suggesting that queerness was located in the city, even while urban renewal eliminated spaces where gay men and women congregated.

Larger than life, Divine was the star of Waters's movies. She was played by Glenn Milstead, a longtime friend of Waters. While most of his actors mumbled through wooden performances, Divine stole every scene she appeared in, beginning with her first important role as

Jackie Kennedy in *Eat Your Makeup* (1968). Milstead soon developed Divine into a unique queer antihero who was so grotesque that she did not fit into any simple category of sexual or political identity. *Pink Flamingos* (1972) and *Female Trouble* (1974) are the apex of this trajectory. Her character would be tamed for more mainstream-oriented films like *Polyester* (1981) and *Hairspray* (1988). In both *Flamingos* and *Female Trouble*, there is a key scene where Divine, "unveiling his 'look' for the world to see," wearing a tight-fitting gown and high heels, unnaturally dyed hair, and makeup that makes her look like a deranged circus clown, "undulat[es] her way down the street with the confidence of a fashion model on the runway. Blowing kisses and smiling to dumbfounded strangers" unaware they were being filmed.[58] Waters and his cameraman filmed from a car driving slowly next to her. So outrageous it seemed real, Divine's "coming out" evoked the growing visibility of gays, lesbians, and transgender people.

Divine's queerness is made visible in these films by pushing African Americans to the background and making them foils whose reactions underscore her outrageousness. As urban renewal and residential segregation displaced black people who already had few options for where they could live, Waters similarly marginalized black Baltimoreans, both as black and as gay. He was not alone in doing so. Cultural nationalism and Black Power in the 1960s and 1970s included many women but idealized heteropatriarchy.[59] Black Panther imagery of unsmiling men with guns and rhetoric condemning enemies as "faggots" put straight masculinity at the center of its movement. As Leerom Medovoi has argued, white and black radicals like the yippies and the Panthers shared this "model of masculinized libido."[60] For their part, white gay activist movements and, later, academic queer studies often didn't acknowledge race in their thinking about politics and identity.[61]

These scenes showed audiences how they should react to Divine by capturing the spectators acting "as if Divine had been dropped from a flying saucer and was having an epileptic fit. Not a soul would think it was a scene from a movie."[62] Who were these spectators? In both *Pink Flamingos* and *Female Trouble*, they are mostly African Americans, unsurprising given the downtown locations that Waters chose for filming. The unaware extras are used to portray the audience's other—the shocked, disgusted, horrified, unhip outsider. As viewers we are "torn between watching her and watching the onlookers," which makes clear that the audience for the film is not the same as the people gawking at Divine inside the frame.[63] During the filming of *Female Trouble*, Waters had more trouble getting the reactions he wanted, perhaps because in that scene Divine is wearing makeup to make her face look like she's been burned by acid. "I think the downtown shoppers were just being polite and didn't want to gawk at someone who was so obviously disfigured. Realizing drastic action was called for, I yelled for Divine . . . and we drove around looking for a more hostile crowd." He finds it with a group of "drunken bums on a side street, warming themselves in front of a bonfire." Divine does her modeling act again. The homeless men grab her, "too drunk to realize the tits they pawed were just foam rubber and the ass they pinched was removable." Waters pushed Divine back into the car. He decided to "later cut the shot because I thought some of the bums might object to making their screen debut in such a potentially embarrassing scene."[64] Was Waters really concerned about the embarrassment of these homeless men? More likely, their desire for Divine did not supply the disgust needed for the scene. Of course, he does not give the mainly African American Baltimoreans in the other scenes the opportunity to stave off embarrassment. That he seems unconcerned suggests that he understood that the audience for his films was mainly young queer and artsy whites on college campuses, going to midnight screenings in New York City, or vacationing in the gay mecca Provincetown. In fact, it was not until 1977's *Desperate Living* that we see a black queer character, played by Jean Hill, in a Waters film.

In the movies that made Waters the bad boy of underground cinema, black people are literally sidelined, depicted, at best, as spectators who help to construct the liberated white queerness of

Divine. Yet, of course, there were black gays, lesbians, and transgender people in Baltimore. Waters himself was amazed that the black drag queen Peaches would perform with the band the Upsetters for appreciative audiences of college frat brothers who would have likely beaten her if they had encountered her on the street.[65] But none of this made it into his movies. Instead, black people haunt the background. In *Female Trouble*, moments before the alley scene between Connie and Raymond Marble, a black family appears. They watch for a moment, hovering at the edge of the shot. The focus remains on the white actors. In the next moment, they're gone. As urban renewal remade Baltimore to the detriment of its black neighborhoods and residents, Waters also pushed them to the margins of his dream version of the city.

**Shooting Dreamland** | How could Waters film transvestism, nudity, drug use, and transgressive sexual acts in public? He ably utilized his whiteness and the zones of desolation created by urban renewal to his advantage. Like for the makers of *West Side Story*, who filmed on location near the site where the Lincoln Center was being built, "the destruction of urban renewal created a spectacular film set rather than the foundation for bettering the lives of those displaced."[66] The urban renewal process took years. Once they suspected that an area was being considered for the site for an urban renewal project, homeowners, renters, and business owners would stop upkeep on their properties. In the Rosemont neighborhood in West Baltimore, the residents argued that "the condemnation ordinance in our neighborhood did not give any incentives for maintaining or preserving their homes." In response, many people left. The vacant homes that remained drew vandalism and crime.[67] In East Baltimore, two hundred homes were destroyed in the early 1960s to build an industrial park, but the land remained vacant until the new post office headquarters was built there in 1970.[68] When urban renewal agencies identified the actual sites for renewal, there would often be an outcry by the public, leading to protests and court battles that had to be completed before demolition, rehabilitation, or construction could take place. Then, as renewal got underway, what were once neighborhoods or commercial areas were overrun by construction crews and equipment. Charles Center took more than a decade to build, unsettling a space of thirty-three acres downtown. While the Greater Baltimore Committee and the Charles Center management team predicted that the project would have a long-term beneficial effect, even they had to admit that, "back when the plan was first announced in 1958, it spelled the 'kiss of death' for a lot of real estate immediately, because people began to realize that this was an area in which the properties were going to be taken . . . There were vacancy signs everywhere."[69] The domino effect continued. As the city condemned buildings and construction tore up streets, fewer resources were given to surrounding areas, making them a haven for subversive or illicit uses. Every step of this process created zones of desolation that Waters could use for filming.

Fells Point was a particularly rich location for Waters's filmmaking since urban renewal had not changed it much since William Manchester described it as Sticktown in *The City of Anger*.[70] It "wasn't built up with concrete and cement, it was wood. Old wooden benches and wooden piers and there was a lot of land that wasn't even touched yet."[71] Factories sat abandoned, and a rusted freighter ship bobbed in the harbor. A fierce battle over the location of a freeway through Fells Point galvanized citizen activism in the neighborhood, bringing working-class residents together with newer middle-class homeowners who had been drawn by the historic housing stock. The fight over the proposed freeway was waged for years. Robert Maier, who worked as a location scout and in production for several Waters films, described the neighborhood as "an end-of-the-world scene, with a bleak future," as portions of it were condemned. As he explained, though, "Such negatives were positives for Baltimore's more adventurous (and broke) students, artists, and bohemians of the 1960s."[72] The bohemian atmosphere and the historic houses meant that, after being spared as a potential site for the freeway, gentrification ultimately displaced many of the residents who were there in the 1960s and 1970s.[73]

Waters's guerrilla style meant that public spaces were his locations. With no permits, he hid or rushed his filmmaking to evade authorities. Even though there was no official structure for giving film permits, Waters had surprisingly few difficulties and only one run-in with the law. "I found the best way to get a location was just to walk in and boldly ask if I could film. If the people were not used to this request, they generally would stammer a confused, 'When?' and I would tell them, 'Right now.' They generally said yes, thinking it would be interesting and would give them something to talk about . . . We'd film immediately, before they changed their minds, and get out. Hit and run."[74] Even the local post office and the Baltimore city jail allowed him to film on their premises. Contrast this extraordinary level of access to the experience of African American filmmaker Haile Gerima, who shot his film *Bush Mama* on the streets of Los Angeles. The LA police harassed Gerima and his black crew, searching them and, in one instance, arresting them on suspicion that they had stolen their equipment.[75] Waters's whiteness protected him from such outrages, except when he stepped onto private, highly surveilled property.

His only arrest occurred while filming *Mondo Trasho* without permission on the grounds of a private university. Waters called it a "gutter film" shot in "alleys, gutters, Laundromats, and deserted areas around Baltimore" suggesting blight and desolation.[76] But the place where he chose to film a key scene only seemed deserted. Pearce, having just had her toes sucked by a foot fetishist in a park, was supposed to stumble out of the brush onto a road. Meanwhile, Divine, driving a red Cadillac convertible and distracted by a naked hitchhiker, played by Mark Isherwood, runs over Pearce, killing her. To give the impression of being in a wooded area, they filmed on the leafy campus of Johns Hopkins University, north of downtown. As they were in the middle of filming, a campus police officer, having spotted the nude man, burst into view. They jumped into their cars and peeled out, hoping to avoid arrest. But the campus police called the Baltimore city police, who picked up Waters and others still in the convertible. Mink Stole was arrested later in her bathtub, noting to the press that "there was more exposure in the arrest than in the incident."[77] Judge Solomon Liss dropped the charges after reading a poem he had written for the occasion:

> Old Baltimore is in a spin
> Because of Isherwood's display of skin
> . . . And so, go then and sin no more
> Disrobe, if need be, but behind the door.[78]

More than a funny anecdote, it proves by contrast the lack of monitoring of downtown Baltimore spaces. Universities were instrumental in the implementation of urban renewal as they took over adjacent neighborhoods.[79] Simultaneously, they tightly controlled the use of public space on their campuses, even if, in this instance, the judge gave them a break.

**Amazing Grace** | If Waters's films ironically benefitted from urban renewal, art also fulfilled a more critical role in the era. From murals to movies, artists expressed anti-renewal sentiments through their work.[80] While many of these efforts were small in scope or locally specific, some Hollywood films critiqued urban renewal. The 1974 film *Amazing Grace*, starring comedian Jackie "Moms" Mabley a year before she died, is a weakly comic film about 1970s urban politics, urban renewal, and black activism that offers a different perspective on urban renewal than do the preceding films. Set in Baltimore, portions were filmed at Baltimore's Morgan State College, around the downtown, and in Philadelphia. Neither the *Baltimore Sun* nor the *Afro-American* lauded the film. R. H. Gardner in the *Sun* thought it "malign[ed] the city government, the newspapers, and by implying that they are so stupid any dishonest politician can manipulate them for his own ends, the inhabitants as well."[81] The *Afro* described it as irreverent but agreed that it "showed Baltimore in a bad light."[82] Regardless, the film, part of a growing number of black-centered movies released in the 1970s, spoke to issues relevant to the black community.

Released the year after President Richard Nixon replaced urban renewal with a community development block grant program, the plot follows Moms as Grace, an elderly woman living in a rundown neighborhood in East Baltimore. At the opening of the film, a newly retired train porter and erstwhile entertainer, played by Baltimore native Slappy White, moves in with her. They notice that Welton Waters, a black man running for mayor, played by longtime character actor Moses Gunn (who would later return to Baltimore on the TV show *Homicide*), and his wife, Creola, have moved in next door. Their upper-class ways raise Moms's suspicions, as does the fact that a black man is running for mayor. It turns out that Waters is being paid off by the white power structure in Baltimore, which Moms figures out when she sees the white campaign manager in Waters's house. As she says, "Ain't no white man got no business in colored folks' houses this time of night." Although he has two law degrees, he's running to take the black vote away from another challenger, ensuring that the current political administration will remain in power. For his efforts, the white mayor will put him in charge of the $10 million urban renewal program. "With all that money in your hands," says the incumbent's campaign manager, "you ought to be able to find a way for some of it to end up in your pocket." Living in this working-class black neighborhood is a ruse to try to prove his authentic blackness with the community.

The plot revolves around racial passing and black people's lack of access to institutional power structures. Waters may be black, but his political commitments suggest that he's only passing as such. His alcoholic wife, Creola, passes for white or Puerto Rican in the film, though when her wig is pulled off, her afro outs her as a black woman. When the white politicians meet in a backroom with Waters, complete with a haze of cigar smoke, the campaign manager says, "I think we all realize that Mr. Waters is black, but I think we can all ignore that. He has." Although Waters is accomplished and highly educated, he has no access to fundraising money because of his race, so he believes that he must sell out his community to ensure his personal success. The white elite, of course, has no interest in the black community except to use it as a pawn to access federal government largesse. Liberal whites are not to be trusted, because their concern is for power, and using black people to get power is completely acceptable. Moms uses her invisibility as a black woman to her advantage, sneaking into the mayor's office as a cleaning woman and eavesdropping on his conversations. The white mayor is a boor, barking into his phone about "liberal fairy liberals" and placating a concerned listener that "there's no one here" even as Moms, having filled in for a friend who cleans the mayor's office (apparently without comment), is dusting nearby.

Moms offers a different view. Like the maternal figures of the early civil rights movement, such as Ella Baker, Moms utilizes a discourse of motherly and Christian concern for her community that draws from a black infrastructure located in churches, houses, and black colleges and populated primarily by the older working class and young students. In swaying youth to vote for him during a scene filmed at Morgan State College, a hotbed of civil rights activism, Waters says that he was "cured" of his racial self-hatred not by radicalism or by a movement but by Moms. Moms sees young people as the future, calling them the "dark meat of God's chicken." It works, of course. Waters wins the election, and the black community in Baltimore is brought into the political mainstream.

Although the movie is set in Baltimore, its political commentary expands beyond a single city. Baltimore stands in as a quintessential black-majority city that is still controlled by institutions that exploit its residents rather than represent them, much in the way that David Simon would later use Baltimore as the setting for *The Wire* to depict problems endemic to any number of other cities. Rather than needing white people to save black neighborhoods as suggested in

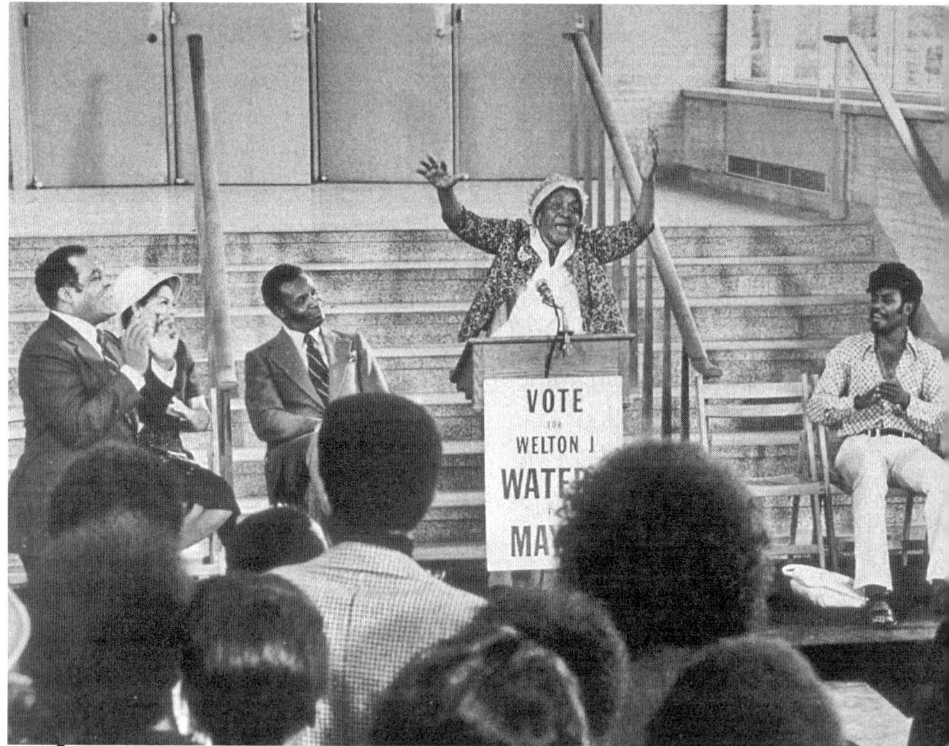


Comedian Moms Mabley rouses a crowd of student activists in her final film, *Amazing Grace*. Set in Baltimore, the movie depicted urban renewal as an anti-black displacement program.
Photofest

*The Baltimore Plan*, black people, inspired by Moms as a neighborhood leader, take care of their own community. In portraying a moment when black political power challenged white politicians, *Amazing Grace* depicts urban renewal as a political bargaining chip. A decade before, and the offer to Welton Waters would have likely been control of the local community action agency. Urban renewal is understood as a political rather than social construction in this film. Both *The Baltimore Plan* and John Waters's early films show blight as something that exists, never acknowledging their own role in defining it. *Amazing Grace* suggests that the urban renewal program is a political game designed not to improve the city but to maintain certain power structures and displace and disenfranchise black citizens through the rhetorical concept of blight. It's not hard to imagine that if Welton Waters had become head of the urban renewal program, the first neighborhood to get condemned would have been the one where Moms lived.

**The Filth and the Fury** | It was cool and dry on April 7, 1968, when John Waters and his ragtag gang of actors, designers, artists, and pranksters drove to Bohemian National Cemetery in East Baltimore. Their friend, Maelcum Soul, born Patricia Ann Soul, was going to be buried there. Only twenty-seven when she died of kidney failure, she had lived an exciting life. She starred in *Roman Candles* and *Eat Your Makeup*, which had premiered only a few weeks earlier; posed as a nude model; and worked as a bartender at famed artists' hangout Martick's. She was a central figure in Baltimore's mid-1960s bohemian scene who painted her face blue to match her outfit, glued spit curls to her face with real glue, and dyed her hair maroon. She influenced Waters's depiction of women on film. And, of course, she was their friend. Nothing would keep them from this funeral. But getting there was difficult. It wasn't a long drive from downtown Baltimore, but it was bad timing. As Waters remembered, "We fought our way to her funeral through the riots following Martin Luther King's death." He reported their shock at what they saw. Soul had been "laid out without her usual makeup."[83]

By the time the National Guard left on April 14, six people would be dead, many more injured, and hundreds of buildings damaged or destroyed. In recollecting that moment, Waters didn't acknowledge any of this. What he remembered was the erasure of his friend's flamboyance, turning her into what none of them wanted to be: normal. Young and insolent, perhaps, but Waters's recollection suggests the deep divide between black and white youth in Baltimore. For one the riots were an impediment, while for the other they were an outcry against poverty, racism, and urban renewal. While Waters was fascinated with black culture, his commitments were to cultural revolution.

Business leaders, politicians, even social workers used the concept of blight to reshape the city through the 1960s. Film was critical to this process. Visualizing blight through films like *The Baltimore Plan* aroused public sympathy for the poor and concern for property values, health, and safety. Stopping blight through neighborhood conservation and urban renewal was meant to ensure that crime and disease did not spread from the blighted areas while providing better housing for the poor and working class, many of whom were African Americans. Enforcement of housing codes, however, often led to the eviction of black tenants. Even when bad housing was replaced with better housing, it was often too expensive for working-class people. Usually, though, housing wasn't replaced at all. Instead, it was turned into office buildings and other downtown amenities designed to draw suburbanites back to the city to boost flagging revenues. By 1968, Baltimore residents had tired of urban renewal's promises. When the city obtained $22 million in federal urban renewal grant funding, it sought voter approval for a bond issue to purchase and clear 240 acres of land in the Inner Harbor. Voters rejected the proposal.[84] It would take more than a decade for the Inner Harbor project to open.

John Waters defined blight differently. First, rough-edged places like Fells Point were cheap enough for artsy young people to live in. Ironically, their living there gave the neighborhood a caché that would prime it for gentrification. Waters's films also shaped the landscape in contradictory ways. He didn't portray blight as a scourge to be eradicated. Instead, he turned blight into filth. These decaying environments allowed filth to flourish. Filth's anarchic queerness and deviance was not simply reducible to a gay identity or a political position. It was a radical overturning of conventional morality. That he expressed this vision on the streets of Baltimore is not accidental.

Because of urban renewal, the city was full of zones of desolation, places where the predominantly white countercultural young could live and hang out. Places where Waters could film Divine having sex with herself, eating dog feces, and parading a massive mohawk hairdo without being bothered by the authorities. In these desolate urban locations, Waters visually portrayed white queerness. His films have been canonized as essential queer cinema, but these early works marginalized black people, literally pushing them to the edges of the frame or using them as spectators for white queer people. It would not be until 1977's *Desperate Living* (filmed in a rural area outside of Baltimore) that he would portray a black queer character. *Hairspray* would take up white racism and the civil rights movement as its topic in 1988. But, before that, Waters helped define Baltimore as queer and bohemian. Ironically, even though Waters thumbed his nose at bourgeois decency, his work helped propel the creation of Baltimore as an arts-driven tourist city.

Of course, black Baltimoreans had their own ideas about urban renewal. *Amazing Grace* positioned Baltimore as a quintessentially black city, with a vibrant community of activists. Through its chitlin' circuit humor, it argued that blight was defined by those in power to help themselves, disputing the official discourses of urban renewal and neighborhood conservation found in innumerable pamphlets, reports, and news articles. Next, I consider a different counternarrative. With funding from the War on Poverty, black Baltimoreans, mainly young people, published poetry, art, and stories about their city in a scrappy magazine called *Chicory*.

# "THE MOST AUTHENTIC MICROPHONE OF BLACK FOLKS TALKING EVER DEVISED"

## *Chicory* and the Poetry of Human Renewal

The twelve-year-old girl named Carol Calloway put it in the context of a fairy tale. "Once upon a time," she wrote, "their [*sic*] was a riot." It "was started by a white person killing Martin Luther King, Jr." If John Waters and his friends saw the fires and destruction from the window of a moving car and journalists descended on still-smoldering neighborhoods to get quotes and leave, she lived it, "was in the house when the riot was going on," and could see "army and troop trucks driving up and down the street."[1] Like an evil witch, the police and military threatened children with arrest if they strayed outside, so she huddled, scared, in her home. J. Allen Jones was there, too. An adult, Jones interpreted things in terms of change over time, something the child could not. Things were bad before the riot. Black people barely had enough food to feed their children. But, afterward, there were "no hungry little brothers" and a "couple drunk big brothers." Even if "one Jew had a heart attack . . . a little brother had his first meal in a month."[2]

These street-level perspectives on the events of April 1968 were offered in the pages of an extraordinary mimeographed poetry and arts magazine called *Chicory*, published in Baltimore by the Enoch Pratt Free Library from 1966 to 1983. Initial funding came through the Community Action Program of the Office of Economic Opportunity, created by President Lyndon B. Johnson as part of the War on Poverty. Inspired by the Black Arts movement, the editors, Sam Cornish, Lucian W. Dixon, Augustus Brathwaite, Melvin Edward Brown, and E. Adam Jackson, made the magazine a space for cultural expression by the residents of some of the poorest neighborhoods in Baltimore. Overwhelmingly African American, they published their poetry and prose with little editing. *Chicory* also published "street chatter," or overheard conversations that captured the poetry of the street in the vernacular. As these examples from the 1968 riot show, neighborhood residents used the pages of *Chicory* to describe their experiences and interpret events that affected their lives. They revealed their visions of the future, views of the past, and political opinions. Within these pages, ideas were discussed and debated. Circulated throughout the neighborhood centers that offered services to the poor and working class, the magazine became nationally known in 1969 with the publication of an anthology of its pieces called *Chicory: Young Voices from the Black Ghetto*. That year, the *Baltimore Afro-American* called the book and magazine "the most authentic microphone of black folks talking ever devised."[3]

Grassroots black cultural productions in the 1960s and 1970s, like *Chicory*, must be understood in relation to the larger political structures of liberalism, especially the War on Poverty as practiced on the federal and local levels. As historian Daniel Widener has argued, alongside the War on Poverty's social and political programs, there was a simultaneous "cultural War on Poverty." Liberal institutions saw "art as a means of generating a greater investment in American society among working-class blacks" but also as revealing "the limits of reform in a radicalizing moment."[4] Blacks Arts and Black Power activists who renounced nonviolence and found strength in their African heritage made strange bedfellows with the architects of postwar liberalism who sought the integration of black people into the postwar consensus. But artists needed resources for their work, and the Community Action Program and the Ford Foundation became two of the most important funders of their efforts.[5] By opening up an "operational space," in historian Devin Fergus's terms, this funding allowed black artists and Black Power activists to develop, promote, and spread their ideas, as long as they toned down their rhetoric.[6] Interestingly, the depth of this connection is underplayed in scholarship. James Smethurst's brilliant *The Black Arts Movement: Literary Nationalism in the 1960s and 1970s* examines the interplay between regional artists and organizations and the national Black Arts movement, suggesting the subtle ways each affected the other. While Smethurst includes civil rights legislation in a timeline of the Black Arts movement in an appendix to his book, he doesn't include the passage of the legislation creating the War on Poverty, even though it funded both Amiri Baraka's nationally recognized and influential Black Arts Repertory Theater/School and less-well-known projects like *Chicory*.[7]

Thousands of projects like *Chicory* existed around the country, thanks to federal or philanthropic funding. Hidden in libraries, archives, and special collections, as well as people's memories and personal papers, most have been forgotten. *Chicory* had been held in storage boxes at the Enoch Pratt Free Library until I asked to look at it in 2014, which led to its being digitized and made available online.[8] But examined within their historical and geographical context, these projects offer important insights into the relationship between arts and policy and between radicalism and liberalism. *Chicory* also gives us a peek into what black Baltimoreans were thinking about their city in a moment of intense change.

*Chicory* existed in a complicated cultural space. On one hand, Baltimore's white liberals funded it because they saw it as part of a larger program of "human renewal," which was the social equivalent of urban renewal. Focused on fighting poverty by helping mainly African American residents become more productive citizens, Baltimore's *Plan for Action* (1964) explained, "it was the analogy to physical renewal that led to the term 'human renewal' . . . The plan would serve to mobilize all resources in a coordinated and comprehensive attack on human problems in blighted neighborhoods." Human renewal would help the African American community assimilate into mainstream society, not uproot it, which the rise of Black Power and black nationalism and the urban uprisings of the mid-1960s suggested was on the horizon.

Part of a spate of African American cultural programs during this era, *Chicory* was seen by white liberals as serving two other important roles. It offered white liberals insight into the conditions of black life.[9] They wanted to understand what black people experienced in order to empathize with them. As John L. Erlich, professor of social work at the University of Michigan and a supporter of increasing black enrollment there, exclaimed in prefatory comments to the *Chicory* book, "A special challenge is offered to those of us who are white: to look to our responsibility for the destructive effects of poverty and racism, and to give full recognition to those who might best interpret their meaning to us."[10] Black people must speak the truth of their lives, while whites must listen and make change. Such surveillance also dovetailed with human renewal's need for data about black populations in order to change them.

Finally, *Chicory* was intended as a release valve. In an era defined by urban insurrections against police brutality, political disenfranchisement, poverty, and racism, liberals imagined self-expression through art as a way that black communities could talk about their problems without resorting to riots. As one disgruntled black worker from Baltimore wrote in the national Black Panther newspaper, "We all know that the federal government only initiates and supports the poverty program in so-called, highly explosive areas. The purpose for this being, is to keep niggers off the street, and into (supposedly) some gainful and constructive environment."[11]

While human renewal tried to reshape the residents of the inner city in Baltimore to be more middle class, the writers and editors of *Chicory* took advantage of the opportunity afforded by the program and the freedom the library gave them to make the magazine that they wanted. For the creators of *Chicory*, which included two librarians, Evelyn Levy, who directed the Enoch Pratt Free Library's community action programs, and Thelma Bell, the first African American children's librarian at Pratt, and its editors (particularly Sam Cornish, the founding editor), *Chicory* was a way to leverage the opportunity presented by the War on Poverty. For the librarians, *Chicory* connected the library with the black community. It was part of an array of programs and services offered to expand literacy and use of the library by African Americans. For Cornish and the other editors, *Chicory* was a black public sphere where authors could debate ideas in its pages. The editors generally published submitted material as it was, rather than going through the editorial process of a traditional literary magazine. While mainstream black newspapers have long been seen as central to the black public sphere, *Chicory* was even more radically open to community members.[12] As gender studies scholar Gwendolyn D. Pough writes of the role of hip hop as a black public sphere, *Chicory* was a space where individuals "discussed issues of collective good, worked toward change and challenged state power" while also "reshaping the public gaze in such a way as to be recognized as human beings" who are also black.[13]

*Chicory* accomplished four goals. Writers regularly criticized the institutions of liberalism through which human renewal was put into practice, like social work, welfare, and community centers. Other state institutions came under fire, especially the police, portrayed as an invading force who abused their power to oppress black communities. Many writers wrote about Black Power, black nationalism, and cultural nationalism in ways clearly inspired by the Black Arts movement. Writers offered varied suggestions for how the civil rights movement should adapt to urban life, what the black community needed to strengthen itself, and the relationship of the black community to white people. Following from Black Power/Black Arts invocation of "black is beautiful," another kind of counternarrative emphasized joy and love instead of desperation and pain. While white liberals sought out images of black poverty and destitution to support their social reforms, *Chicory* writers depicted the strength and beauty of the black community. *Chicory's* editors used the opportunities created by human renewal to spur black cultural production in and about Baltimore.

**Rooting *Chicory* in Human Renewal** | In Baltimore, human renewal grew out of the Baltimore Plan, which emphasized "rehabilitating the people" who lived in the pilot area along with their surroundings.[14] "A Letter to Ourselves," written by Gordon Manser, executive secretary of the Baltimore Area Health and Welfare Council; George B. Brain, superintendent of public instruction; and David Wallace, urban planner, took these ideas and outlined the basics of human renewal for Baltimore with the hope that the Ford Foundation would fund the project. That the letter was addressed to a group of elite civic leaders as "ourselves" suggested that human renewal was envisioned as a top-down process. The purpose would be "changing the attitudes and behavior of people" through specially designed programs so that they would "become responsible, achieving beings with respect to their personal and communal affairs."[15]

After the Ford Foundation passed on funding, the proposal was reworked as Baltimore's *Plan for Action*, the blueprint for how the city would use War on Poverty funding. The *Plan for Action* positioned human renewal as the counterpart of urban renewal, which was simply insufficient for ensuring the city's vitality. Without efforts to "deal with human problems," the authors worried, "the essential nature of the City would not change."[16] The built environment was not the city, they argued. In fact, its "essential nature" is determined by its people. But beneath this humanist rhetoric was antagonism to the poor themselves. From its genesis, human renewal was beset by its own internal contradictions, which made the poor the problem to be solved and the recipient of its compassion.

With the declaration of the War on Poverty in 1964, Baltimore quickly gained the funding it needed to put its ambitious plans to reshape its populace into motion. Government had long sought to mold its citizens. The Progressive Era settlement house movement hoped to make immigrants more American, while the postwar period saw the rise of human-oriented disciplines of social work, human relations, and mental hygiene. Title II of the Economic Opportunity Act of 1964 codified human renewal as "human performance" with the goal of "improving human performance, motivation and productivity."[17] Service providers would help reshape the poor, while also giving them other needed services, like day care or remedial education classes. Nationally, the goals of human renewal ranged from job training to countering "physical and emotional illness."[18]

Even though the letter acknowledged the lack of coordination among and insufficient resources of the city's social service agencies, it blamed poor people themselves for their condition, saying they lacked motivation for improvement. Their own behavior was "chronically disorganized," and they had low levels of "social functioning."[19] Echoing social scientists like Oscar Lewis and Daniel Patrick Moynihan, the environment had negatively affected their behavior. But poor people's attitudes and their subsequent behaviors could be changed. "We believe," wrote Manser, Brain, and Wallace, "it possible to motivate and enable individuals to achieve happier, better adjusted personal lives and wider and more fruitful participation in community life than they do now."[20] In the midst of a publicly declared war on it, poverty—at least as colloquially and economically defined—receded from focus. Instead, "people's happiness" came to be seen as "an element of state strength" and an appropriate aspect of its interests, no different from education, welfare, or the census.[21] Programs from Character Building Youth Services to the Consumer Protection Program to the Neighborhood Youth Corps sprouted up, some run by the Community Action Agency (CAA) and some by existing agencies.

To enact the plan, Baltimore needed data about its impoverished citizens, community buy-in, and outreach to local neighborhoods. Communities learned about the new programs for the poor through

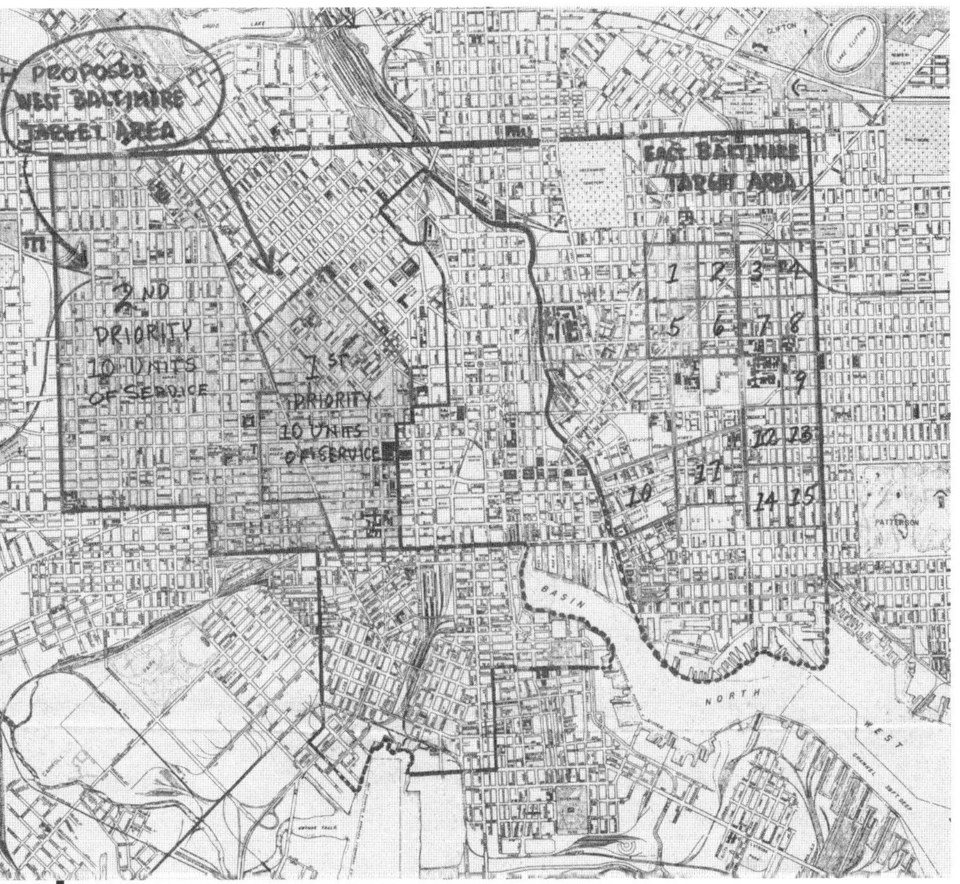


To utilize federal funding from the War on Poverty, Baltimore officials created the East Baltimore Target Area. Neighborhood centers offered services throughout, including spaces where *Chicory* editors collected poems and artwork from residents.
McKeldin Administrative Files (second term), 1963-1967, Baltimore City Archives

newspapers, events like the Human Values in the Emerging American City discussion program at Goucher College, and local television programs like *The Man from Nowhere*, which examined issues of poverty in the city.[22] Census data provided enough information to identify a section of East Baltimore as the action area where the CAA would focus its efforts. It would later expand to West Baltimore. A follow-up survey identified the resources that already existed within its boundaries. The residents of the action area were envisioned as key informants about the realities of poverty. Through interviews, residents identified nine types of problems facing the action area. While some were external, like unemployment and lack of suitable housing, other problems were more emotional in nature: "apathy, lack of initiative or motivation," and "absence of good morals."[23] These "environmental" issues fed into the larger problems of the area.

But social workers and teachers were already trying to fix such problems, with little success. Perhaps community members, called "indigenous leaders" in the *Plan for Action*, would have more impact. These indigenous leaders, like Sam Cornish, would "have an intimate knowledge of the assigned neighborhood" and would be able to connect personally with residents because of their shared cultural background.[24] With a hierarchical structure, the CAA subdivided the action area into fifteen smaller units, each with a neighborhood center. These centers would hire professional counselors who, in turn, would identify local residents to serve as emissaries between the center, the CAA, and the community, developing a sense of trust between the residents and the center. Success would be measured by how many neighborhood residents participated in approved activities, as a means of creating a culture of surveillance where residents would "exert positive influence on one another."[25]

While the War on Poverty was supposed to support the "maximum feasible participation of the poor," in this early phase, Baltimore sought to use the poor merely as guides to their communities, rather than integrate them more fully into decision making. This structure would later cause conflict between black activists and the city's anti-poverty initiatives. While community cohesion was the stated goal, only certain types of community organizations were deemed appropriate. Gangs were not. The Street Club Program, for example, was designed to stop juvenile delinquency.[26] Political activity, too, was narrowly defined; "it is not intended that these groups" at the neighborhood centers "engage in aggressive social action."[27] Instead, indigenous leaders were supposed to convince local residents to participate in normalizing institutions in order to create social pressure that would result in changed behavior among poor people of color. Out of this uneasy alliance of influences, *Chicory* was born.

**_Chicory_ and the Black Arts Movement** | The first neighborhood center opened in the East Baltimore target area in a former police station that had sat empty for five years. Other centers soon opened in more likely spaces, including a library branch located at 606 South Ann Street in Fells Point, housing projects, or in row houses, like the one at 112 North Wolfe Street. Thirty-three were operating by 1968. Once youth corps workers cleaned and repaired the spaces, service providers moved in. Evelyn Levy and Thelma Bell provided racks of paperback books with no due dates, space for Volunteers in Service to America (VISTA) to tutor young people, and a station wagon outfitted with a screen to show movies outdoors.[28]

Led by liberal administrators in this period, Pratt staff were interested in issues of racial injustice and in connecting with poor and working-class people in the city. In 1964, the library created Resolving Racial Tensions: Program Planning and Library Materials for Community Leaders, which drew sixty community leaders to the Patterson Park branch to learn what kinds of materials the library owned to help with racial understanding.[29] One month before Martin Luther King Jr.'s assassination, activist Walter Lively gave a lecture for the library, describing how, without structural change, the United States would become two nations divided along race lines.[30] Its newsletter, the *Staff Reporter*, published numerous articles in which librarians considered how they should deal with issues of social justice. The major motivation was to connect to members of the community with little or no familiarity with the library. Rather than expecting the community to come to the library, the library reached out to the community in ways that attempted to eliminate class and racial difference. Pratt contracted with the Community Action Commission in Baltimore to provide library services to the target area in East Baltimore.

Sam Cornish, a poet, was hired as a library aide to the neighborhood centers to work with young adults. Born in 1935, in the 1200 block of Druid Hill Avenue in West Baltimore, Cornish, who was African American, built bridges between the library and the poor, predominantly black residents of the area. Hassled by his peers for liking books as a teen, he hung out at bookstores and the Pratt Library.[31] He dropped out of Douglass and Booker T. Washington High Schools, preferring to learn from the books that he devoured. After serving in the US Army Medical Corps from 1958 to 1960, he returned to Baltimore. In 1961 he published his first book of poetry, *In This Corner*. Self-described as "flamboyant," his writing showed a variety of influences, including the realist novelists of the 1930s that had inspired William Manchester and the Beat poets of the 1950s.[32] While his work often used African American history and explicitly discussed African American life, he had a contradictory relationship with the Black Arts movement.

The Black Arts movement began in the mid-1960s, after the assassination of Malcolm X. This movement sought to prove that "African Americans possess a distinct aesthetic, sense of values, and communal ethos."[33] If, as literary scholar James Smethurst has argued, the Black Power movement can be understood as the "political wing of the Black Arts movement," it was because they sought similar goals—the liberation of African American consciousness, the empowerment of black people, and the creation of an internal black nation.[34] Black Arts and Black Power were, in many ways, inseparable. The important anthology *Black Fire* (1968), "full of black rage and black dreams and black love," defined the movement's ideology.[35] Through its essays and poetry it proclaimed that Black Arts was "telling it like it is," meaning not adapting white or obscurantist literary language but speaking plainly.

As writers like Amiri Baraka, Sonia Sanchez, Larry Neal, and June Jordan asserted, poems are political. Publishers, like Broadside Press in Detroit, used eye-catching short publications called broadsides to bring poetry to the street.[36] Popular artists, such as James Brown and Nina Simone, took the ideas of Black Power and spread them widely. Through these various public spheres, discussions of black identity took place around the nation in venues large and small. While Cornish published poems in *Black Fire*, the *Journal of Black Poetry*, and *Liberator*, he "felt somewhat at odds with the separatist impulse in Black Arts ideologies and institutional practices."[37] However, *Chicory* would grow from these influences. A small magazine like the ones beatniks produced, it spoke in the voice and cadence of the people who wrote for it, not professional writers.

With this background, Cornish began working with young people at the neighborhood centers. Looking for texts that would encourage residents' literacy, Cornish introduced them to Warren Miller's *The Cool World*, a novel about young gang members in Harlem, which resonated so deeply the group discussed writing a play inspired by it based on their lives.[38] Instead, Cornish proposed the library fund a small literary magazine to publish the unedited writings of residents and snippets of "street chatter" heard by Cornish and his group of editors-at-large. They called the magazine *Chicory* to reference the "perennial plant . . . with bright-blue flowers" that had long been used in southern and poor communities as a substitute for coffee.[39] Like this hardy weed, *Chicory* would blossom even in the rockiest soil.

His editors included VISTA volunteers working in the centers, including Thomas B. Edsall, who went on to an illustrious career as a journalist and author; Jerry Morton, who also became a journalist; Christine Henckel; and Claire Bergan. *Chicory*'s first issue was published in November 1966, featuring work from what Cornish called "your paycheck community, or your unemployed community, your people who are down and out."[40] The goal was to create a space where Baltimoreans who were excluded from the public sphere by their race and class position could write freely "about experience, about being poor, about being alive."[41] Each issue included a mix of poems published anonymously; with only a first, last, or nickname; or with a full name, sometimes with other identifying information, like age. Men and women both contributed as well as many children (all the editors, however, were men). The library loved the magazine and made producing it part of Cornish's official duties. Even after federal funding ended, the library continued the magazine until 1983. Issues were freely available at the community centers. Contributors would get their own copies. The library mailed issues to those on a mailing list, which included African American activists and cultural luminaries such as Ossie Davis and Ruby Dee.

For Enoch Pratt librarians, *Chicory* helped the library become more responsive to the community and gave them insight into the needs of working-class African Americans during a turbulent time. The riots taking place around the country made them question the role of the library in a city like Baltimore. What was the purpose of an institution that was originally built thanks to the largesse of a wealthy white man as a place of uplift?[42] Theoretically open to all, librarians in this era confronted the fact that they needed to overcome barriers to people coming into the library to fully be a community resource. The neighborhood centers were an experiment in changing the way the library worked. *Chicory* fit well within this model of experimentation. If the library wanted to be useful to the community and the community wanted to write poetry, then *Chicory* was useful. And if the librarians wanted to understand what people in inner-city Baltimore thought and felt, then *Chicory* documented that, too. When the Enoch Pratt Library attended the American Library Association conference, *Chicory* was the most popular item on its table. Clearly, other librarians were also wrestling with these issues. Yet, the Community Action Agency was only dimly aware of its existence. *Chicory* doesn't appear in the voluminous documents in the mayor's papers on the Community Action Agency. But this doesn't mean that it wasn't significant. Indeed, because of its low profile, *Chicory* was able to survive well beyond most of the cultural programs and Black Arts institutions of this era.

In 1969, the Association Press, an arm of the YMCA, published *Chicory: Young Voices from the Black Ghetto*, a collection of poems and street chatter that had been previously published in the magazine. Edited by Cornish and Dixon, the magazine's second editor, this book was part of a spate of publications of poetry by inner-city people, often youth. Budd Schulberg's *Out of the Ashes*, written by black people in the Watts section of Los Angeles after the riot there in 1965, was perhaps the most famous, though not the only one. *The Me Nobody Knows*, an anthology of writings by young students of color in New York City was published in 1969 and adapted as a musical that premiered off Broadway in 1970. June Jordan and Terri Bush edited a collection of poetry called *The Voice of the Children* (1970). *Somebody Real: Voices of City Children*, edited by Nicholas Duva, collected the writing of students in Jersey City, New Jersey. These books gave white liberals, confused and concerned by the riots that had taken place in Watts, New York, Detroit, and Baltimore, the chance to peek into the lives of poor people of color, especially children. Liberals wanted to counter the radical ideas percolating in cities with large black populations. When the *Saturday Evening Post* and *Life* magazine published feature stories on Maulana Karenga's cultural nationalist organization, US, in 1966 after the Watts riots, they accompanied their articles with photos of black youth being trained in military-style drills.[43] Stories about the Black Panther Party's breakfast program emphasized that young people were also taught about Marxism and anti-colonialism.[44] In comparison, published poetry collections like *Chicory* suggested a different path forward, one where white liberals learned from black youth and helped stave off insurrection or violent conflict. As the editors explained in their introduction, *Chicory*'s intent was "to inform other people within and without that area of a way of living. It exposes honest, often harsh feelings about our local schools, policemen and poverty programs. It expresses the feeling of what it is to be black and in trouble."[45]

If in Baltimore the magazine circulated within the black community as well as to the library staff, the book seemed poised to be read predominately by a national white liberal establishment. Ads for the book appeared in the *Baltimore Sun* and the *New York Times*, suggesting its national reach. It was not reviewed widely, though the reviewer for the *Hartford Courant* noted that the more literary poems seemed "pretentious." If poetry is defined as writing that shows "craft, knowledge, sophistication," then "nothing in this volume qualifies as a poem." The most effective in his view were the "simple, the ignorant, the genuine" pieces that expressed more than a "loud lament" about the conditions of poverty.[46] While the Black Arts movement lauded vernacular black language as poetry because it refused to conform to the rigid standards of academic poetry, it did not see this work as simple. It was a beautifully complex method of expression that reflected histories of surviving under oppression using coded language. But this writer, who gave the book a positive review, had no way of interpreting these poems in this nuanced manner. By disconnecting them from the Black Arts movement, Black Power, and the questions plaguing black artists in this era, he liked best those poems that discussed inner-city life in ways that fit into preconceived notions of black authenticity.

For neighborhood residents, *Chicory* offered an opportunity to define their lives and experiences publicly and, importantly, in print. Horace "Turk" Hazelton, a seventeen-year-old high school dropout, published a poem in the first issue of the magazine and quickly became a regular contributor. With his joker's grin, dark sense of humor, and keen observational eye, Turk, who earned his nickname by virtue of his November birth, wrote (or dictated to Cornish) pieces that captured the world around him, from encounters with police to analyses of the flaws of Baltimore's educational system. Turk made such an impression that Cornish wrote a poem called "Turk" about him. Speaking as Turk, he skeptically addresses liberals who were suddenly interested in him because your "concerns / project you / instead of me."[47] While Cornish, who smartly navigated liberal interest in *Chicory* to ensure the publication's success, critiques liberals for the shallowness of their interest, for Turk, *Chicory* gave him a chance to share his thoughts with the world.

Publishing in *Chicory* and interacting with editors like Cornish and his successors opened new life paths for him and others. As Turk told a reporter in 1966, "I gotta write a book some day. I got some ideas that won't wait."[48] Alongside a poem she published in 1968, Marion Reid described herself as identifying "readily with the black people of the community, especially black women like herself . . . aspir[ing] to become a professional writer, chiefly a poet."[49] For others, it could lead to wider notoriety. A woman named Tina Brown published several poems in *Chicory* before having her work published in the *Baltimore Afro-American*. Renowned poet Afaa Michael Weaver published in the magazine in 1980–1981, before winning prestigious national grants and awards. Terry Edmonds, who would later become the first black presidential speechwriter for President Bill Clinton, wrote several pieces in *Chicory* as well. If *Chicory* was intended to funnel the energies of black people into productive uses, in these cases it worked.

Cornish left his editorial position in 1967. From October 1967 to June 1969, Lucian Dixon, who would coedit the anthology with Cornish, took over. Cornish returned as editor from September to December 1969. In January 1972, Melvin Edward Brown became editor. *Chicory*'s longest-serving editor, he helmed the magazine until October 1980, when E. Adam Jackson took over as editor until the magazine's last issue in the winter of 1983.[50] Brown, also born and raised in Baltimore, attended Columbia University and received an MA from Johns Hopkins University writing seminars. He published his first book of poetry, *In the First Place*, in 1974. Brown conceptualized *Chicory* differently than Cornish had. In 1976, he argued, "There was this whole sociological thing with *Chicory* when it first started as if outlets such as *Chicory* could take off some of the pressure. . . . People talked about brilliance in ghetto writing and how new voices should be listened to and all that crap. I think that was all a kind of game. I

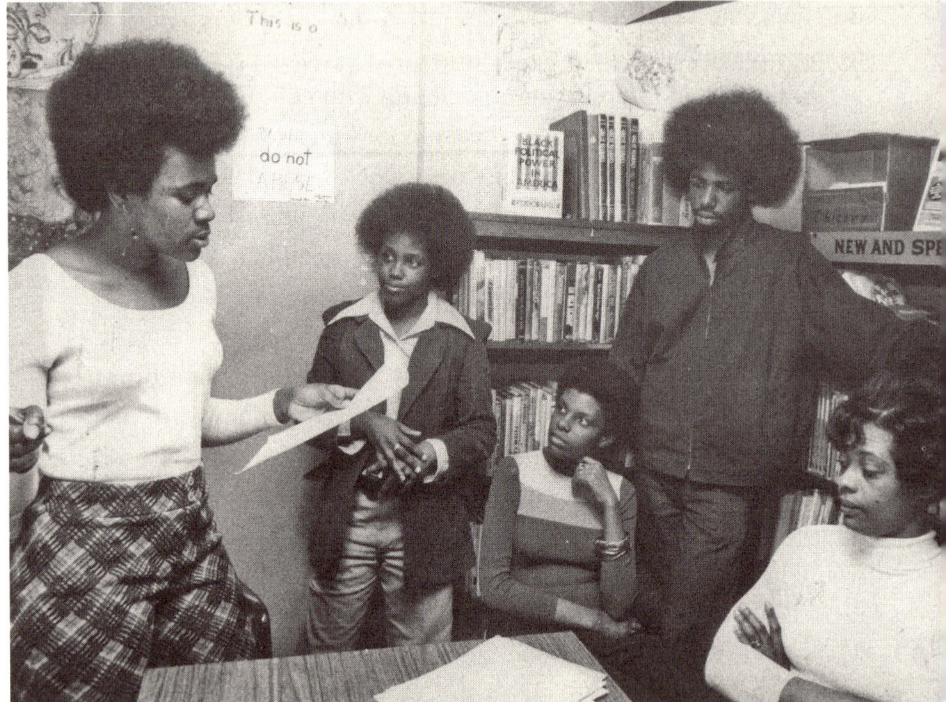


Phyllis Jones, a contributor to *Chicory*, reads aloud in the magazine's office in the early 1970s. *From left*, Annette and Kathleen Stockett, John Givens, and Frances Proctor.

Permission from Baltimore Sun Media

don't really think about that at all now." *Chicory* would still function as a public sphere, but "I think the values it has are to the people who contribute to it themselves."[51] Rather than speaking to liberal power structures to change society from the outside in, for Brown, the goal was to start by changing the self (understood as politicized) and moving outward into the community. Often this meant critiquing the black community as well as white people.

As a public sphere, *Chicory* allowed for the expression of varied ideas. If white liberals saw the magazine primarily as a way to peek into the black ghetto, its contributors saw it as a platform to create debate within the black community and to *confront* white America. In the July 1968 issue, two women, Dellyse Maxine Harris and Jannis R. Rhodes, used the pages of *Chicory* to speak back to white liberals and organize the black community across class. Their essay was titled "A Message from the Ghetto." The direction was clear—they were speaking from their position within Baltimore's black neighborhoods to listeners who didn't live there. They proclaimed their identities as African Americans who have lived their lives in Baltimore. Their experiences give them the clout to "help you see the truth as we do." The "you" included both white liberals and the black middle class who had lost connection with the urban black experience. The essay intends to "inform you of the shameful condition of American life." It catalogs the injustices, like bad schools and unsafe housing that define ghetto life before switching to addressing black people who must "stand as one to overcome." They offer a call to action to spur the black community to come together across class in racial solidarity. Harris and Rhodes included their addresses at the end of the essay to prove their local credibility and give people an opportunity to write them in response. The poem uses the surveillance of white liberals as a stage from which to claim justice, while also calling together a community who must "not fight among ourselves but work together for freedom." It ends with the authors thundering that "the destruction of America is imminent because of its racial problems. WE ARE AMERICANS AND DEMAND OUR RIGHTS."[52]

*Chicory* was messy, often offering contradictory ideas in one issue. Several themes stand out. Writers present counternarratives to sociological theories like the culture of poverty and to urban and human renewal, while other pieces support them. Many poems critique the institutions of the state. Unsurprisingly in an era when police brutality was a major civil rights issue, the police are the subject of much discussion, though schools and politics are discussed as well. If the police represented the hard power of the state, then welfare and social work were the soft power of liberalism. These critiques are paralleled with discussions of Black Power and cultural nationalism. Finally, writers countered common narratives of black life as defined by poverty and desperation. These pieces show that there is also beauty and joy there.

**Soft Power** | *Chicory* narrated the African American community's complicated interactions with human renewal and liberalism through city institutions, like the welfare office, and authority figures, like social workers. While liberal institutions tried to help black residents, "city officials became adept at making compromises that, even while expanding representation of the poor and raising public awareness of inequalities, preserved existing municipal authority structures."[53] This became increasingly clear with the creation of Baltimore's Community Action Agency and its mandate to promote "maximum feasible participation of the poor."

Governed by an eleven-member board, the Community Action Agency, appointed by the mayor with city council approval, was a political football caught between local politics and a growing Black Power movement. The fact that federal dollars were being pumped into the poorest neighborhoods of Baltimore at the same time that black militants were becoming more visible in those same areas meant that there would be very public battles over these resources. These militants mobilized the impoverished, a community ignored by the middle-class civil rights organizations in the city, like the powerful Baltimore NAACP chapter, in order to gain political power.

The creation of the agency led immediately to critical questions. Who was qualified to lead an agency directed at helping the poor? More to the point, who would be allowed to by the city council? City council president William Donald Schaefer, who would later be elected mayor with the support of black voters, disavowed black radicalism. A. Eugene Chase, from the Antipoverty Action Committee, argued that many of the nominees, like Morton Macht, a wealthy developer, "have contributed to the perpetuation of poverty and discrimination. They haven't dealt with the poor and aren't of the poor."[54]

These tensions caused the first director of the CAA, Melvin J. Humphrey, a professor at Morgan State College, to resign within months of his appointment.[55] Parren Mitchell, who would become the first African American congressman from Baltimore, was named head of the CAA in September 1965. In 1966, Bernice Burton wrote an ode to Mitchell in *Chicory*, called, simply, "Parren Mitchell," suggesting that residents saw him as a fighter for the black community.[56]

Mitchell became more committed to grassroots organizing over the course of his tenure. In January 1967, the anti-poverty activist group U-JOIN (Union for Jobs and Income Now), which came out of Students for a Democratic Society, protested at a city council meeting for more representation by the poor. While he tried to prevent U-JOIN from taking over a housing program, he made sure that poor people were represented on the Community Action Agency, although their numbers remained small. He allowed the neighborhood centers to start a voter registration drive against the wishes of the city council. By 1968, though, Mitchell moved more fully into militancy as he began using the neighborhood centers to organize the poor politically, bringing eight hundred people to the Poor People's Rally in 1968, directing picket lines, and holding a demonstration at city hall at which as many as seven hundred people appeared.[57]

All of this came to a head in 1968, following the riots. Baltimore experienced three days of upheaval that April, with black leaders trying to calm the situation. When Governor Spiro Agnew summoned them, including Mitchell, to a meeting, they expected to be thanked for their help. Instead, Agnew proclaimed that they had allowed black militants to cause the riots, dressing them down in such a condescending fashion that many walked out. Mitchell cited Agnew's actions as spurring greater black militancy rather than diminishing it. As he explained, "I think that temporarily that Agnew confrontation provided the platform on which a much tougher, militant Black group, Black leadership could become . . . Had he not done this, and I'm not saying that it was right or wrong for that new tough Black militant group to emerge, but he provided a forum for it."[58]

By that fall, Mitchell had resigned from the CAA, citing a "strangling bureaucracy" and "the failure of the D'Alesandro administration to coordinate programs for the poor through the poverty agency."[59] Thirteen members of the Community Action Agency resigned in protest. They refused to return unless Walter P. Carter, a well-known civil rights activist who was chief community organizer for the Model Cities Program, was appointed to the position. By doing so, it would not only end the conflict with the members, whose absence meant that the agency was out of compliance with federal mandates; it would also help connect the CAA and Model Cities more closely.[60] However, thanks, in part, to a failed attempt in 1967 to elect more black members to the city council, Carter's nomination was blocked. Given Mayor D'Alesandro's vocal support of Carter, this was a bloodbath, in which the council, led by Schaefer, actively defied the will of the mayor. Carter argued that the battle over the CAA was part of "a war against forces and institutions that must be changed. These are forces of evil and dilapidation, oppression and cultural depression . . . These forces were not committed to eliminating poverty, and after the riot they were more defensive than responsive."[61]

What was the impact of the human renewal policies called for by the city's liberal elites on the black community? How did black Baltimoreans feel about liberalism and its institutions? Donald Grafton Gwynn, a regular contributor to *Chicory*, published "White Liberals (Most of Them or All of Them, I Think Sometimes)" two months after the riots and in the same month that Parren Mitchell resigned as head of the Community Action Agency. He argues that white liberals "come into our neighborhoods/with lots of charities and lots of gifts/and they never really help us to help ourselves."[62] Hypocrites, they want to be assuaged of their white guilt by black people without making substantive changes. Using the discourse of community action and maximum feasible participation, Gwynn accuses white liberals of breaking their promises to poor black people in Baltimore.

While Gwynn speaks in broad terms, other writers focus on specific social institutions like welfare. In the late 1960s, activists, with the help of neighborhood legal services, successfully fought egregious rules that attempted to control welfare recipients' labor and, for women, their sexuality.[63] Catalyzing this activism was, to quote the title of one *Chicory* poem, "what welfare does to you." Welfare is described as a byzantine system of undisclosed rules and regulations that "leaves you no choice but to lie, cheat, and steal."[64] If conservative discourse argued that bad behavior led to someone being on welfare, June Booth, this poem's author, argues that welfare forces individuals into bad behavior. This mistrust of the institutions of liberalism appeared in several *Chicory* pieces. In July 1967, for example, a street chatter piece included lines like "my worker treats me like a dog" and "wonder what lie my worker going to tell me today."[65] Like *Claudine* (1974), a black-produced film starring Diahann Carroll as a single mother on welfare, these pieces in *Chicory* expressed a critical black perspective on one aspect of liberalism's soft power.

In its insistence on the creativity of black residents of all ages, *Chicory* resisted a basic assumption of the human renewal program in Baltimore—that black people had been so deprived of arts and culture that they were unable to express themselves. The *Plan for Action* argued that "disadvantaged children, because of limited experiences during their pre-school life, are quite limited in all forms of communication skills" and "are not prepared to learn to express thoughts and ideas in writing."[66] But *Chicory* assumed the opposite. Children of color from low-income families were expressive but in ways that were not validated by the larger white middle-class culture. By publishing young people's writing, they asserted their value as writers and as citizens who could speak about their experiences with authority. Street chatter, a clear outgrowth of the Black Arts movement's belief that "when I hear a group of brothers or sisters talking I hear poetry—sometimes a very complete poetry" further asserted black expressiveness.[67]

*Chicory* also published work by social workers and neighborhood assistants, giving them the chance to describe their experiences on the front lines of the War on Poverty. For the Community Action Agency, these individuals were critical to the success of human renewal. They were needed to gather data on residents, encourage them to sign up for social services, and help win trust for city bureaucracies. While they tried to connect with the local residents, fear and class differences impeded their efforts. Much like the college students who moved into poor urban areas in the Students for a Democratic Society's Economic Research and Action Project, the neighborhood center workers could only attempt to bridge these gaps.[68] As the author of "on being a neighborhood assist" wrote, "oh you are scared . . . we are scared as hell," but the knowledge that the "people on this street have it a lot worse than we do" motivates her to "give people a chance" even when they "don't smell good."[69] As a safe public space, the community center drew people with addiction or other problems, and although the staff personally recoiled from these individuals, it was important to treat them with respect, which would, in the long run, create strong bonds with the community. These individual interactions, however, did not address structural inequities. In "Community Notebook: Life with Community Action," a center worker realizes that the children who come to the center have never seen a lemon, because the stores in their neighborhood don't sell them. She takes them on trips to raise their awareness of the world outside the boundaries of their neighborhood. Yet such activities were unlikely to change their social situation.[70]

Of course, not every piece in *Chicory* critiqued liberalism. The neighborhood centers did incorporate working-class and poor black residents into the larger system in the ways that human renewal intended. A 1968 poem by Daniel Johnson called the Baltimore City Council a "bunch of old fuddys [*sic*]" who use democratic procedures to hide their true goal of enriching and supporting white communities.[71] Voting is the best recourse to ensuring proper representation for black residents, a liberal solution to municipal problems in a time of rising Black Power activism. Another piece, "Thugs United," describes a group of Baltimore youth, all of whom are the leaders of small gangs who meet in the Community Action Center to jointly try to help the community. Rather than identify herself as from West Baltimore, the writer, Bernadette Hall, says she's from Area #56, using the numbers assigned by the CAA. In this small way, we see how some people adopted the CAA's geographical designations. Hall writes about how this group of young men living in a nearby housing project come together at the neighborhood center to discuss how to better their lives and their community, which is plagued by drugs, imprisonment, and lack of education. These indigenous leaders question society calling them thugs, noting that the word is a way for them to be written off and forgotten. Instead, the group invites the police to the center to make sure they understand that their meeting has a social purpose—to find activities for young people that will take them off the street, especially resonant in the months after the riot when this essay was published. While there are no later pieces that report on whether this group continued, in this instance human renewal worked as intended. It brought marginalized people into the centers, where they worked to determine their own liberal solutions to neighborhood problems.[72]

**Hard Power |** If social workers and welfare represented liberalism's soft power, the police were the clear representation of governmental "hard power" in the pages of *Chicory*.[73] Police brutality and harassment of black Baltimoreans was the subject of several poems. Rather than seeing incidents as the actions of individual cops breaking the rules, *Chicory* writers connected police harassment to larger structural issues of race, poverty, and masculinity. One month before the 1968 riot, *Reader's Digest* published an article, "How Baltimore Fends Off Riots," detailing the changes that Police Commissioner Donald Pomerleau had made in the city, including ordering his officers to be friendlier with the community and forcing them to take courses in black history.[74] Such acts of community policing are cited as the reason why Baltimore, unlike Newark, Watts, or Detroit, had not experienced a riot. The prematurely congratulatory tone is contradicted by the words of neighborhood residents. In the first issue of *Chicory* in November 1966, Turk published a poem called "Going Home." In it he tells the story of a run-in with the Baltimore police when walking home at night after dropping off his girlfriend. He is harassed by white cops, and he asks why they're questioning him, which they see as insubordination. One of the cops "starts to feel my behind." This threatened sexual violence emphasizes how little control Turk has over his own body on a public street simply because he is black, male, and young. When Turk jumps in response, the cop uses this as an excuse to pull out his gun, emphasizing his masculinity and power. He tells Turk to run but that if he does "i going to blow your head off." Turk, who had likely experienced this abuse before, "saw now how it was going to be for me." He waits for the cop to holster his gun and then runs. His language turns the neighborhood into a place that is simultaneously familiar and strange. While he is "smelling the streets" to find his way, he is also "bumping into dark gates," symbolic of his inability to truly find safety.[75] While Pomerleau was touting his community policing, young men like Turk were publicly discussing their victimization by the police.

"Prison Camp," from the June 1969 issue, uses the metaphor of a prison camp to describe life in Baltimore's inner city. Rather than cells, there is "slum housing"; rather than "prison chow," there is "welfare food." And rather than prison guards, there is the "honky cop," joined, at times, by "the national guard" and "the riot patrol." No matter what their name, these agents of the state are linked to a common project: control of black people through intimidation, violence, fear, and poverty, which works in tandem with the police to keep them in the ghetto, an analysis that Black Power organizations also espoused. Even after "the riot patrol's gone," it is replicated by the city police, the "prison guard, in this prison camp/this ghetto, this slum, this airtight cage/of poverty."[76] The poem ends with a call—"I want my freedom . . . I won't stay in the prison camp"—but there is no indication of how the author will achieve this end.

"Helmeted policemen" also links kinds of state violence. It weaves together popular cultural representations of masculinity and heroism with the war in Vietnam and policing at home. Beginning with a quote from a *New York Times* article about helmeted police officers clearing anti-war protestors with tear gas and clubs, it asks the reader whether she recognizes them from other kinds of demonstrations, like those of the civil rights movement where the police also beat and dispersed protestors. The author imagines the reader turning "the channel when it was over to 'Gunsmoke,'" asking, "did you ever stop to think who that hero on the tv is? that white man hero military Western sheriff city cop?" Although the western portrays the protagonist as fighting against evil characters (often Indians), in reality "he's a national guardsman in your home in Newark/he's a city policeman who shoots suspects in the back."[77] "Helmeted policemen" was written by someone identified only as simba, a Swahili word used in Maulana Karenga's cultural nationalist US organization to describe young people involved in his movement.[78] Although it is unclear whether this author was influenced by the US organization, the use of this name suggests a cultural nationalist perspective. This complicated poem criticizes the ideological function of popular culture that normalizes white male authority that protects property and inflicts violence on poor and nonwhite people.

Black women also explore their interactions with the police in *Chicory*, from points of view ranging from powerless witness of police overreach to victim of unending bureaucracies. In "troubled sleep (night in the city)," the writer is woken up by noise. Looking out her window, she sees two police officers chase two young men, followed by shots and an ambulance's siren. No dream, she can only observe this intimidation, which although not directed at her fills her with fear.[79] Interactions with the police could also be mundane. When a woman finds her car has been stolen, she asks the police for help, but they're off duty and refuse with the wearying blankness of the career bureaucrat. When she does find a police officer to help, she doesn't have her driver's license, so he also refuses her.[80] These kinds of frustrating interactions with bureaucracy, which appear in other black texts like the novel *The Bluest Eye*, by Toni Morrison, and the film *Killer of Sheep*, by Charles Burnett, degrade black women and erode their relationship with the police as well.

**Black Power** | An umbrella term, Black Power included black liberationist ideas and activities. As Peniel E. Joseph has argued, "Black power defined a movement for racial solidarity, cultural pride, and self-determination."[81] Beyond this overarching goal, however, there were many ways to put this into practice, especially on the local level. The Black Panther Party and the Revolutionary Action Movement espoused revolutionary nationalism, anti-capitalism, anti-colonialism, and solidarity with freedom struggles around the globe. Maulana Karenga's US organization and the Black Arts movement advocated cultural nationalism. They argued that liberation required black people to change their ways of thinking, finding strength in their heritage and history as descendants of Africa. Black capitalists wanted to create a black-run economy, while black separatists like the Nation of Islam wanted land to build their own state.

By the mid-1960s, Black Power activists worked within a contradictory political climate in Baltimore. The Republican mayor Theodore McKeldin was committed to civil rights and even spoke at the Congress of Racial Equality's 1966 conference in Baltimore. These actions were seen by some as merely a way to defuse radical black activism without truly changing the status quo. His successor, Thomas D'Alesandro III, who took office in 1967, was also committed to civil rights, but he was confronted by the intransigence of Governor Spiro Agnew, especially after the 1968 riots, which limited what he could do. The city council was less warm to Black Power and civil rights. Even harsher, Donald Pomerleau, the police commissioner, took a hard stance against Black Power, particularly the Black Panther Party, whose members were harassed by the Baltimore police.[82]

As historian Rhonda Y. Williams, the foremost expert on Black Power politics in Baltimore, has shown, within this political context, Black Power activists worked throughout the city in a band stretching from the cultural national Society of United Liberators (SOUL) School in West Baltimore to East Baltimore, which was a hotbed of radicalism where a number of organizations were headquartered. In 1966, CORE named Baltimore its Target City, holding its conference and catalyzing several actions there. This drew national attention to the situation of black people in Baltimore. It also "spurred new alliances as well as divisions and inflected the political context in which people lived and organized."[83] More middle-class civil rights organizations, particularly the Baltimore NAACP, refused to work with Black Power groups. Other civil rights organizations in Baltimore, like the Interdenominational Ministerial Alliance, were surprised by CORE's decision to make their city their target but found ways to work together on issues around housing, welfare, and poverty.

The grass roots mobilized in multiple ways. Walter Lively, a well-known Black Power activist who led U-JOIN, helped to found Mother Rescuers from Poverty, Baltimore's first welfare rights organization. As Williams has shown, women in public housing in Baltimore organized around tenants' rights as well, taking advantage of training opportunities offered through the Community Action Agency. They fought for the hiring of a black manager at a public housing project and held a sleep-in at the Department of Social Services to demand better treatment.[84] These acts, rooted in these women's lived experience, counter still common images of Black Power as male dominated and focused on displays of armed power.

Soon after, the Baltimore branch of the Black Panther Party opened in East Baltimore at 1248 North Gay Street.[85] After the first head of the chapter was expelled by the national organization for treating it more like a social club than a political organization, John Clark was sent in from California to lead the group.[86] The chapter started a free breakfast and lunch program at a local Catholic church, a free dry cleaning service, a short-lived food co-op, and political education classes. Because of Maryland's laws, they did not carry guns openly as in California, but "the Panthers were seen by many as the only black leaders who had not in some way been co-opted by the White establishment, particularly as that establishment acted through government."[87] Police harassment of the Panthers took several forms. In the December 1969 issue of *Chicory*, amid poems about Christmas, a piece of street chatter reported that the police were harassing the Black Panthers by having the utilities turned off at their headquarters. They emphasized the power of the Panthers by noting that "there were three hundred cops / after eleven panthers." In May 1970, police raided several Panther offices and homes, arresting six for the murder of a former Panther and suspected informant.[88] Even after the chapter dissolved in the early 1970s, its impact was still felt in Baltimore through the work of people like Paul Coates, a former Black Panther who ran a bookstore and started Black Classic Press to publish black nationalist books and whose son, Ta-Nehisi Coates, has become one of the foremost writers on the black experience in the United States.

*Chicory* served as a public sphere where information about Black Power activities was reported and ideas about what Black Power meant in Baltimore circulated within the community. Importantly, if *Chicory* served in part to tell white liberals about life in the black ghetto, when discussing Black Power, the conversation shifted to an internal one. *Chicory*'s editors established relationships with Black Power organizations. Artwork and writing intended for *Chicory* could be dropped off at the neighborhood centers or at the offices of local branches of civil rights organizations like CORE or the Student Nonviolent Coordinating Committee. The September 1968 issue included several pieces that were reprinted from the SOUL School's newsletter, *The Liberator*. Benjamin "Olugbala" McMillan, a CORE member, opened the SOUL School in West Baltimore near the Murphy Homes. Cultural nationalists, the SOUL School focused on arts and literature and black pride. Suggesting the ways that Black Power principles spread through interpersonal contact, the Murphy Homes tenants' association invited the SOUL School to present student artwork. When the school realized that the group was not exclusively black and that the building manager was white, representatives told the black tenants that they should get rid of the "blue-eyed devils." Soon after, the tenants replaced the white manager with a black one.[89]

*Chicory* published an explanation of the SOUL School's mission of "increasing the Black Man's awareness of his long, proud heritage. Much stress is also placed on understanding the present powerlessness of Black communities and the creation of ways and means to change the condition."[90] The issue included poems written by SOUL School participants. "To Be Black" defined black identity as beautiful, wonderful, and real. "Slave Woman," by Beverly Havard, imagined the pain of an enslaved woman, particularly that of sexual assault and impregnation by white men.[91] Such imaginings were part of Black Arts' engagement with black history. But, as in much cultural nationalist art of this era, black women were defined through their reproductive capacity. While women were deeply involved in the day-to-day activism of Black Power on the ground in Baltimore, this poem and others suggested that their value centered primarily on their ability to give birth to black children and to support black men.

Although it is impossible to distill what *Chicory* writers said about Black Power into a few themes, one of the clearest messages was the need for black unity in the face of white racism and internal differences. At times, this was linked to a global anti-colonial struggle. Two poems from 1973 are exemplary. Black Power organizations struggled in the early 1970s. Maulana Karenga was in prison, devastating the US organization. The national Black Panther chapter ordered the closing of most branches, including the one in Baltimore, so that members could move to Oakland to support the political campaigns of Huey Newton and Elaine Brown. A larger shift toward gaining traditional political power dominated the movement in many ways. Black Power advocates won a huge political victory with the 1970 election of Kenneth Gibson as the first black mayor of a large northeastern city, Newark, New Jersey. The National Black Political Convention in Gary, Indiana, in 1972, drew thousands of black leaders who debated whether black people should try to make the Democratic Party support more black nationalist goals or start their own party. What was the role of the grassroots community member in these discussions of political campaigns?

In Baltimore, *Chicory* writers reemphasized the key ideas of Black Power as self-determination, racial solidarity, and cultural pride. "The Difference," by Joyce P. Williams, refuses to let outsiders use the differences between black people to split the black community. The Black Panthers are feeding the poor while the black nationalists are "restoring manhood." The black Muslims are praying to Allah while African revolutionaries are rising up. Even drug dealers in Harlem are destroying their drugs. Rather than holding one of these methods as superior, she claims that "our blackness makes us one," which should be kept secret from whites, who will be surprised by the fact that "we've come together."[92] The title "Chains, Chance, Change, Challenge," from November 1973 pays homage to Amiri Baraka's *Raise, Race, Rays, Raze* (1971) to suggest black empowerment. The poem describes the chains that are no longer on black people's wrists or neck but on their mind. But change is coming "not because crackers is more lenient (liberal?)" but because of black activism. This activism, however, is not "the pallid features/complexion civil rights protest" but the activism of a list of global black forebears, from Kwame Nkrumah to George Jackson to Queen Nzinga. Through unity, or *umoja*, freedom will be gained, which will end "foreign control monopoly of African energy."[93] With this pan-Africanist politics and use of Swahili words adopted by cultural nationalists, Vincent A. Johnson, the author, shows how the anti-colonial struggle worldwide is linked with the lives of black people in Baltimore.

Even if Black Power did not win political campaigns in Baltimore as in other cities—Baltimore's first black mayor would not be elected until 1987—Black Power ideas circulated from the community through *Chicory* and back again. As Smethurst has argued about the Black Arts movement, poems like these emphasized "the need to develop, or expand upon, a distinctly African American or African culture that stood in opposition to white culture or cultures."[94] As we will see in the following chapters, white Baltimoreans would reach back into their own white ethnic heritages to make claims on the city. In these examples, black writers in *Chicory* constructed their own heritage claims, but ones that linked the global to the national to the local.

**Black Joy** | Perhaps most radically, *Chicory* countered the image of black life as wholly consumed by desperation. For white liberals and the media, images of black destitution proved the need for political intervention in the inner city, much in the same way that depictions of blight were the excuse for urban renewal. In "____ on white people looking at the poor," published in May 1967, the writer notes, "They always coming down here to see how poor and dirty we are," ignoring the many poor white people who are never shown in the same way.[95] While this piece directly confronts the media for its narrow portrayal of black people and neighborhoods, other pieces did so more implicitly.

While, as we have seen, many poems used a realistic aesthetic to comment on contemporary black experience, others did not. Some writers published clearly fictional pieces. Others offered surrealism and humor. "The Soul Fish" from February 1972 is about the writer on a boat floating past a fish listening to R&B singer Roberta Flack. It even includes a drawing of the man and the fish, complete with sunglasses and a transistor radio next to where its ear would ostensibly be.[96] A piece like this has no direct sociological value. It does not give readers any idea of how to help end poverty or what the community needs. But it shows *Chicory*'s function as an outlet for the imagination.

Another type of poem stresses that African American life, even in Baltimore's poor neighborhoods, contains beauty and joy. This is a critical rejoinder to the discourses of the era, when black life and culture were condemned by government officials and in sociological theory as inherently flawed. As feminist scholar bell hooks argues, black communities and families are sources of strength and healing in a racist world.[97] Unsurprisingly, many poems are about love and relationships. Writers penned odes to their lovers, singing their praises as black men and women, as in the poems "The Man I Love" and "You," which both appear in the December 1973 issue. The former is written by a young woman to her older boyfriend, while the latter seems to be written by the boyfriend to her. In these poems and others, we see black people asserting their love for each other as both individual romantic partners and as members of a larger community.[98]

The community could also be a source of joy. Poet Lucille Clifton, who lived in Baltimore and was a supporter of *Chicory*, wrote the introduction to the June/July 1975 issue, which was by Eastern High School students, noting

> how many of these poems and stories talk about "joy" and "good" and "great" and that most difficult, most real and necessary of things, "the real me." Notice how often they talk about Love . . . I have walked among them and felt them swinging down their halls, and the vibes have kept me going through more than one day. The girls of Eastern High School; the women of Eastern High School are our tomorrow and hey, hey it's a bright day! Dig on it![99]

Public spaces became sites for black culture. "Africa at the Park: July 23, 1972," uses the placement of words on the page to suggest a tumbling motion that matches the description of dancers and drummers. These folks have found joy with each other during the long, hot summer, a summer not just of untimely death due to oppressive heat but one of community. Even as other *Chicory* authors acknowledge how segregation limits public space for black people, author Phyllis Jones depicts a gleeful claiming of public space:

all rejoicing at the spirits
all endorsing all the spirits
all enforcing every sound
reaching realms that Blackness found
Get down Brothers and Sisters,
Get Down!"[100]

**The End of Action** | In 1971, the neighborhood center at 112 North Wolfe Street closed. Fittingly, residents learned of this closing when the sign that read "Action" was removed from the building. Other centers closed, too, victims of urban renewal efforts that reduced the population of the area from four thousand to fifteen hundred. The War on Poverty was ending, a casualty of a never-declared war in Vietnam that sapped the national will to fight an enemy as elusive as poverty and of a political shift to the right on the federal level. While cities like Baltimore remained firmly in Democratic hands, they had to learn how to work with and against President Richard Nixon, whose New Federalism gave state governments more control over federal funds. Ever clever, artists and municipal officials found ways to leverage these ideological shifts to support cultural work through new policy programs like the Comprehensive Employment and Training Act. Private foundations and philanthropics became increasingly important as well. But the high point of federal support for arts and culture under LBJ would not be seen again.

*Chicory* represented a complicated cultural text, one that was created as the social arm of urban renewal. Human renewal proceeded on the assumption that black people were poor because of their behavior, not because of social structures. While it was seen benignly as a program to "enhance the social and economic opportunities of poor blacks," it did so through efforts to reshape black people themselves.[101] *Chicory* meant something different to each group involved in its creation. For its white liberal creators and readers, it offered a peek into the ghetto so that they would know better how to help the people living there. It also was an outlet, designed to let off the steam that might otherwise erupt into another riot. But, for its editors and writers, *Chicory* was an opportunity to use the funding flowing into Baltimore to create a public sphere where black people could write counternarratives of urban crisis, debate Black Power, and describe the city that they lived in as well as the one that they dreamed of. But, like all spaces for resistance, it was hard to summarize its point of view. Instead, it offered a wide range of perspectives, exactly like those that existed in the black community itself.

*Chicory* kept publishing for another twelve years after the first neighborhood centers closed, thanks to the continued support of the Enoch Pratt Free Library, which paid the magazine editor's salary and financed publishing and distribution. Unlike many other arts projects created with War on Poverty funding, *Chicory* lasted long after the truce was called. But to do so, it had to change, becoming more focused on community organizations than on neighborhood residents and moving, at times, beyond Baltimore.

*Chicory*'s editors continued to publish work by marginalized people, but they began to define those people in new ways, collaborating with incarcerated men, pregnant teenagers, and elderly people. These writers still grappled with questions of Black Power and life in the city of Baltimore. While, as Suleiman Osman has argued, black nationalist activists were deeply interested in neighborhood control, *Chicory* shows how, throughout the 1970s, they saw their struggles as part of larger, global battles against white supremacy, colonialism, and capitalism.[102] These links bridged the local and the global. "A visit to Johannesburg, South Africa," by Joyce P. Williams, published in the June/July 1976 issue, uses martial language to describe how white supremacy and capitalism created apartheid and how it will be defeated.[103] Daki Napata, a West Baltimore minister and activist who ran for mayor against Kurt Schmoke, connected civil rights battles in the United States with anti-colonial activities in Angola, Cuba, and Zimbabwe, invoking Frantz Fanon's theories on colonialism.[104] In January 1979, Peter Harris wrote "In a Name (for Ketema Jawara

Keita)," an ode to his child (who is also pictured on the cover of this issue). Harris explains they gave him an African name to give him "ancient ties, to do modern battle." This name "reattached his cord to history."[105] While the Black Arts movement is usually defined as ending in the mid-1970s, *Chicory* shows its continued importance in people's lives, particularly as part of a cultural nationalist desire to connect a mythopoeic African past and a revolutionary present and future.[106]

But the role of art and culture in Baltimore was changing. As we will see next, Mayor William Donald Schaefer used the arts to promote a singular image of Baltimore as unique, quirky, and nonthreatening. *Chicory*, the voice of the poorest black communities in Baltimore, was messy, often mediocre, at times brilliant. It was uncompromising in its depiction of the problems that plagued neighborhoods and in its celebration of black culture and life. It was multivocal. Under the autocratic Schaefer, city government, business, and civic leaders had one voice, which continued to repeat one message: Baltimore was Charm City. But few people who wrote for *Chicory* would see themselves as residents of that Baltimore. Their Baltimore encompassed the housing projects, community schools, and public spaces of a downtown populated by residents and workers, not tourists. Their Baltimore leapfrogged the suburbs to connect to a global black diaspora.

# HOLLYWOOD EAST

## William Donald Schaefer Animates Neoliberal Baltimore

John Waters had a complicated relationship with the state. From getting arrested for filming a naked hitchhiker on the grounds of Johns Hopkins University for *Mondo Trasho* to having *Pink Flamingos* and *Female Trouble* censored by Mary Avara, head of the Maryland State Board of Censors, he earned official condemnation. But, by the late 1970s, his location filmmaking in Baltimore intersected with the strategy of Mayor William Donald Schaefer to make the arts part of the city's efforts to manage the shift to a postindustrial economy. When Waters met Schaefer at a dinner, the visual contrast between the two could not have been starker: young, skinny Waters, dressed in his "thrift-shop-pimp-meets-hillbilly" style, and the stocky, balding, ruddy Schaefer, in his everyday suit and tie.[1] Schaefer claimed to be a fan. He "told me 'to continue making films in Baltimore,' . . . I doubt whether he's ever seen my films, but I think he's read about them and decided that if they get any image of Baltimore around the world—good or bad—it has to have a positive effect on the city. It makes it a lot easier to work, knowing the city is behind your twisted vision."[2]

Beyond their surface differences, the two men shared a deep love of Baltimore, a flair for showmanship, and a desire for complete control over their visions. For Waters, this meant cultivating a pencil mustache and filming acts like Divine eating dog feces for real on camera. For Schaefer, it meant absolute loyalty from his subordinates

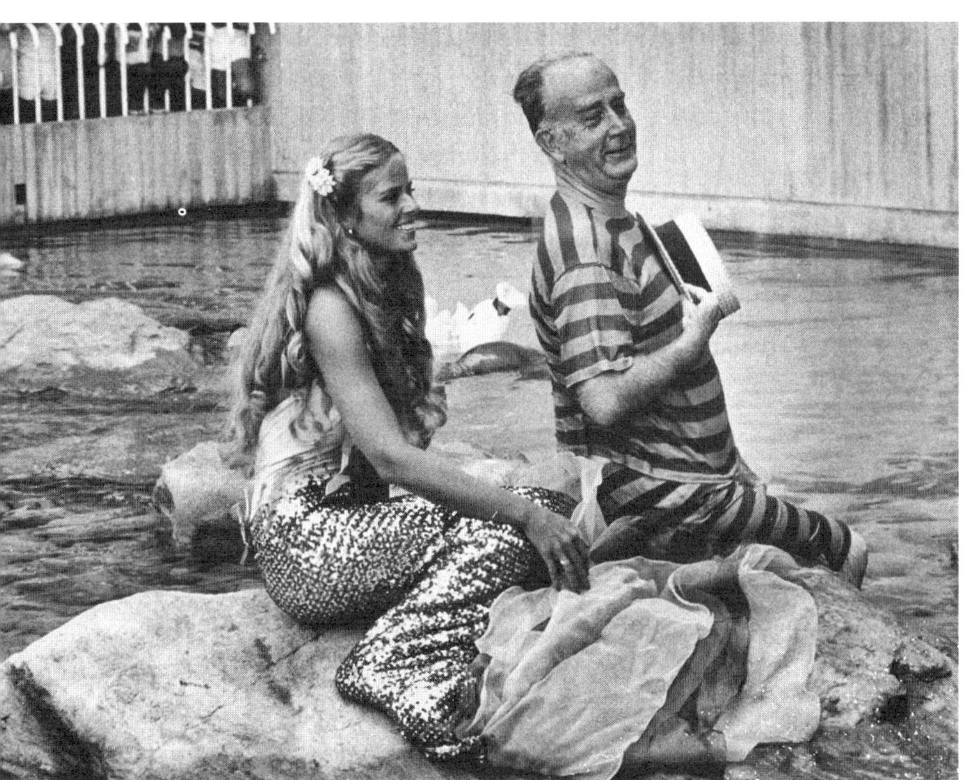

Mayor William Donald Schaefer poses with a mermaid for the opening of the aquarium in Baltimore's Inner Harbor. Schaefer's public relations stunts brought visibility to his efforts to animate the city.

Permission from Baltimore Sun Media

(or they would feel the wrath of his legendary temper) and a penchant for publicity stunts, like posing in an old-fashioned bathing costume with a mermaid for the opening of the National Aquarium in 1981. Elected in 1971, Schaefer, like Waters, was a tireless booster for the city whose idea of how to represent Baltimore was surprisingly catholic. Even though Waters's films exhibited extreme characters and transgressive acts, they could also be a promotional boon, if they raised the visibility of Baltimore and helped it compete with other cities for tourists and investment.

Over the course of his four terms, Schaefer used his power as mayor to reimagine Baltimore as an arts and culture capital appealing to upwardly mobile residents, tourists, and businesses. In doing so, he created a template for postindustrial cities around the nation and world. Cities in the 1970s responded to deindustrialization, federal and state disinvestment, and crime by pinning economic development to both tourism and the creation of a pro-business environment through changes in everything from tax policy to interest rates.[3] He justified the shift from 1960s-style managerialism, where city governments provided services to residents, to entrepreneurialism, where cities competed for investment through risky financial ventures and public-private partnerships, as Baltimore's only path to a postindustrial economy.[4]

While Schaefer is remembered for large-scale urban renewal projects like the Inner Harbor, those had been started under previous mayors. Even the public-private partnerships that defined his tenure were initiated by Mayor Thomas D'Alesandro Jr. and the Greater Baltimore Committee when they created the Charles Center–Inner Harbor Management Corporation. What distinguished Schaefer from his predecessors was his rebranding of Baltimore as a renaissance city. This rebranding encompassed three key components. First, he made Baltimore more entrepreneurial to woo investors and corporations to the city through tax breaks, public-private partnerships, and sweetheart development deals. Second, he understood that Baltimore's image was a hurdle to investors, so he first needed to give it both positive and unique associations. The creation of a city film commission hit both marks. As a pro-business agency, the commission helped film producers cut through bureaucratic red tape, making it easier to film in the city. In turn, those films spread images of Baltimore far and wide.

But image was only part of the story. Finally, there needed to be more activity to ensure that tourists, upwardly mobile residents, and business owners and their employees found the city exciting. Other cities used a variety of strategies that Baltimore learned from. Old factories in San Francisco became Ghirardelli Square in 1964, a complex of upscale stores, restaurants, and offices, all with a view of the bay. By preserving historic elements and incorporating out-of-the-ordinary retail, the space exuded a carnival atmosphere designed to draw urbane customers.[5] When John Lindsay became mayor of New York City in 1966, he quickly encouraged filmmaking by streamlining the permitting process. He appointed Thomas P. F. Hoving, a former director of the Metropolitan Museum of Art, parks commissioner. After Robert Moses's dour tenure, Hoving experimented with making the parks into sites of whimsy and playfulness designed to draw people in.[6] In Cleveland, inspired by San Francisco and Pittsburgh, there were parallel efforts to preserve a historic theater to attract middle-class audiences and preserve the city's history at Settler's Landing Park.[7] Baltimore, like these and other cities, used a combination of historic preservation, nostalgia, retail development, and arts and culture for revitalization.

Under Schaefer, arts and culture boomed in Baltimore. Before Schaefer, the arts were supported through Baltimore's museums, theaters, and universities; underfunded initiatives like *Chicory*; or were self-funded, like John Waters's early films. After Schaefer became mayor, city funding and support flowed more freely. In 1980, the city helped fund thirty quasi-public arts and culture corporations in Baltimore, from the Baltimore Arts Festival to the Baltimore Theater Project.[8] More than just increasing the number of arts activities in the city, Schaefer's administration reimagined the purpose of the arts. Rather than uplift or personal expression, the arts became the key to making visitors and upwardly mobile residents feel safe on public streets. Unlike suburbs, where streets were empty except for cars, the "sidewalk ballet" that had so captivated journalist and urban renewal activist Jane Jacobs could be engineered through public arts and culture funding.[9] Spaces needed to be animated. Cities had to be fun. Baltimore created bustling activity on public streets through specific kinds of noncontroversial arts.

Schaefer and his administration developed a municipal infrastructure that, like in New York, "was at once visual and material, combining intensive marketing . . . with neoliberal political and economic restructuring" around tourism and economic development, including film and television production.[10] Turning the city into a playground required significant municipal funding and labor. This arts and cultural infrastructure developed alongside a real infrastructure created through urban renewal. It equally changed the city. Schaefer's ambition and impatience made his sixteen years in office a turning point for Baltimore. He leveraged the sense of crisis that had been growing since the 1940s to disrupt how city business had been done. By competing with bigger cities for visitors and investment in the 1970s and 1980s, Schaefer helped create a neoliberal Baltimore where image, investment, and economic development trumped providing social services for residents.

**Baltimore's Biggest Booster** | Born in Baltimore in 1921, Schaefer was a contradictory character. While he espoused deeply traditional values, like living with his mother until moving to the governor's mansion in his sixties, he was also an audacious politician who reenvisioned Baltimore as a tourism center, rather than the industrial city it had been for generations. Before elected office, Schaefer worked as a lawyer. His political career began with another contradiction. He lost two races for the Maryland House of Delegates but polled enough votes that he got the attention of Irvin Kovens, the legendary fundraiser and Democratic political boss. Kovens offered to run Schaefer for city council in the Fifth District. Schaefer agreed but only if it was understood that he would always vote the way he wanted. When Schaefer won in 1955, it was clearly thanks to Kovens's machine, indebting him to longstanding political structures. He became city council president in 1967.

Schaefer built his reputation and amassed a group of loyal associates, like Joan Bereska, who would be one of his chief aides throughout his career, and Sandy Hillman, who would lead Baltimore's promotional efforts. In his tenure on city council, he supported urban renewal projects like the 3-A Expressway and voted to repeal the egregious tavern exemption that allowed Baltimore establishments that sold more liquor than food to remain segregated. The latter earned him sufficient support in the black community to make him a contender for mayor, especially after the riots following Martin Luther King Jr.'s murder damaged Mayor Thomas D'Alesandro III's reputation enough that "the increasing powerlessness of the big city Mayor . . . to close the pandora's box of urban troubles" was enough to keep him from seeking another term.[11] Schaefer became mayor in 1971, a post he would hold until 1987, when he moved to the governor's mansion.

Schaefer loved Baltimore, its townhouses with marble steps, grungy waterfront, and seedy red-light district called the Block. He understood the economic problems facing a city where manufacturing employment had dropped more than one-third between 1967 and 1977 and the population had peaked more than twenty years earlier.[12] Even so, he imagined that others might love Baltimore as much as he did. Why couldn't Baltimore draw visitors the way San Francisco or Philadelphia did? His vision of tourism as the engine of Baltimore's renaissance surprised others. As Bailey Fine, one of his aides, remembered, "He'd talk about downtown and a revamped inner harbor . . . and tourism. People would turn and look at each other. Tourism? It was like working for a crazy person . . . It just wasn't going to happen. But he said it over and over."[13]

Although tourism was in its early stages as an industry in the city and state, others were exploring its possibilities. The state legislature debated tourism bills. Governor Spiro Agnew named it the topic of the Governor's Conference on Economic Development in 1965.[14] Eric I. Weile, chair of the Legislative Council Committee on Tourism, argued in a 1970 speech to the Maryland Hotel & Motor Inn Association that "the travel industry is one of the biggest, if not the biggest business in the United States and it is growing by leaps and bounds . . . [W]e are talking about a sector of the economy that provides a vast number of jobs, and pays enormous sums in federal, state and local taxes."[15] By 1968, the Greater Baltimore Committee had created a Convention and Visitor's Council, which, in 1969, developed a summer boat tour of Baltimore's harbor, which was the fourth largest in the nation. An article in the *New York Times* described its highlights, including a view of the nation's oldest warship, the frigate *Constellation*, and Fort McHenry, where Francis Scott Key wrote "The Star-Spangled Banner."[16]

But boat tours and conventions wouldn't be enough. The perception of the city had to change. Urban crime terrified people in the late 1960s and early 1970s. Buildings set on fire during riots burned their way into the consciousness of the audiences watching the nightly news. The homicide rate rose precipitously during the 1960s and only continued to climb in the next decade. Still, Baltimore officials believed that people could be wooed back to Pratt or Charles Street, if only there was something to do there. Charles Center, the first major urban renewal project completed in Baltimore, "at night is dullsville," said one respondent to a 1973 marketing survey about the city.[17] Another noted acidly, "It is definitely not a cultural center. I don't know of anyone who ever went to Baltimore for a vacation or for fun; if they did I have my suspicions about their sanity."[18] The marketing survey, completed by Hill and Knowlton, became a blueprint for Baltimore's rebranding. Amazingly, just five years after the riots, the anonymous respondents in the city and the greater Baltimore area thought that race relations were good, the labor force was stable (and unlikely to strike), and crime was not a major issue. What was needed was simply more activity, which would be put under the purview of revitalized tourism and economic development agencies. While urban renewal had resulted in a rebuilt downtown, buildings alone had not supplied a central ingredient for a successful city: people.

Under Schaefer, the city government began to treat Baltimore like a product to be sold, starting by commissioning that marketing survey. Sandy Hillman, the head of the Baltimore Office of Tourism and Promotion under Schaefer, described their ideal city as one that was "animated." Animation would merge with and build on urban renewal. As she explained in nearly countercultural language, "We began creating animation—creating happenings, turning the city on to itself, using public programming as a means of bringing people back downtown again . . . And we did it in these brand new public spaces" created through urban renewal.[19] The term "happening" had been coined by artist Allan Kaprow to describe improvisational and participatory arts events, the first of which took place in New Jersey in 1958.[20] The counterculture borrowed it to describe spontaneous events, often in public, with a theatrical or performance aspect. In both cases, the intent was political, breaking out of rigidly circumscribed arts events to allow for fluidity and whimsy. For Hillman, though, happenings turned experimental artistic practice into something benign. The goal was to find "common denominator entertainment" rather than edgy explorations of self and community.[21]

Here again, the arts fulfilled a variety of functions. For William Manchester and social realist writers, literature presented a mirror to society that exposed its flaws and urged new social and political policies. By the time of the Cold War and Great Society, the arts were envisioned as a way for the United States to promote democratic values abroad.[22] At home, the arts, as with *Chicory*, were tools for community self-expression that were hopefully less explosive than rocks thrown at police cars. But, by the 1970s, the arts had "special importance for the central city . . . because of the contribution [they] can make to the attractiveness of the city and therefore to its economic viability."[23] Arts activities made spaces seem safe and fun, drawing people to them as members of ephemeral audiences. But how, the mayor's administration wondered, could it animate city streets without the fear of out-of-control public behavior? Two years after the 1968 riots, another riot spurred by racial conflict erupted at the usually staid Flower Mart, an annual street festival in Mount Vernon Square. Black and white youth disrupted the festival with brawling, reminding officials that public spaces could be animated in ways counter to the mis-

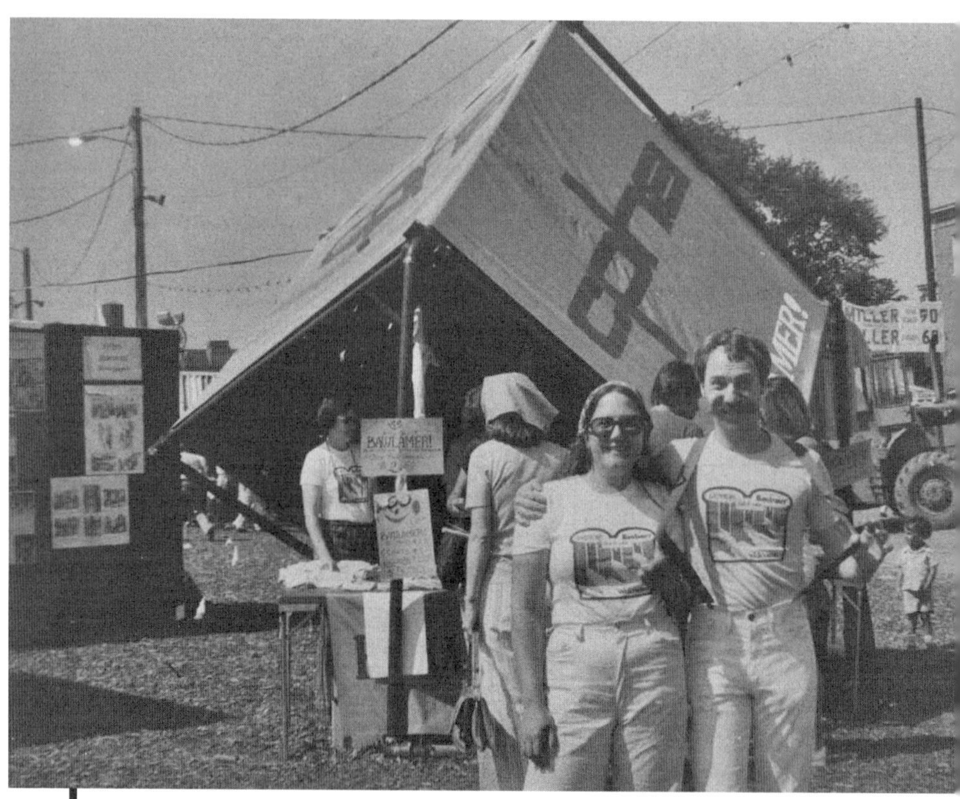


The City Fair drew thousands downtown. Organizations like the Citizens Planning and Housing Association rented booths alongside neighborhood associations.

CPHA—City Fair Booth, 1976; Citizens Planning and Housing Association Records; R0032-CPHA, Box S8-B1, Folder 58—Photographs and Media, 1941-1997, University of Baltimore Special Collections and Archives

sion of the municipal leadership.[24] The administration responded by tightly controlling public space through managing the kinds of art that would be sanctioned there. Noncontroversial street performers, like jugglers or mimes, who especially appealed to families with children, were auditioned, scheduled, and monitored by Hillman.

Her first major success in putting the theory of animation into practice was the Baltimore City Fair, held at Charles Center. In contrast to the spontaneous street activity that occurred during the riots, the fair was controlled. Each neighborhood had a booth that highlighted its unique characteristics. Attendees, who numbered in the hundreds of thousands, strolled from one to the next as they wished but with a clear path and purpose. Ethnic festivals (formerly held in neighborhoods but now moved to the Inner Harbor), concerts, theater, and son-et-lumière spectacles would soon follow. As Hillman wrote, "When you talk about 'image,' perception is equal to—if not more important than—reality, whether you're talking about selling soap or selling cities."[25] The municipal bureaucracy carefully managed the arts, as part of a larger urban symbolic economy, to draw specific audiences and encourage them to act in sanctioned ways in public spaces. Such efforts at control were never complete, though. Local groups leveraged the public visibility of these new events for political activity. The Movement against Destruction, an umbrella of neighborhood groups fighting the 3-A Expressway that threatened to demolish several neighborhoods in South Baltimore, reserved a booth at the 1973 city fair. The booth displayed maps and distributed promotional items like posters that read "Stop the Road."[26] Through these acts, MAD countered the image of the neighborhood as an apolitical source of personal identity and gave a political edge to the city's animation activities.

**The Infrastructure of Image** | Image and infrastructure worked in tandem. A promotional campaign could not bring visitors to a city with no attractions, but attractions needed to be married to a narrative that sold the city's unique qualities. While infrastructure projects had teams of people working to make sure that permits were filed and building codes met, image projects needed the same to ensure a consistency of vision. This required creating new agencies of government and promoting public-private partnerships as a counter to unwieldy government bureaucracies. Following the lead of the Baltimore Chamber of Commerce in the early twentieth century, the Greater Baltimore Committee created the Convention and Visitors Council in 1968 and the Promotion Subcommittee in 1970. With Schaefer's election, city government became involved. Clearly patterning itself after Atlanta's rebranding campaign called "Forward Atlanta," Schaefer replaced the ineffective Convention and Visitors Council with Baltimore Forward Thrust, which would "be more aggressive in luring conventions and visitors to the city."[27] By the next year, it would be renamed the Baltimore Promotion Council, which "combined state, city, and corporate funding to promote the city to national media outlets and more effectively recruit conventions, leisure travelers, and potential businesses looking to expand or relocate."[28] Combining public and private funding, whether for urban renewal or for branding the city, defined Schaefer's term in office.

Three examples show how Schaefer's administration quickly worked to control the image of Baltimore. In January 1974, producer and director James Goldstone approached the Baltimore Promotion Council about filming a TV show about an aging doctor living in a Baltimore marked by rapid demographic and social change. Called *Dr. Max*, the script for the pilot begins with the doctor being awakened by a call from a friend whose ill wife has taken a turn for the worse. Max rushes to meet them at the hospital, a journey that allows the camera to show the city. Max's stately house is surrounded by homes being divided into apartments, the neighborhood a "last bastian [*sic*] of tidy, predominately white, fading middle class stability . . . each house with its ascending marble steps, these stone steps a trademark of residential Baltimore." Nearing the small community hospital, he sees "brownstone tenements. Modern high rises. Crumbling condemnation. Rubbled lots. Towering glass and steel edifices."[29] The nonsynchronous juxtaposition of the old and new shows the city as it changes. Dr. Max, a representative of an older style of medicine, is also a figure of that fading city, which the script emphasizes through these deliberate exterior shots.

City officials were not smitten with this symbolism. Hillman asked Bereska to examine the script and give approval. Within a few days, Bereska responded with concern about the portrayal of Baltimore.

"There are several scenes involving rundown tenements, decaying neighborhoods, etc., and this aspect of the program could be stressed," by the director, "more than its positive scenes."[30] She asked for assurance from CBS about the ultimate portrayal of Baltimore in the show before giving approval for filming. *Dr. Max*, starring Lee J. Cobb and filmed in Baltimore, aired on CBS later in 1974. A failed pilot, it never spurred a TV series.[31] The debate over how this program depicted Baltimore, however, demonstrates that urban economic development is never divorced from image control. While Baltimore struggled economically in the 1970s, the city did not simply welcome all filming opportunities with open arms, though; as we will see later in this chapter, it increasingly became convinced of the importance of film production to its economic health and its image. Instead, the Schaefer administration had a complicated vision of how the city of Baltimore should be portrayed and exercised control over its portrayal through agencies like the Baltimore Promotion Council and the film commission.

In 1975, another television show attempted to depict Baltimore in ways counter to its promotional priorities. Famed producer Norman Lear, known for using television to raise liberal social issues, adapted Lanford Wilson's 1973 play, *The Hot L Baltimore*, for TV. Wilson's play told the story of a ragged group of elderly people, prostitutes, and outcasts living in the formerly grand Hotel Baltimore (the *e* in the neon sign had burned out), slated for demolition thanks to urban renewal. Wilson, who had built his reputation in the Off-Off-Broadway scene writing with sensitivity about marginalized people, created a theatrical vision of "a nation of transients looking for a past and a wake-up call."[32] He won a Drama Critics' Circle Award for Best American Play. Lear's version was set in the same hotel and included a diverse set of characters, including a black man, an undocumented immigrant woman from Colombia, and two gay men. Two women sex workers were also regular characters. Running for only thirteen episodes, the show is remembered most for being the first to include a gay couple as regular characters, though not by residents of Baltimore. WJZ-TV refused to air the show on the city's affiliate station. As station general manager Joel A. Segall explained, "We find it is not acceptable to station or community standards for air. On top of that, we are concerned with the image of our city as shown in the program."[33] Although there's no way to know whether the station management made this decision after being pressured by the city, the refusal to air the show suggests that the city government's vision of an appropriate image for Baltimore became hegemonic, followed by those, like the station manager, who were not directly under its control.

Slogan and branding campaigns designed to shape the impressions of potential visitors also required a municipal infrastructure. A failure at the time, the Charm City campaign of 1974 eventually gave Baltimore its most popular nickname. Like other cities, Baltimore officials repeatedly attempted to "replace negative perceptions" through slogan and branding campaigns intended to instill pride in residents and woo tourists.[34] Even back in 1915, the Merchant and Manufacturers Association of Baltimore assured its readers that "Baltimore has long been known as *The* Convention City—not a Convention City" because of its unique attributes, including "that indefinable quality called character; charm."[35] As competition between cities for conventioneers and tourists heated up in the second half of the twentieth century, cities differentiated themselves by promoting their unique, but not too-out-of-the-ordinary features.

The Baltimore Promotional Council created the Charm City, USA, campaign. It emphasized Baltimore's embrace of its history and heritage, even though the city had aggressively pursued urban renewal. As a press release noted, the campaign's message "expresses Baltimore's commitment to preserve and enhance its history, charm and tradition while giving itself a progressive, modern appearance." An ad in the *New York Times* and other national publications asserted that, "while the wrecking balls of other cities have been busy leveling tradition in the name of progress, Baltimore has been meticulously re-routing progress around its history in the name of tradition. Therein lies the charm of Baltimore."[36] Charm, in this context, evoked the cultural, historical, and architectural uniqueness that differentiated Baltimore from colder or more modern cities. The 1976 Baltimore annual report noted that "age can have its positive side. It can give a city charm and identity . . . the kinds of vestiges of the past—that help give a city its roots, its collective sense of self, its uniqueness."[37]

Charm was also racialized as white. The *New York Times* ad, for example, shows the ubiquitous white marble steps leading to a house with a painted screen in the window. A Baltimore folk art mostly found in the white ethnic neighborhoods of East Baltimore, the screens allowed those inside to get air into their houses over the summer without letting passersby see in.[38] The ad, which depicts no people of color or sites associated with them, "charmifies" the painted screen, taking it from being a living practice to a symbol of a city where quaint, premodern activities can be found. As we'll see in the final chapter, white ethnic neighborhoods and culture defined charm, ignoring the majority African American population of the city.

**Hollywood East |** With a municipal promotional infrastructure in place and a strategy to use the arts to animate the downtown, Schaefer's team was almost ready to reinvent the city. The final piece of the plan was the creation of new agencies and organizations to support arts and culture to appeal to corporations, tourists, and upwardly mobile residents. Schaefer creatively leveraged federal money, like Comprehensive Employment and Training Act (CETA) funds, and developed quasi-public agencies that used public money to pay for these activities. He created the Mayor's Advisory Committee on Art and Culture in 1974, which financially supported arts activities in the neighborhoods while also taking "advantage of the opportunities provided by the revitalization of downtown Baltimore for introducing a wider range of cultural activities."[39] The Schaefer administration even privileged cultural organizations over industrial ones, seeing them as integral to the new Baltimore being created. It evicted a chemical manufacturer that employed sixty people from its location near Penn Station to allow the Lyric Theatre to expand.[40] In the new Baltimore, a theater mattered more for economic development than a smelly chemical manufacturer.

Schaefer's patronage of the arts earned him a begrudgingly positive comparison with a Renaissance prince by the often-critical local alternative weekly paper.[41] He even pressed Baltimore Museum of Art director Arnold Lehman into giving him a tour so he could learn about contemporary art to better understand the museum's holdings.[42] A mural program brightened city walls and buildings. He convinced the Mechanic family to engage new theatrical productions on the way from DC to New York at the Morris Mechanic Theater and supported holding an international theater festival, which drew performers and audiences from around the world, in Baltimore from 1976 to 1979. By 1986, Baltimore was the site of the International Theatre Institute's Theatre of Nations Festival.[43]

While Schaefer's administration embraced a wide variety of arts, film became central to animating the city. After all, "according to no less an authority than the Museum of Modern Art, John Waters has 'put Baltimore on the film map.'"[44] This initiative would not only create a positive image for the city as a place of lively activity but could also provide direct economic benefits. Not only would film productions pay extras, buy food, and fill hotels; they would "increase favorable awareness of Baltimore" with business executives and the general public nationally, in the hopes of drawing them to do business with or visit the city.[45]

While Waters proved that independent, feature-length, profitable films could be made in Baltimore, Schaefer hoped to reach into Hollywood's deep pockets. Cities found Hollywood filmmakers particularly open to their advances in the 1970s. The New Hollywood, led by auteurs like Martin Scorsese and Francis Ford Coppola, used location filming in cities to tell complex stories of a post-Watergate, post-Woodstock America of despair and ennui. Another popular genre, blaxploitation, also filmed in cities. Unlike the New Hollywood films, these films featured African American actors and stories of hypermasculine antiheroes, a reaction to long-standing stereotypes of blacks in films as servile or criminal.[46] Location filming for Hollywood productions required securing permission from various city agencies for closing streets, using buildings, and diverting traffic, among other things. Such permissions necessitated entering a labyrinth of municipal bureaucracy and could take weeks or months for resolution. In the late 1970s, cities and states around the country began creating film commissions that would mediate between film producers and city bureaucracies. Easing the process saved productions money. Having a commission could give one city an advantage over another in an increasingly competitive marketplace.

To attract productions, Schaefer created a city film commission located in the mayor's office and run by Fontaine Sullivan, the head of the volunteerism office. The film commission would work with production companies to cut through the city's own bureaucratic red tape. It was part of a larger constellation of efforts by Schaefer to make Baltimore more business friendly and augured the future of Democratic politics locally and nationally. He promoted public-private partnerships that existed in legally gray areas with little to no public oversight, as with his hiring of local developer Francis Knott to run the 1978 referendum on developing the Inner Harbor. Schaefer had been city council president when voters rejected the 1968 Inner Harbor proposal. Seeing the project as integral to Baltimore's future, he refused to let that happen again. Knott got the referendum passed. For his efforts, his remodeling company received city loans.[47] According to geographer David Harvey, the success of this referendum meant that Baltimore had fully become an entrepreneurial city, more attuned to corporate than citizen needs.[48] Most damning, Schaefer created a revolving loan fund of $100 million that was used for development and to bail out failing projects without city council or public oversight.[49] Two trustees controlled what was essentially a shadow bank. When reporter C. Fraser Smith exposed these activities in a series of articles in the *Baltimore Sun* in 1980, Schaefer responded that it was the only way to spur Baltimore's renaissance.

"Speed and flexibility are an asset," Schaefer argued. "If you've ever tried to get through some government red tape, if you've ever tried to get through all the bureaucracy, you can see the need for the ability to move."[50] Although voters were supposed to have a say through public referendums on issuing bonds to pay for large-scale projects, Schaefer's administration found ways to work around the city charter in the name of economic development.

This anti-bureaucracy attitude extended to film production. In return for making it easier to get around city rules, production companies would spend desperately needed money in the city, even, at times, filling in gaps left by shrinking public funding under President Nixon's New Federalism. In filming the Norman Jewison–directed and Barry Levinson–written *And Justice for All*, for example, the crew had to install new lights in a real courtroom, an improvement that remained after they left. An indictment of the serious financial needs of the city, Sullivan boasted that it was a smart way to use private dollars for public benefit in the *Baltimore Sun*.[51] While the Baltimore film commission began as an arm of city hall, by the early twenty-first century it was a private nonprofit that worked closely with, but was not officially a part of, the city.

The roots of the Baltimore film commission began with the blaxploitation drama *The Hitter* (1979), starring Ron O'Neal, who had played Youngblood Priest in *Superfly*, one of the most famous films of the genre. James Beek, an aide to Schaefer, worked with Gary Herman, the producer, to find suitable locations and arrange for their use. Filmed in several locations in Baltimore in 1977, including warehouses, garages, and the Armistead Bar, which was attached to the infamous single-room occupancy Armistead Hotel, *The Hitter* told the story of a down-and-out boxer fighting for his next break.[52] With scenes shot on the Block, the location of Baltimore's strip clubs, and on the Inner Harbor, *The Hitter* is a document of a city on the verge of being reimagined for tourists. Shortly after filming, the Armistead Hotel would be torn down to make way for the Municipal Employees Credit Union headquarters in a deal that seemed to enrich some high-ranking bureaucrats.[53] In just three years, Harborplace would open at the Inner Harbor with huge fanfare, catapulting Baltimore to national attention as a city entering its renaissance after the economic and social dislocations of the 1960s and 1970s.

Soon after *The Hitter*, two other Hollywood movies were made in Baltimore. *The Seduction of Joe Tynan* and *And Justice for All* (both 1979) were filmed in the city, though in the former Baltimore was made to stand in for Washington, DC. With *Joe Tynan* (at the time called *The Senator*), the mayor realized that there was no centralized method of permitting and assigned Fontaine Sullivan, volunteer coordinator, to work with the production. By mid-1978, before the film was finished, Schaefer created the Commission on Motion Picture and Videotape Productions, located within the Mayor's Office, to formalize this relationship. The Maryland legislature debated the creation of a statewide film commission in 1979, a spur to Baltimore to quicken its pace since the state, unlike the city, could offer tax breaks.[54] The mayor offered other perks. As Schaefer noted in a letter to film producer Gary Stromberg, his control over the commission benefitted filmmakers. "Commission members are responsible only to and directly to me," he wrote, explaining that it "is their job immediately to answer your needs for manpower, equipment, physical facilities, supplies, and materials. They well know that in movie production time means money and that by eliminating red tape, bureaucratic hassle, and false starts, they will save your company precious time and money."[55] The job of the city was increasingly becoming helping private businesses deal with the city.

The commission had sixteen members, including Leon Back, president of the Maryland Association of Theater Owners; Dallas Weigle, slide show expert; James W. Curran Jr., a WCBM radio personality; and, most interestingly, Pat Moran, best known as a producer of and sometime actor in John Waters movies as well as a small business owner. Many people advocated for the mayor to hire Moran as the director of the commission, replacing Sullivan. As a memo to Schaefer's closest aide argued, "The future could be dazzlingly bright if Pat Moran and other energetic and savvy Baltimoreans can be fully utilized. Unfortunately, the Mayor does not seem to be inclined to create a couple of CETA positions and allocate a modest sum of money to support film promotion. I hope I am wrong in this. If the Mayor shows a genuine commitment to this project and puts knowledgeable people like Pat in charge, the economic benefits to the city will be great."[56] As was the case with urban renewal, federal funds, this time from CETA, could be used to promote municipal growth but in the area of cultural development. While Moran was not given the job, a few years later, another Dreamland actor, Joseph "Turkey Joe" Trabert became head of the Baltimore Film Commission from 1987 to 1990. Once criticized by the city, the municipal infrastructure incorporated Waters's outré outsiders.

If Baltimore had become "Hollywood East" by the late 1970s, as Sullivan argued, then it seemed only appropriate that it should hold its own version of the Oscars to honor filmmakers working in Baltimore.[57] Called "the Don," after Schaefer's middle name, the award ceremony was envisioned as the red carpet event of 1978. As its tagline stated, "Anyone Can Go to Hollywood and Earn an Oscar, but You Have to Be in Baltimore to Earn a 'Don.'"[58] Chaos reigned behind the scenes, as few tickets were sold and little money was raised.[59] Even the local television stations refused to broadcast the event.[60] Nonetheless, the event would highlight Baltimoreans working in film both in the city and outside of it and announce the creation of the mayor's film commission. The list of potential Don awardees included Levinson, a native son who had written the script for *And Justice for All*, and Betsy Slade, who acted in *Kojak*. John Waters was mentioned as "the best independent film maker in the country today," whose films had been shown at the Cannes Film Festival.[61] Members of the *And Justice for All* cast were promised to appear, though Sullivan noted that Al Pacino was "temperamental" and it was hard to know whether he would show after all.[62]

Interestingly, the directors, producers, and actors in *Amazing Grace* and *The Hitter* were completely ignored by the organizers of the Don, even though Tom Cripps, a professor at Morgan State University, was to be honored for his book on the depiction of African Americans in film, *Slow Fade to Black*. Films made by and starring white people—a spectrum spanning works as varied as those by avant-garde provocateur John Waters and middlebrow Barry Levinson—were suitable representatives of Baltimore's efforts to promote itself as a film capital. Baltimore's cultural representations mirrored the city's residential segregation, a process that would continue through the remainder of the twentieth century and into the twenty-first. Cultural productions by African Americans remained separate from those of white Baltimoreans, rarely receiving the same level of promotion, funding, or visibility. The *Baltimore Afro-American* made this point in an article condemning *And Justice for All*. After positioning the film within the context of the beginnings of the mass incarceration of black men, the author asks why the only black actors hired for the film play extras in courtroom and jail scenes, while whites play judges and lawyers. Continuing on, the author asks, "Were all the charges of police brutality swept under the rug just in time to cash in on Hollywood gold?" The parallels between racist law enforcement in Baltimore and Hollywood filmmaking are clear. To be acceptable to Hollywood filmmakers, Baltimore had to hide its internal problems to woo economic development opportunities that tended to portray African Americans in stereotypical ways as criminals, if at all. With a deep bitterness, the article ends by noting that "the film company is expected to leave $1.25 million in B-more. It just might leave something else. A sense of shame, which might force the city to clean up its act."[63]

**A Pattern Is Forming** | A weekend storm felled tree branches and interrupted the annual German festival. Owners of shops with whimsical names like the Seldom Scene and Embraceable Zoo scrambled to get their inventory in order before opening day. But when July 2, 1980, dawned hot and cloudless, there was no possibility for delay: Baltimore's Harborplace, the centerpiece of the three-decade-long project to renovate the Inner Harbor, was finally ready to open.

Image and infrastructure had merged in the process of renewing Baltimore and resulted in a gargantuan project that was as much about changing the narrative of Baltimore and animating the waterfront as it was about a new economy based on tourism and leisure. A pattern was forming for Baltimore—a compelling story of rebirth married to the creation of new arts and building infrastructure paid for through public-private partnerships.

Schaefer emphasized a different kind of pattern. "Stay absolutely within the pattern," he argued, "and we would have down at the Inner Harbor a nice rat-infested place, the neighborhoods would be the way they were fifteen years ago."[64] Baltimore's renaissance required entrepreneurial action by the city. But the public bore the cost of such entrepreneurship. The vast majority of the funding for Harborplace came from public coffers, while management of the site—and its profits—stayed in private, corporate hands, a new kind of quasi-public arrangement.[65] Critics complained that the money spent on the downtown could help the residents of Baltimore's impoverished neighborhoods, who felt ignored by the push for development. Nothing symbolized this better than the failed attempt by two hundred public housing residents to meet with Mayor Schaefer. On July 1, 1980, nearly six hundred unionized maintenance workers began striking against the Housing Authority for better wages, leaving fifteen thousand residents in the city's public housing projects without hot water. While a federal mediator worked with the union to resolve the issue, a small group of residents marched from Lafayette Courts to city hall, demanding to see Schaefer and even pounding on the closed door. When they learned he was at a reception in the Inner Harbor to celebrate the next day's opening, they marched the several blocks to intercept him there, but he had left moments before their arrival.[66] The message was clear. The mayor focused on downtown elites, developers, and tourists, rather than the regular citizens who had elected him.

But, surprisingly, city leaders did not envision tourism as the major purpose of the Inner Harbor in its early incarnations. In the

1960s, the GBC imagined the Inner Harbor as another Charles Center, a complex of offices with some cultural amenities. Skeptical citizens only narrowly approved the loans for the first phase of the project, which allowed the Charles Center–Inner Harbor Management (CCIHM) company to acquire a thousand properties and relocate seven hundred businesses to make space for the new office buildings that would anchor the 240-acre area.[67] By the late 1960s, the Harbor was a grass-covered park area, beloved by the surrounding neighborhoods.

CCIHM and Schaefer refused to give up on their vision. A park was not going to be the economic engine of Baltimore's renaissance, nor was it going to change the image of the city. Martin Millspaugh, president of CCIHM, brought in developer James Rouse to reimagine the space as a festival marketplace, a type of shopping center he had developed in Boston's historic Faneuil Hall in 1973. Eschewing cookie-cutter anchor department stores for small vendors with offbeat items, shoppers would be entertained by buskers, musicians, and those suddenly-in-demand jugglers. To reference the past, Rouse incorporated ersatz architectural features into the design, giving it a vague sense of history not deeply connected to a specific historical period. Unlike a mall, it offered "the experience of the preindustrial city in which the historic open market—the nostalgic point of reference for the new festival marketplaces—had provided a locus of social relations and public discourse seemingly absent from both the suburban shopping center and the previously abandoned postwar city."[68] Immediately successful, Rouse went on to build New York City's South Street Seaport and the Gallery at Market East in Philadelphia, among many others.

To prove the viability of the Inner Harbor, Schaefer pushed his Office of Promotions to animate the area. The city fair, organized by Sandy Hillman, was moved from the Charles Center to the Inner Harbor in 1973. The Tall Ships that docked in Baltimore harbor during the Bicentennial celebration in 1976 drew droves of tourists, suggesting the area's potential. This critical mass of activity convinced Rouse to pursue a festival marketplace that would trade on the waterfront's history to bring tourists and visitors looking for fun, unusual consumer experiences.[69] As food writer and journalist Calvin Trillin joked, "the problem of Baltimore's lack of any old warehouses whose brick could be artistically exposed" was "solved by beginning new buildings from scratch" that were designed to look old.[70] The neighborhoods around the Harbor, though, resisted the plan, preferring to keep the park. In 1978, the forces of development won a public referendum.

Harborplace opened in 1980, while the National Aquarium and a Hyatt hotel did so in 1981. "Profit," Rouse stated, "is the thing that hauls dreams into focus."[71] The Inner Harbor became the profit machine that clarified the dream of a tourism-centered neoliberal Baltimore. While locals still used the space, including black youth involved in early hip hop, it kept tourists away from the rest of downtown.[72] Separated from downtown by multilane Pratt Street, to this day a walkway from the Renaissance Baltimore Harborplace Hotel allows its guests direct access to Harborplace without stepping foot on the street. Indeed, all the major tourist attractions are aligned on one side with Pratt Street acting as a moat separating it from the downtown. The culmination of decades of planning, millions of dollars of investment, and acres of demolition, the Inner Harbor fulfilled the promises of the GBC and Mayor Schaefer. Four hundred thousand people came for the opening, and in the next year eighteen million visitors came, more than the total number who went to Disney World. It seemed to realize Rouse's goal to make the city "a warm and human place, with diversity of choice, full of festival and delight."[73] The former industrial heart of Baltimore was now a tourist mecca that produced no goods but, instead, employed people in service sector jobs to cater to visitors drawn by the narrative of a renaissance city. Thanks to the Inner Harbor, the *New York Times* called 1981 "the year of Baltimore."[74]

But how to heal those divisions between the neighborhoods and the downtown, between the working-class folk and a city hall that seemed to be perpetually looking for the next big thing? Schaefer, yet again, turned to art and animation. The Baltimore Theater Project, founded by Philip Arnoult, had created a musical show called *Baltimore Voices* out of hundreds of oral history interviews recorded for the Baltimore Neighborhood Heritage Project (BNHP), developed by Ted Durr, a professor at the University of Baltimore, and undertaken by a team of oral historians. Coming out of the new social history and the work of progressive public historians, *Baltimore Voices* attempted to change the representation of Baltimore in a time of urban renewal, deindustrialization, and demographic change. The show, funded through CETA and grants, emphasized the vibrancy of working-class neighborhoods through song and dance. Its progressive political commitments to the contrary, it, too, became part of the selling of Baltimore. The city saw its usefulness as a tool of the larger project to connect downtown and the neighborhoods. *Voices* was performed during the 1980 city fair, while the University of Baltimore booth displayed a traveling BNHP exhibit there and sold the book *Baltimore People, Baltimore Places*.[75] Every Friday in August 1980, the cast performed a forty-minute version of *Baltimore Voices* at the top of the World Trade Center in downtown Baltimore for the tourists and sightseers.[76]

While Schaefer capitalized on the work of public and oral historians and theater professionals to co-opt *Baltimore Voices*, city agencies spurred another partnership between local and nationally known artists. Before Harborplace opened, the city commissioned Helen and Newton Harrison, married conceptual and environmental artists from California, to undertake an art project called the Baltimore Promenade. Funded by the National Endowment for the Arts, the project was managed by codirectors representing two entities that would have been unlikely to work together just a decade earlier: Larry Reich, head of the Baltimore city planning department, and Fred Lazarus, president of the Maryland Institute College of Art. The city provided planners and landscape architects to work with the Harrisons as they surveyed the city, while MICA hosted an exhibit of their large-scale photos of the city and gave them an opportunity to teach a workshop, "Urban Promenade: A Baltimore Case Study."

The Baltimore Promenade project demonstrated the tensions between the stated goals of public art and its true value to the city as a handmaiden to economic development. The NEA grant specified that the goal was to "create a new—a renewed—unity between sections of the city."[77] Although the Harrisons, outsiders to Baltimore, consulted with the public over the course of the project, their vision was privileged. The grant proposal suggests, too, that economic development was paramount. It notes "current commitments for over $350 million of construction in this area in the next seven years, and the prospect for at least $150 million more."[78] Continuous development as much as the need to heal social divisions gave the project national impact.

The central theoretical conceit of the project was the promenade. The Harrisons argued that a promenade is "both an activity and a place, a stage on which people in a community meet and mix."[79] Rather than walking with purpose, this leisurely strolling meant that there was a "high level of amiability and conviviality" on the promenade that created a self-regulating ephemeral community that would discourage running, shoving, or behavior that would break the mood.[80] Perhaps most importantly, the "promenade is the only public adventure where you have permission to stare."[81] The promenade aligned perfectly with Schaefer's vision. Art and municipal government could work together to reimagine public space to appeal to visitors and businesses looking to invest in the city. Indeed, the Harrisons' project resulted in a series of suggestions for how to connect four areas of the city—the waterfront, Lexington Market, Antique Row, and Patterson Park—through small changes like creating a walking path around the Patterson Park pond and signage. The goal was animation. People would become the focal point, drawing other people. Rather than the pointed staring at Divine that John Waters captured while filming her promenades through the city in *Pink Flamingos* and *Female Trouble*, this would be warm and friendly. This panoptic gaze

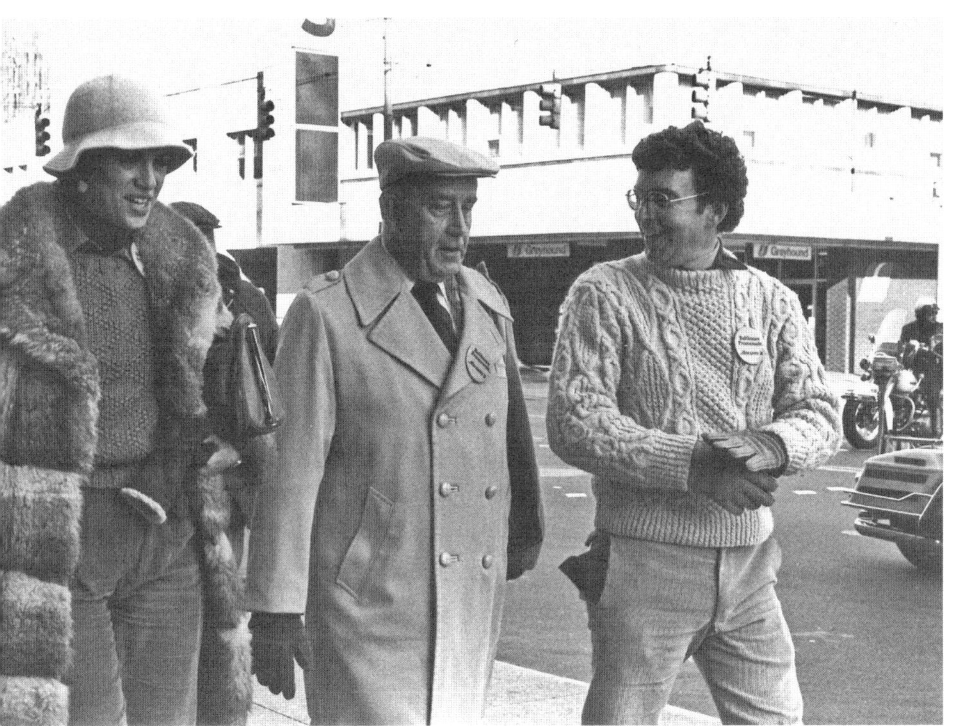

Sandy Hillman (*left*) and Mayor Schaefer (*center*) take a stroll during the Baltimore Promenade in 1981, claiming the streets for city-sanctioned leisure as part of an NEA-funded art project.
MICA Archives, Decker Library, Maryland Institute College of Art

of everyone looking at everyone would ensure a safe, comfortable space for the majority. During the inaugural promenade on December 13, 1981, approximately two hundred people, including Mayor Schaefer, "followed a handful of Pied Pipers playing flute and violin music along a trail sometimes strewn with trash or broken pavement—on a quest for a unified Charm City." Yellow balloons streamed along the route and cheerleaders, unicyclists, and jugglers entertained the walkers. A police motorcade "made many of the walkers feel secure in areas where some conceded they might not have wanted to walk by themselves, even by daylight," suggesting that the everyday life on these streets simply scared people from outside those neighborhoods.[82]

Who is a city's downtown for? As the Baltimore Promenade project showed, the downtown "has been not only the linchpin of urban real estate and conspicuous consumption but also an idealized public place and thus a powerful symbol . . . invested with civic meaning."[83] By the early 1980s, Schaefer perfected a formula to renovate downtown Baltimore for a new economic moment. He used the arts to animate public spaces to woo tourists, business owners, and the upwardly mobile to interact with each other in contained activities where they were both audience and entertainment, to define the city as both modern and charming. One of the taglines for the Baltimore Promenade project was "a pattern is forming." With the yoking of art to neoliberal renewal, the control of both the image of the city elsewhere and the use of space within it, a pattern was forming that would define Baltimore for decades to come. Art would not be used to heal civic wounds but, instead, to animate space. Artists, whether filmmakers or muralists, worked with the municipal apparatus to construct a Baltimore that was open, amenable to tourists, and, most importantly, business friendly. Renewal expanded from projects to build highways and skyscrapers (displacing people of color in the process), to include cultural activities under a growing municipal government. While responsible for Baltimore's much-lauded renaissance, these changes also led to feelings of dislocation and alienation, even among the white middle class, whose members expressed their ambivalence in many cultural representations set in Baltimore in the 1980s.

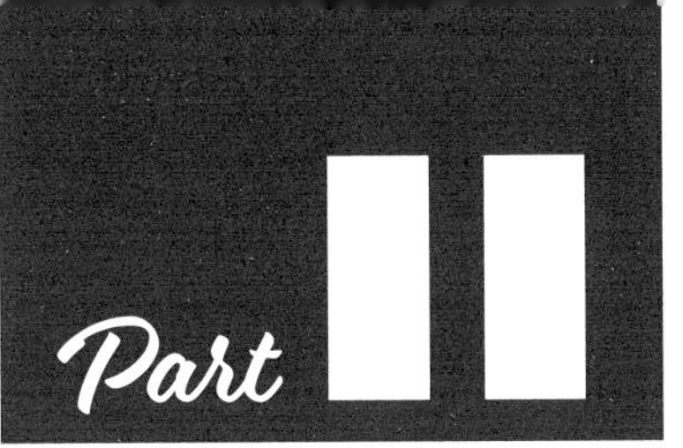

# Part II

# GOOD MO(U)RNING, BALTIMORE

# ACCIDENTAL TOURISTS

## Alienated Whiteness amid Renaissance

The Baltimore of working-class African Americans faced off against white working-class eccentricity with the publication of two books within a few years of each other. Part of the urban fiction boom of the 1970s, Jerome Dyson Wright's self-published *Poor, Black and in Real Trouble* (1976; republished by Holloway House) followed Philip Avery, a successful criminal, whose "violent behavior is caused by the unfairness of an oppressive system," who proves his masculinity through sexual control over women and by punishing male homosexuality.[1] Growing up in West Baltimore in the 1950s, Avery understands that to be poor and black is to be in real trouble or locked within a system that is designed to keep black people disenfranchised psychologically, socially, and economically. After carrying groceries to a white woman's home, he is attacked and robbed by a group of white teens in front of a white police officer who ignores his request for help. While the civil rights movement takes place in the background of the novel, he doesn't participate in nonviolent protest. His protests are in the form of "terroriz[ing] white businesses."[2] Like *The Autobiography of Malcolm X*, the novel details the political and racial awakening of its main character. It refuses to be nostalgic about the past, identifying overlapping systems of oppression for black Baltimoreans.

The Citizens Planning and Housing Association's tenth edition of *Bawlamer: An Informal Guide to a Livelier Baltimore* in 1981 was quite different. This cheeky guidebook, which had grown from 64 to

223 pages over the course of a decade, encapsulated what was becoming the overarching image of Baltimore—offbeat, quirky, and white. On its cover, the word Baltimore shifts to Bawlamer, the colloquial white working-class pronunciation of the city's name. Inside, a glossary offers out-of-towners tips on how locals pronounce words like "flower" (flar) and "trash" (traysh). Welcoming to tourists, Baltimore "is really like a small-town hometown—with just the right amount of Big City panache."[3] Published by a nonprofit organization, *Bawlamer* merged with and expanded on the policies of the Schaefer administration. It promoted the image of eccentric whiteness that would become dominant in the cultural representations of Baltimore in the 1980s.

A spate of high-profile films and novels, and lesser-known ones, rode the wave of Baltimore visibility in the 1980s. Thanks to the film commission and state efforts to win productions, Maryland ranked ninth in the nation for film and television revenues by the late 1980s.[4] In 1988 alone, three films shot in and about Baltimore, *Hairspray*, *Talking to Strangers*, and the never-released-for-home-viewing *Stage Fright*, appeared at international film festivals from Berlin to Cannes.[5] From Anne Tyler's *The Accidental Tourist* (novel, 1985; film, 1988) to Barry Levinson's *Diner* (1982), *Tin Men* (1987), and *Avalon* (1990) to John Waters's *Hairspray* (1988), filmmakers represented Baltimore more in this era than ever before. Alongside these well-funded mass productions, others proliferated. Robert Ward's novel *Red Baker* (1985) tells the story of an unemployed steel worker. Rob Tregenza's film *Talking to Strangers* (1988), which Jean-Luc Godard reviewed positively in the catalog of the Toronto Film Festival, explores the existential crisis of an artist. Steve Yeager made a film homage to the burlesque theaters that had occupied Baltimore's red light district, titled *On the Block* (1990).[6] Although varied in tone, genre, and medium, each work depicts characters disoriented by a changing city. While a film version of *Poor, Black and in Real Trouble* floundered for a lack of funding, these other works, which centered whiteness and a nostalgic desire for the Baltimore of the past, most often the 1960s, won acclaim.

The main characters in each become "accidental tourists" in their own lives and city. Anne Tyler coined the phrase "accidental tourist" for the title of her novel, but it explains the relationship between people and places more widely. If a tourist is someone who purposefully consumes unfamiliar cultures, observes unknown peoples, and enjoys unusual experiences, then an accidental tourist is thrown suddenly into unfamiliar territory. As Baltimore competed for upwardly mobile professionals and as its economic and social landscape marginalized blue-collar industrial life, longtime residents and native sons and daughters found themselves accidental tourists in a city quickly shifting away from their needs. Rather than the "anticipation . . . of intense pleasures" that tourists feel from visiting "sites outside the normal places of residence and work," these accidental tourists' primary emotional response was alienation.[7]

Each of these works centers whiteness. Even in *Hairspray*, a film about the civil rights movement of the early 1960s, the lead characters are white. Whiteness is constructed in two primary ways. White characters are shown to be either eccentric, charming reminders of a way of life that is being supplanted by modernity, or they are alienated, bitter, and angry at change. Unsurprisingly, it is the white eccentric that becomes the most popular image, one that helped to sell Baltimore as different from other cities like Washington, DC, or New York that are wholly modern. In the other works, working-class white people direct their anger at people of color, precluding acknowledgment of shared economic marginalization. Finally, nostalgia suffuses all these portrayals. A complicated emotion, nostalgia is often defined as a desire for the past, but it is equally about place. The creators of these cultural texts located Baltimore's heyday in the early 1960s, a moment defined by security, stability, and order—though *Hairspray* reminds us of segregation's role in maintaining that order. While these are not the only images of Baltimore from this period, they are the most important in their popularity, critical acclaim, reach, and visibility.

**The Accidental Tourist** | Although she had published several novels and earned critical praise before moving to Baltimore, it was when Anne Tyler began setting her finely drawn, poignant stories of familial love and heartache there that her books became best sellers and award winners. Born in Minneapolis to socially conscious Quaker parents in 1941, Tyler and her family moved to the Celo Community, a Quaker commune in North Carolina in 1948. The rural isolation of the community shaped her sense of herself as an outsider, giving her a deep interest in observing others.[8] An artistic child, Tyler began writing in college, majoring in Russian at Duke University. She published her first novel, *If Morning Ever Comes*, in 1964, followed quickly by her second, *The Tin-Can Tree*, in 1965. Soon after, she and her husband, an Iranian child psychiatrist, moved to Baltimore, where she has lived in the Roland Park neighborhood since. With the publication of *Dinner at the Homesick Restaurant* (1982), she was a finalist for several major literary awards. It was not until *The Accidental Tourist* (1985) that she won the National Book Critics Circle Award and was a finalist for the Pulitzer Prize. The novel's success led to its adaptation as a film, directed by Lawrence Kasdan in 1988. The film earned rave reviews and was nominated for four Academy Awards. Her next book, *Breathing Lessons* (1988), won the Pulitzer Prize for fiction. In 2018, she published her twenty-second novel. Like John Waters, Baltimore has been the setting for her work since moving there. She's become so associated with the city that, in 2003, the British newspaper the *Independent* printed a suggested Baltimore travel itinerary for fans of Tyler's novels.[9]

Tyler sets *The Accidental Tourist* in a Baltimore bifurcated into two specific classes—the upper and lower class—which are easily identified by geography, taste, and worldview. The upper class is rigid, locked into social rituals and etiquette divorced from emotion, while the lower class is passionate and humming with life and energy. These classes are represented through the main characters: Macon Leary, a writer whose son has been murdered and who is separated from his wife, and Muriel Pritchett, whom he hires to train his out-of-control dog.

Macon Leary, a travel writer who hates traveling, represents an aristocratic Baltimore. After his carefree, adventurous mother sent him, his brothers, Porter and Charles, and sister, Rose, to live with her parents in a stately house in an upper-class Baltimore neighborhood, the Learys learn to inhabit a controlled, narrow-gauge world. Rose alphabetizes the groceries; Macon, after his wife, Sarah, leaves him, begins washing his clothes in the shower while he bathes in the name of increased efficiency. Their disconnection from the outside world manifests fully in the siblings' inability to get around the city that they grew up in. This "geographic dyslexia" renders the city outside their house unfamiliar territory, a strange and disorienting landscape.[10] Yet their obsession with order is also a function of their upper-class milieu. The Learys manage well enough until Macon's son is murdered. The tragedy shatters Macon, but he is unable to express grief in publicly acceptable ways, instead isolating himself from his friends and neighbors and driving his wife away with his lack of emotion

In the midst of a changing Baltimore, the Learys represent an earlier way of life. "Quietly and harmlessly nuts," they are cocooned eccentrics who have fashioned a world in stone.[11] Macon's publisher, the suave Julian, lives in a singles apartment building and boats on the weekend, part of the new Baltimore of young professionals. He finds the Learys fascinating, a remnant of a different generation. Acting as a tourist in the Leary house, Julian observes them, commenting favorably on their strange habits (eating bland, early dinners that always include baked potatoes), and eventually marrying Rose for her old-fashioned qualities. By seeing them through Julian's eyes, Macon understands his family to be eccentric. "He has this one-sided notion of us," Macon tells his sister. "I just pray none of us says anything unconventional around him" (116). This eccentricity either pushes people away, like Sarah who finds him stodgy and unemotional, or draws people to them, like Julian or Muriel, the woman who forces Macon to break out of his shell.

Muriel, as is to be expected in a romantic comedy, is Macon's opposite. A single mother, she is working class, holding several low-skill jobs at once to make ends meet for her and her sickly son. Macon meets Muriel at the veterinary office where she works when he boards his increasingly aggressive dog there. Realizing he is single and wealthy, Muriel offers her services as a dog trainer. Class difference is, of course, a central trope of romantic narratives, whether the female lead is Cinderella or Julia Roberts. For Macon's family, Muriel's hand-to-mouth lifestyle explains her interest in him—she is simply looking for a man who can ease her economic burdens. To be fair, Muriel understands that, in the face of an economy with few well-paying jobs for a single mother with a high school education, marriage is her best way to rise into the middle class. She lives on the fictional Singleton Street in a poor section of South Baltimore, which seems to Macon a "labyrinth of littered, cracked, dark streets" with "too many murky alleys and stairwells full of rubbish and doorways lined with tattered shreds of posters" (181). By entering her world—represented by the easygoing communal nature of Singleton Street—he learns to express his grief and find joy. It is the place as much as the person who changes him: "In the foreign country that was Singleton Street he was an entirely different person. This person had never been suspected of narrowness, never been accused of chilliness; in fact, was mocked for his soft heart. And was anything but orderly" (194–95).

Eccentricity defines the "kooky, yakkety animal trainer" Muriel, but it is of a different kind than the Learys'.[12] Muriel dresses in an eclectic combination of colors, patterns, and thrift-store style, often paired with long, fake nails that the film, especially, lingers on. Unlike the prim and respectable Sarah, she is sexual, with a "larger-than-life vitality, an abundance, a willingness to disregard convention and the opinions of others."[13] She speaks in malapropisms.

Outgoing and extroverted, she has no boundaries with strangers, telling them her life story, as she does with an embarrassed Macon. When she and Macon are mugged in her neighborhood, she whacks the thief with her purse, sending him on his way. When she follows Macon to Paris, he's concerned that she'll be lost in the strange city. Instead, she quickly makes friends, finds out-of-the-way shopping nooks and vintage treasures, and consumes the city with gusto. Muriel's eccentricity represents a different Baltimore, one rooted in white ethnic community-based life.

The greatest difference between Macon and Muriel is their ability to deal with the demographic and social changes happening in Baltimore and, by extension through Macon's travels, the world. As international capital transformed cities including Baltimore around the world in the 1980s, these global flows brought increasing racial, cultural, and linguistic diversity. While stiff, stolid Macon falters in their face, Muriel, who is racialized throughout the novel, fares better in part because her class and gender give her no choice. Macon finds it comforting that he can tell his readers where to buy Kentucky Fried Chicken in Stockholm but is disturbed that they now expect to know where to find pita bread, which "had grown to seem as American as hot dogs," as well (10). When he travels to a once-familiar hotel in London, he sees "cone-shaped ladies in long black veils." Although he "hated to sound narrow-minded . . . his readers did avoid the exotic" (32–33). In the face of these changes, he feels dislocated, his sense of stable identity shaken by these interactions. Although American cultural hegemony turned the world into an extension of self and home in the post–World War II period, rapid globalization threatens this hierarchy.

While Tyler has shifted her depiction of black characters over time from being repositories of wisdom and common sense to more directly confronting white racism, in her books the "predominant racial theme is the proposition that equality and harmony between the races are not only desirable but achievable."[14] However, neither the novel nor the film *The Accidental Tourist* includes any characters of color. People of color haunt the margins as representatives of the changing world. Muriel, instead, is depicted in terms coded as nonwhite. Macon describes her upon their first meeting as a "thin young woman in a ruffled peasant blouse. She had aggressively frizzy black hair that burgeoned to her shoulders like an Arab headdress" (25). After she complains about taming her hair, Macon suggests she buy an Afro pick, but she is embarrassed at the thought (92). On one hand, using these phrases in relation to the white Muriel underscores the lack of actual characters of color in the novel or film, even though Baltimore by the 1980s was a majority black city. On the other, it suggests her position within society. A single mother with a series of low- or no-skill jobs, she lives on the margins, racialized by her class position. Unlike Macon, nonelite women do not have the luxury of feeling dislocated. Instead, they must become part of a growing class of migrants, nannies, caretakers, and factory workers, buffeted by the needs of capital.[15]

For Macon, self-realization comes through crossing class and geographic boundaries. Accidental or not, his view is very much that of the tourist. His gaze turns Muriel's world into a miniature, like a dollhouse or cartoon tourist map. It blots out the despair and striving (in the film, the sudden death of one of Muriel's neighbors is not even mentioned) and reimagines it as charm. In Macon's mind Singleton Street is "full of gaily drawn people scrubbing their stoops, tinkering with their cars, splashing under fire hydrants" (325). Their plucky resolve and flexibility in the face of change become a source of strength for him.

Reviewers ignored these questions of race, class, and economics but did acknowledge the importance of geography. John Updike's review described Baltimore as "rich in characters and various in locale, yet with a cloistered and backward-gazing quality like that of a less drastic Yoknapatawpha County, with the same convenience to a microcosm-maker."[16] *People* magazine also identified Baltimore as important to a novel that is "about common people" dealing with "genuine tragedies—from random violence to personal alienation."[17]

Reviewers enjoyed the offbeat characters depicted here and in other works. Wallace Stegner described Tyler's characters as a "Dickensian gallery of oddballs, innocents, obsessives, erratics, incompetents and plain Joes and Janes" who "all see the world a little skewed."[18]

**Red Baker** | If *The Accidental Tourist* spread an image of white, quirky Baltimore that unexpectedly supported municipal prerogatives of tourism and economic development through commodifying white eccentricity, then Robert Ward's PEN Award–winning novel *Red Baker* revealed the inner life of white working-class men as alienated and enraged by this partnership. Ward, born in 1943, grew up in Baltimore raised by his grandmother, a social justice activist who was the inspiration for his 1990 fictionalized biography, *Grace*. He attended the University of Arkansas's writing program and lived in the Haight-Ashbury district in San Francisco before returning to Baltimore in the late 1960s. He published his first novel, *Shedding Skin*, in 1972, and began working as a journalist. After *Red Baker*, he wrote for the TV police show *Hill Street Blues*, launching a career writing for movies and television.

*Red Baker* begins by alluding to the narrativization of his home city. "There never was a story with a happy ending in Baltimore," title character Red Baker muses, even though the novel does have a seemingly happy ending—but one that, pointedly, does not take place in Baltimore. Red is a steel man, a longtime worker at the Larmel steel factory. Layoffs set him on the downward spiral that the novel recounts. Although *The Accidental Tourist* never mentions specific contemporary events in Baltimore, *Red Baker* locates itself immediately within the economic dislocations of President Ronald Reagan's first term in office. Red fumes at the hypocrisy of the "president and his band of television writers . . . telling us the economy was on the big climb" when 60 percent of Larmel's workforce is laid off with one week's notice.[19]

*Red Baker* is not a political novel, however. It is a Springsteen song in the form of a book—the story of a man's disillusionment with a world that promised him stability in exchange for adherence to codes of white masculinity but then hoodwinked him. After losing his job, he vacillates between low-paid demeaning jobs and periods of alcoholism and drug use. He fantasizes about leaving his wife and son and moving to Florida with a stripper named Crystal. Instead, his wife leaves him after he drunkenly hits her and his son. He eventually agrees to work with a crooked cop who orchestrates a robbery of one of Red's enemies. The sure thing, of course, backfires. Red's best friend Dog is killed, but Red makes it out with the money.

That this story takes place in Baltimore is important, because so much of the public discourse around the city in this era was dominated by a renaissance-not-rustbelt narrative. The renaissance narrative focused on the upwardly mobile tourist or eccentric whiteness, not the economic troubles of white working-class men like Red. The centering of alienated white masculinity here and in the films *Diner* and *Tin Men*, to which we will turn in a moment, ignores potential coalitions with women or people of color, further isolating white men. "Red Baker's Philosophy: You're usually up to your head in mud, but as long as you can keep breathing you're ahead of the game" is a survival strategy but not one that changes or even substantively questions the system (14). Red, an accidental tourist in a deindustrializing Baltimore, can make tentative steps toward success only when he leaves, meaningfully, for the Sunbelt, a center of suburban conservatism. His story of white working-class male alienation is also a story of place, but, in this case, Baltimore has turned its back on these men, who must leave it behind. Understanding this trajectory tells us about the men who harbor intense rage at cities and progressive racial policies, which they see as ignoring their needs to help the undeserving.

Staring "half dead out the window at the bright new city, with its huge office buildings all lit up and empty," Red feels "it was a strange place—not Baltimore at all." How could someone who had lived his entire life in the same city feel this dislocation?

> Because I lived in Highlandtown, because I had my job, my family, and my friends, I hadn't noticed how much it had all changed . . . none of that really affected me or my family. But now for the first time I saw things as they really were. I saw the city had been pushing me and my friends all along, and we had been so caught up in just staying alive, that we had never once pushed back. (235)

Disconnected from a local political structure run by machine Democrats for generations, the white working-class people have been blind to the changes happening around them, cushioned by the promises of their class and racial position and neighborhoods that prioritized racial homogeneity over adaptation. Like many white ethnic neighborhoods in Baltimore and elsewhere, African Americans were kept out of Highlandtown, though they lived in bordering areas. As black civil rights activism made gains and street protests turned into riots, Highlandtown residents became obsessed with law and order. During the 1968 riots, for example, one neighborhood landlord made a loaded shotgun accessible to his tenants, "in case the blacks decided to mount an assault on Highlandtown."[20] For Red Baker, Highlandtown connected him to a rich past, but its isolation and narrowness obscured reality. Red and his friends play football with his son and his friends, creating a bond that "connected, one generation to another, and it felt good and filled" him with joy at the consistency of this white male sociability (54). But such hopefulness is fleeting in the face of the macro changes happening around him. With the slipping of economic stability (defined only as secure, well-paying work that allows for a male-headed household), Red finally realizes that the city has changed.

He lashes out at the aggressive marketing of the renaissance city by throwing a trash can with "Balmere is Best" written on it into a parked luxury car, a fruitless effort (83). He begins to understand the process of memorialization that will turn him and his blue-collar brethren into kitsch to appeal to young professionals. He goes to the Angry Oyster, a "new mall bar," whose logo "had a picture of a little demon oyster popping out of a shell with a rough-and-ready look on his face. The new Baltimore" (43). Prioritizing consumerism and decorated with ersatz portholes and fake wood, the Angry Oyster commodifies the symbolism of the Harbor's past to sell it to outsiders who find it quaint. The demon oyster is an image of a blue-collar worker like Red or his hard-fighting friend Dog, "rough and ready." But only as a logo, not as real men, as they find out when the waitress chastises the rowdy Red and Dog: we "got our policies, ya know?" about how patrons should act (44). While the real tourists, the college kids wearing trucker hats, are comfortable, Red is at sea, a tourist in his own city and class position.

Red's alienation from place, class, and family turns to rage, the kind that the New Right tapped into, "a populist grab bag of resentments based on region, race, economics, and sexuality."[21] With the loss of large employers like Bethlehem Steel and the McCormick spice company, men like Red have few transferable skills in the new economy. Yet their ideologies of whiteness and masculinity make them see certain jobs as beneath them. Service work, the only growing sector of the economy, is fine for women, who are supposed to serve others, but not for white men.

Race also structures what jobs are seen as suitable. When he goes to the unemployment office, the African American woman working there, whom he refers to internally as "Ms. Motown," tells him that a job as a maintenance worker at Harborplace is the only job available. The insult to Red's masculinity is layered. First, his wife works at Harborplace, meaning that she could see him doing this low-paid work. It also puts them in the same class of occupation—service work. But, more pointedly, Red is disgusted at what he sees as the racial implications of this job. He sees it as "Nigger work for Red. Thirty-nine years old, working as a trash man" (43). While the employment agent explains that this initiative is "part of the special task force the mayor has instituted. The Baltimore Full Employment Brigade. Kind of like the old CCC Camps," placing it into a political history of working-class employment measures, Red refuses (42). Nonetheless, he repeatedly finds himself competing with African American men for jobs with no benefits or stability.

He ignores his white privilege. For example, the owner of a parking garage, who knew him as a young man, hires him as the supervisor and lets him pick the other hires even though he has no more experience than the black applicants. His ignorance and anger represent the forces pushing the United States rightward in the 1980s. This is the legacy of *Red Baker*. While the steel mills may have closed, "the workers are still out there," but "women, immigrants, minorities, and, yes, white guys, all make up the 'new working class' . . . but there is no discursive, political place for them comparable to the classic concept of the industrial working class."[22]

***Diner* and *Tin Men*** | Where *The Accidental Tourist* and *Red Baker* were set in present-day Baltimore, several films about Baltimore were set in the early 1960s. Released during the 1980s, they suggest a Reagan-era desire to return to an earlier moment of seeming cultural cohesion. Ambivalence about changes wrought by civil rights activists, feminists, and gay rights activists empowered the New Right, which organized around a vision of a return to an era of white male dominance. While, as we will see, *Hairspray* complicates this narrative because of its engagement with civil rights, the critically regarded and popular *Diner* and *Tin Men* depict a segregated white lower-middle-class Jewish Baltimore where the biggest threats to white male dominance are aging and changes in work caused by technocratic government and reduced conspicuous consumption. The men of *Diner* and *Tin Men* are also accidental tourists, but, unlike Red Baker, they are not angry. They are confused and wistful even though they are also superfluous to a modernizing city.

Based on Levinson's own stories of growing up in Baltimore, *Diner* was a smash success. In a year dominated by science fiction slickness from *Blade Runner* to *Tron*, critics saw *Diner* as filmmaking at a human scale, with small stories leavened with the idiosyncrasies old friends come to expect from one another. Set in Baltimore during Christmas 1959, the episodic story follows six friends as they contend with the existential and material questions posed by adulthood. Eddie, played by Steve Guttenberg, is so afraid of commitment that he forces his fiancée to pass a quiz about the Colts football team before he will marry her. Roguish charmer Boogie, played by Mickey Rourke, is a hairdresser whose schemes to earn some quick cash get him in hot water with an impatient bookie. Rich kid Fenwick, played by Kevin Bacon, battles a drinking problem. Shrevie, played by Daniel Stern, is married to Beth, played by Ellen Barkin. He can't stand his dead-end job and is more comfortable spending time with his old friends than his wife. Tim Daly plays Billy, the only character with a future, who learns that his girlfriend is pregnant. Indecisive Modell, played by Paul Reiser, offers colorful commentary on everyone else's plights. Every night, they gather at the Fells Point Diner to relive their youth, banter, kvetch, and sop up French fries with gravy.

With their motormouth joking and eccentricities, the men of *Diner* broaden the template of charming white working-class identity to include Jewishness by ignoring racism. Jewishness is depicted as a marginalized identity, reflecting the reality of anti-Semitism in Baltimore. Although the characters are aware of social divisions around religion, they are blind to racial conflict. Set before Baltimore became a black majority city, the film's absence of black characters reflects the writer and director's viewpoint. As Barry Levinson said of his memories of Baltimore, "There was very little prejudice. The diner brought together people from various backgrounds. Jews and gentiles, middle-class and lower-middle-class guys all became friends."[23] Levinson's memories to the contrary, the fate of blacks and Jews in Baltimore were intertwined, as in many places. The end of restrictive covenants allowed Jews to move to new areas of the city. Black people began to move into these formerly Jewish neighborhoods.[24] Unsurprisingly, perhaps, Levinson reports that he had no conception of such issues growing up in the city. When the *Baltimore Afro-American* interviewed Levinson about the film, he acknowledged that "there were only about a dozen blacks at our school [Forest Park]" but that he did not "have an awareness" of issues around integration or block-busting.[25] Another *Afro-American* article tartly noted that "what this pix reflects is when Baltimore was a segregated city and blacks attended either Douglass High or Dunbar High."[26]

Place is critical. Levinson filmed on location in Baltimore, thanks in part to the efforts of the fledgling Office of Motion Picture and Television Development.[27] Unlike John Waters in his early films, Levinson and his crew worked closely with the city. The location filming made the film seem authentic, while the city touted the money brought in by the production, though it also wooed the producers and cast with a promised $1,000 wrap party.[28] In *Diner*, as Levinson suggests, the diner itself crystallizes the film's themes. Supposedly a place where people from radically different backgrounds and worlds could interact, in reality, like the lunch counters that became the focus of so much civil rights activism, diners were spaces where such possibilities were often foreclosed. African diplomats traveling between "the U.N. headquarters in New York and the nation's capital" found themselves barred from eating "in Maryland's Jim Crow diners."[29]

In naming the film's diner, Levinson showed the importance of place. Called the Fells Point Diner in the movie, the diner was modeled after the Hilltop Diner on Reisterstown Road (the actual diner building, however, came from even farther afield: New Jersey). By naming it the Fells Point Diner, the film connected it to the white ethnic working-class enclave of Fells Point, a neighborhood that had successfully used historic preservation for gentrification. After the film's success, Baltimore TV station WBAL bought the diner building and gave it to the city. Four years later, when the diner was on the brink of closing, Mayor William Donald Schaefer vowed to save it.[30] It became the Kid's Diner, staffed by Baltimore vocational education students.

*Tin Men* takes place a few years later. B. B. Babowsky, played by Richard Dreyfuss, and Ernest Tilley, played by Danny DeVito, are aluminum siding salesmen in 1963 Baltimore. Known as tin men, they scam, hustle, con, and cajole lower-middle-class homeowners into buying siding for their homes. The film opens with B.B. buying a new Cadillac and immediately getting into an accident with Tilley. Neither will take responsibility for the fender bender, which begins a feud that leads to escalating acts of revenge, from breaking car windows to B.B. seducing Tilley's wife, Nora. Unexpectedly, when B.B. calls Tilley to tell him about the affair, Tilley is delighted, telling B.B. to take his wife, please. While the tin men spend their time scheming revenge, they are threatened by the government, which creates a Home Improvement Commission (a real historical event in Maryland) that intends to eliminate their shady practices.

While the transition from adolescence to adulthood defined *Diner*, the changes here come from external social forces. The Home Improvement Commission will, essentially, put the tin men out of business while protecting consumers. The coming of law and order marginalizes these self-made men, making them accidental tourists in their city. In the end, as B.B. and Tilley become friends, they struggle to comprehend these changes. B.B. asks, "You want to know what our crime is? We were nickel and dime hustlers. We got caught because we were nickel and dime." While Tilley mentions a new Cadillac with different fins that will be coming on the market, B.B. understands the coming fad of simpler living, represented by a VW Beetle driving past.

Through these details and the antics of its hustler protagonists, the film adds to the image of Baltimore as a town of white eccentrics. Levinson, echoing John Waters, argues that Baltimore is a "great, colorful city with a lot of great, colorful characters and we tried to capture that."[31] Calling his characters Runyonesque, Levinson connects himself with a tradition of making hustlers lovable scamps—as long as they're white. He remembers the real tin men of his youth with "big cars and fancy kind of clothes, they always had a lot of pocket money, loved hanging out at the track and going to shows and clubs . . . They're sort of like rebels in a way, but they're not like rebels the way we think of rebels . . . Within the framework of a working-class mentality, they are sort of like the gunslinger of their trade."[32] If *The Accidental Tourist* depicted white female eccentricity, in *Tin Men* and *Diner* we see its male variation. Although Levinson admits that *Tin Men* could have been set in other white ethnic working-class locales, like Philadelphia or New Jersey, its connection to Baltimore was important. In fact, in one scene B.B. and his partner sell siding to a woman who lives in the house where Levinson grew up.

Reviewers related to the deep connection to place, seeing the film as innately about Baltimore. Columnist George Will raved about the movie as an evocation of a lost time when men congregated together in ways that feminism changed. While the time may be lost, the place was still accessible. People may not see Baltimore as a beautiful city, he argued, but, "today, Baltimore is one of America's most livable cities and tin men are a vanished species . . . [P]eople and places need not be lovely to be loved."[33] Of course, the nostalgia that suffuses this depiction is most important to the city for its ability to draw new investment. Clarence "Du" Burns, the first black mayor of Baltimore (he rose to the position when Schaefer became governor), noted that filming *Tin Men* brought $3 million to the city. "It means an awful lot to us. Not just for the money, but for people around the country, and even in foreign countries, seeing us. You couldn't pay for this kind of advertising."[34] Depicting a historic Baltimore of eccentric characters with a seemingly unchanged built environment helped economic development.

***Hairspray*** | In his beloved, popular, and culturally influential cult film *Hairspray*, John Waters rewrites the cancellation of *The Buddy Deane Show* from the point of view of Tracy Turnblad, a chubby white girl played by Ricki Lake who leads an interracial group of activists to successfully integrate the show. Merging the teen comedy of the 1960s and the message movie, *Hairspray* tackles the virulent debates over racial integration in early 1960s Baltimore. Set a year before Levinson's *Tin Men*, which ignores civil rights in its focus on white masculinity, *Hairspray* depicts a city where contestations over racial boundaries happen daily, particularly around young people's access to culture and each other.

The film follows Tracy as she becomes an unlikely dancer on *The Corny Collins Show*. When she realizes that segregation means that black teens can't dance with whites, she begins her crusade to integrate the show, with help from her best friend Penny Pingleton, whose overprotective, racist mother tries to stop her, and her new friends Seaweed, a black teen whose mother is Motormouth Maybelle, a local radio DJ played by African American R&B singer Ruth Brown, and his sister Lil Inez. She also vies against Amber Von Tussle, the thin, conventionally pretty, and wealthy girl who wants to win the Miss Auto Show 1963 crown while keeping the show segregated. Tracy's working-class parents, Edna and Wilbur, played by Divine and Jerry Stiller, support integration unlike the Von Tussles, played by Debbie Harry and Sonny Bono, who vow segregation forever.

Although this PG-rated comedy was Waters's first foray into mainstream filmmaking, some cultural critics deem *Hairspray* subversive. Dana Heller, for example, argues that *Hairspray* is Waters's most subversive film because it overturns cultural expectations about normative female bodies in the context of a family film.[35] Other scholars have argued that its over-the-top campiness allows viewers to read it against the grain to subvert the generic plot.[36] However, Waters's film is mainly subversive when considered in comparison to the other Baltimore depictions of this era. Unlike these others, *Hairspray* does have black characters. More importantly, Waters offers a sharp cultural analysis of the intersection between geographic and cultural space and race in Baltimore, depicting black spaces of cultural production and community building. Unlike the earlier representations we've considered, his intersectional approach looks at the way that gender, whiteness, and class produce his characters. Most radically, he depicts intraclass interracial alliances in which white and black working-class people see themselves as having a shared future. But, ultimately, for the majority of viewers *Hairspray* is not subversive for two central reasons. First, having a white woman at the center of a civil rights narrative ultimately marginalizes the black characters and makes them vehicles for a white coming-of-age story. Second, the film's visual texture of pastel colors, huge hairdos, and period details overwhelms the narrative. A hyperbolic Baltimore of the 1960s, which grows even more exaggerated in later iterations of *Hairspray*, becomes the main takeaway.

An astute cultural analyst, Waters understood what made *The Buddy Deane Show* popular and threatening. Its combination of sexual experimentation and spread of working-class and African American styles and culture beyond parental controls terrified adults, in much the same way that rock and roll and comic books did. He suggests as much with repeated shots in *Hairspray* where the film camera moves through a television or television camera to end up in a geographically distant location, like the Turnblads' Baltimore living room. TV's space-time compression, leaping miles and hours instantaneously, suggests the powerlessness of white authorities to control white youth engagement with black culture. As a woman picking up laundry at the Turnblad house says when she sees Corny Collins on TV, "Delinquents if you ask me. It ain't right to be dancing on television to that colored music." Waters grew up obsessing over *The Buddy Deane Show* and idolizing its dancers. Although he appeared on *Deane*, he never became a member of the elite Committee. But, through these young people, a different kind of Baltimore entered his consciousness. Unlike his family's upper-middle-class suburb, these kids "wore sports coats with belts in the back from Lee's of Broadway . . . pegged pants, pointy-toe shoes with the great buckles on the side, and 'drape' (greaser) haircuts that my parents would never allow."[37] These styles visually distinguished working- and middle-class youth from each other. Ironically, the segregated show also introduced white Baltimore to black music, which Waters indicates in the film through radio DJ Motormouth Maybelle, who also hosts the show's Negro Day.

Waters depicts the racialization of space in three scenes. At the record hop, Corny Collins, played by Shawn Thompson, tells the group of sharply dressed teens that it's time for the "hottest tune of the day," "The Madison." As the kids line up, plucky, dance-crazed Tracy arrives with Penny. Momentarily angered when a black teen couple is turned away at the door because "this is a whites only establishment," Tracy forgets their ordeal as she becomes engrossed in the sounds, sights, and proximity to her teen idols. Tracy pushes her way to the front of the Madison line, adding flourishes to the simple steps, like mimicking Wilt Chamberlain and Jackie Gleason, quickly proving herself a standout. The audience chooses Tracy and her partner as the winners, making Tracy the queen of the hop. The racial politics woven throughout the scene are complex. Segregation creates a geographical space in which Tracy can prove herself to be a model teen, knowledgeable about style and dance steps. If she or any other white teens had to compete with black dancers, would they still win? Although black youth are excluded, black culture and celebrity are the foundation from which these young whites can perform their identity. Maybelle is cheered by the crowd for her rhyming couplets and sassiness. They dance enthusiastically to black musicians like Chubby Checker. They even mimic a black athlete in the middle of a dance appropriated from black musicians.

From a whites-only space, Waters takes us to a space of black community and cultural production. First, however, the white and black characters meet each other in an interstitial space—school detention. Seaweed meets Tracy, who has been sent to detention because her beehive hairdo is so large it's blocking students' view of the blackboard. With their shared love of dancing, Seaweed is soon teaching her dances popular in the black community and invites her and her friends to a dance at his mother's record store. Accidental tourists, Tracy, Penny, and Link travel to North Avenue in an African American section of Baltimore. The white teens are welcomed by Seaweed and his sister L'il Inez as they integrate the all-black dance party, presided over by Maybelle. Link and Tracy dance the "dirty boogie," a sexually suggestive dance, while the others watch, implying that this black space frees them to express desire. Penny's mother bursts in with a knife, pulling her daughter, who is dancing with Seaweed, out.

Waters shows us what bell hooks calls a "homeplace," "a safe place where black people could affirm one another and by so doing heal many of the wounds inflicted by racist domination."[38] The camera enters the dance before Tracy and her friends do. We see a group of black teens, watched over by Maybelle, joyously dancing to music created by black musicians. When Tracy, Penny, and Link arrive, however, they stop, become suspicious—who are these white people coming into their space?—until Seaweed greets them, giving them access to it. The attention shifts to them, but, in those prior moments, Waters gives a glimpse of life in black Baltimore missing from the other depictions of the city in this era.

In the third space, integration is resisted by violent whites. Tilted Acres, a fictionalized version of Gwynn Oak Park, a privately owned amusement park, is a white-controlled space of leisure off limits to African Americans. Collins decides to record a show there, which is peacefully picketed by civil rights activists. The TV station owner, Arvin Hodgepile (played by Glenn Milstead out of drag), tells Collins that if "one black face gets on camera, this show's off the air." When a white segregationist woman throws a cherry bomb into the black protestors' crowd, a riot starts as people burst in through the park's gates to escape the chaos. Unlike the real-life Baltimore Area Youth Opportunities Unlimited protest in which whites integrated Special Guest Day, *Hairspray* "reverses the scene so that it is once again black students who must be granted entry into a previously all-white enclave."[39] Police beat Seaweed as Penny, locked in her room by her parents, screams "police brutality" at the TV. If black spaces could be integrated by whites at will, Waters suggests that white spaces would and did fight integration with all the resources at their disposal.

But Waters also suggests the possibility for interracial and intraclass coalitions. Historically, poor and working-class whites were often por-

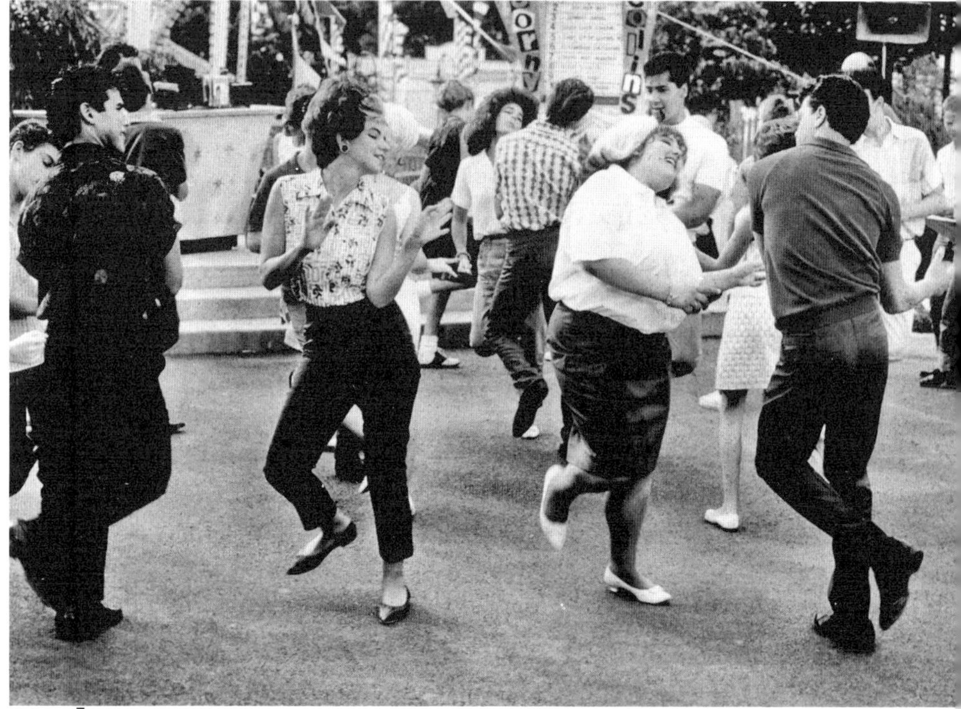

Teens dance at the Tilted Acres Amusement Park before a riot breaks out over integration in this scene from John Waters's 1988 film *Hairspray*.
Photofest

trayed as close to African Americans, both physically and culturally. Franklin Von Tussle calls Tracy "white trash," while Velma underscores how class makes her racially liminal by suggesting that she could even be "high yellow." Whiteness is not monolithic in *Hairspray* but is instead deeply complicated by class position. The Turnblads and the Von Tussles represent two different class positions within whiteness—the working or lower middle class and the upper class. Wealth mires the Von Tussles in the segregationist system. As Franklin Von Tussle proclaims, he's the "richest man in East Baltimore." Fearful of losing money if they integrate their amusement park, they staunchly defend their outmoded views. Velma, the ultimate overbearing stage mother, tells Amber to "at least act white on television," meaning choosing white singers to dance to and maintaining a thin, neat, controlled body, unlike Tracy's or Edna's corpulence. Tracy's own consciousness raising happens in part because school authorities treat her as white trash: she's put in special education classes because her hairstyle shows her working-class background. Just as high schools in the 1950s built large vocational wings to segregate working-class white and students of color from middle-class students destined for college, Tracy is tracked into a dead-end educational space that unwittingly allows for coalition building between black and white students. But Waters also pokes fun at white liberal do-gooders who fetishize African American culture. When Tracy breathlessly confesses to her boyfriend, Link, that she wishes she were "dark-skinned," or when Penny is seen reading *Black like Me*, it's clear that Waters is gently critiquing white cultural appropriation.

Stripped of civil rights themes, *Hairspray* is simply another Cinderella story of a plain girl becoming queen of the dance. But because it is placed within the context of the civil rights movement, Waters's choice to make a white teen the protagonist is significant. For Waters, the fact that she is chubby makes the story subversive: "Normally, the fat kid, the ugly kid, or the gay kid is the sidekick in the movies, never the star. But that kid is always the star in my movies. And the regular hero or heroine is usually the villain."[40] Waters lumps together black youth, poor whites, and fat women as outsiders in *Hairspray*, slyly offering a kind of coalition against elite whites that, at the same time, ignores the actual power differentials between these groups. Indeed, the first integration that happens in the film is Tracy integrating nonnormative body types into *The Corny Collins Show*. While it is a powerful message about body acceptance (and one of the reasons for the story's enduring popularity), there is a world of difference between lookism and actual policies of segregation. When Tracy, who is viciously made fun of by other teens, realizes that the show won't let black and white teens dance together, she sees a shared story of marginalization. For most viewers, this surface reading of an underdog triumphing over her detractors defined the film. In fact, the remakes of *Hairspray* build on this aspect of the story line, ultimately downplaying the queer campiness in the original and becoming even more popular by doing so.

Several Baltimore films in this era showed black characters helping white youth mature. Barry Levinson's 1999 film *Liberty Heights* tells the story of integration from the point of view of a teenage Jewish boy. *Clara's Heart*, another film shot in Baltimore and released in 1988, shows black characters helping the self-actualization of white characters. Based on a novel of the same name, the film stars Whoopi Goldberg as Clara, a Jamaican maid and nanny for a wealthy white family struggling after the death of a child. Clara becomes the closest friend of the lonely remaining child, David, helping him deal with his parents' selfishness and divorce. Even when David breaks into her suitcase to read private letters about her own lost son and calls her a "nigger" when she leaves the family, Clara remains a calm and maternal figure, constantly putting her needs aside to help him grow and mature.

Like these films, *Hairspray* turns the civil rights movement into a subplot in a white teen's coming-of-age story. When Inez meets Tracy, she exclaims that she is her "favorite dancer on Corny Collins!" Seaweed educates Tracy that Negro Day is simply another form of segregation and teaches her his dance steps. While Maybelle begins the movement to integrate *Corny Collins*, she recedes as the focus becomes freeing Tracy from juvenile detention, with "Free Tracy Turnblad" as the integrationist rallying cry. To be sure, Waters incorporated black cultural producers into the film's production. Besides casting Ruth Brown as Maybelle, another R&B singer of the 1960s, Toussaint McCall, makes a cameo appearance. Two black choreographers created the dances for the film, and black actors were used extensively as part of a Screen Actors Guild affirmative action program.[41] But the final shot of the film literally centers Tracy, seated on her throne as Miss Auto Show, with the only black person in the frame, Seaweed, at her feet.

Perhaps even more than the plot, the exaggerated early 1960s look and sound of the film came to be the most influential aspect for Baltimore. While the *Los Angeles Times* review argued that "*Hairspray* is more than just a nostalgic romp full of ratted hairdos and goofy dance hits," it also notes that art director Vincent Peranio "had a field day decorating the von Tussles' glitzy pasteled row house."[42] "No teen realism here," wrote Richard Corliss in *Time*, "just a romp through the pastel homes and matching mother-daughter outfits of a more naive era."[43] As Janet Maslin argued in her review, *Hairspray* wallows in the minutiae of hairstyles, fads, and quirky gimmicks, creating "the vibrant, even hallucinogenic spell of Mr. Waters's nostalgia."[44]

With Barry Levinson's Baltimore trilogy of *Diner*, *Tin Men*, and *Avalon* and Waters's *Hairspray*, Baltimore was repeatedly depicted in the 1980s in the image of its past. Just as the Inner Harbor replaced real historic architecture with ersatz flourishes, these films used a combination of historical events and collective and individual memory to locate the narrative heart of the city in the mid-twentieth century. While his previous film, *Polyester*, had cost $300,000, investors pitched in $1.5 million for *Hairspray* to pay for expensive music rights and costumes.[45] In fact, Waters's exaggerated depiction of his early 1960s female characters became, as we will see in a later chapter, one of the catalysts for a popular Baltimore festival that led to virulent public debates over who accurately represents Baltimore's heritage.

Waters rewrites history, like the momentary integration of Special Guest Day undertaken by BAYOU, so that the elitist, racist segregationists are the ultimate losers. By doing so, Waters whitewashes Baltimore's racist history. By recuperating the history of Baltimore into a tourist-friendly package that promotes a sunny, eccentric image of the city, he even earned congratulations from the government that once censored him. Mayor Kurt Schmoke proclaimed February 16, 1988, Hairspray Day in Baltimore, while Governor William Donald Schaefer designated February 14–20, 1988, John Waters Week in Maryland.[46]

***Talking to Strangers* and *On the Block*** | Two films picked up the themes of alienation and nostalgia in a changing city at the end of the 1980s: Rob Tregenza's *Talking to Strangers* (1988) and Steve Yeager's *On the Block* (1990). Although very different in tone and topic—*Talking to Strangers* is a formalist art film while *On the Block* is a sleazy exploitation film—taken together they evoke a sense of loss as a counternarrative to the constant cheerleading that emphasized Baltimore's progress. For *On the Block*, the patrons and dancers of a strip club must watch as urban renewal and redevelopment destroy the communal space they've created in the red light district. In *Talking to Strangers*, Jesse, the romantic artist protagonist, wanders through Baltimore as an alienated flaneur floating through stratified urban spaces that privilege atomization rather than connection. *On the Block* mourns for the gritty urban underside that has to be swept away for gentrification to happen, while *Talking to Strangers* shows the alienation caused by the move toward a city rooted in symbolic economics, gentrification, and cultural capital.

Baltimore filmmaker Steve Yeager began his career in experimental theater, directing productions at the experimental Corner Theater ETC, an offshoot of underground theater grande dame Ellen Stewart's Cafe LaMaMa theater in New York. Best known for his documentary about underground film, *Divine Trash*, *On the Block* was his first feature film. A 1952 guide titled *America's Cities of Sin* claimed that the Block was the longest honky-tonk area in continuous use in the country, an area where male amusements from burlesque shows to cheap bars to naughty books were available.[47] Theaters like the Gayety, where attendees dressed in tuxedos and gowns, butted up against joints like the Oasis Cabaret, which billed itself as the "World's Worst Show."[48] Even William Donald Schaefer frequented the Block, especially the Two O'clock Club, owned by famed burlesque performer Blaze Starr, before his political career.[49]

Not everyone loved the area. Letters from concerned citizens to Mayor Theodore McKeldin condemned the vice, pornography, drug use, and crime bred by the bars and nightclubs.[50] CORE, which named Baltimore its Target City in 1966, focused some of its civil rights efforts at integrating the Block. Although Baltimore had passed an open accommodations ordinance two years prior, many bars on the Block refused service to black men. Acting Police Commissioner George M. Nelson intervened, convincing twenty-two bars to integrate. Ritter's Tavern, which remained recalcitrant, was the site of a large demonstration by the Congress of Racial Equality and a counter-demonstration by the Ku Klux Klan on Memorial Day in 1966. Following the demonstration, the bar switched to serving black men only rather than integrate, another example of cultural blockbusting.[51]

In the film version of the Block, the bars are integrated. Urban renewal and redevelopment are the existential threats, as shown in Yeager's film. The movie's main plot follows Libby, a stripper who gets a job at the Two O'clock Club and quickly becomes the love interest of two men, a tormented police vice squad lieutenant and Hugo, an awkward handyman at the club, who saves Libby from the officer's attack.

In the secondary plot, the club is threatened by an African American real estate developer, who wants to condemn the area and tear everything down to put up municipal buildings. As he says, "We're talking prime real estate. Baltimore is in the middle of a renaissance," referring to Baltimore as a "model of urban renewal." City leaders did redevelop the Block in the 1970s, as a way to contain it. In 1977, the city council passed a law, patterned after a Boston ordinance, creating an adult entertainment zone that would prohibit the growth of the Block beyond the 400, 500, and 600 blocks of East Baltimore Street.[52] Plans to build a new municipal office tower in the mid-1980s caused the area to shrink again as "skyrocketing real estate values have created pressure to transform sex districts into skyscrapers."[53]

Inspired by Italian neorealism, *On the Block* captures the area as it fades. Shot on location, it shows places like the Two O'clock Club, the Edison Hotel, and Chez Joey and includes people from the Block as extras.[54] While the main female leads don't strip completely (Libby has trained as a dancer, so her routines are higher quality), the other strippers do. In one scene reminiscent of the Oasis, patrons greet an obese stripper with moos. She reveals a fake penis to the crowd. Nonetheless, nostalgia and mournfulness pervade the film, much like the *Hot L Baltimore*. Without the clubs, the patrons will have lost a space of community, becoming accidental tourists in their own city. The owner of the Two O'clock Club explains to Blaze Starr, who appears in a cameo, that the Block was a utopian space for many, like a man with Parkinson's disease who came to the club every day to sit next to a pretty lady. "Where the hell's the harm down there," he asks, although we also see a young stripper, Mimi, nearly die from an overdose. Even Barry Levinson indulged in nostalgia for the Block as a symbol of homosocial Baltimore public spaces threatened by the arrival of television rather than urban renewal in *Liberty Heights*. The community cohered by the Block is threatened by the forces of economic modernization, which are shown to be their own kind of perversion. In one scene, a white male assistant massages the black real estate developer, hinting at their own clandestine desires. While elites hide their desires by condemning other people, the patrons of the Block are honest. When Mimi's father confronts the club's manager, he retorts that his family must be terrible if "his girl prefers to be a stripper than to be at home." The father slinks away.

If *On the Block* and *Red Baker* show how these changes made the working class and down-at-heel into accidental tourists, *Talking to Strangers* suggests that alienation follows even for the new consumers of the city. Cities have often been depicted as lonely, anonymous spaces. Director Rob Tregenza shot the film in Baltimore as nine ten-minute-long segments filmed as single takes with no editing. While the constantly moving camera fluidly shifts from street level to high above the street, connections between people are strained or absent. The opening aerial shot follows Jesse as he wanders the streets near Hollins Market, changing his mind about getting on a bus, waiting at traffic lights. The people are mere dots, moving across and around each other, accompanied by accordion music played by a real street musician.[55] The camera swings toward the downtown in the distance, suggesting that it is the epicenter of change. Ensuring viewer recognition that this is Baltimore, Jesse visits the Inner Harbor to ride a water taxi.

In the context of rising inequality and job loss around the country, Jesse is an aimless unemployed wanderer, like Red Baker. He sees himself as an artist, an identity that he is also ambivalent about because, in the context of the Baltimore renaissance, art is commodified for urban development. Because of this, spaces are bifurcated deeply by class while racial difference is mostly ignored. An older white man accosts Jesse at a soup kitchen, calling him a spy who is scavenging among the real poor to get material for his art. Jesse protests but is eventually thrown out. In the next scene, a man surprises Jesse while he is taking photos of an abandoned area under a bridge. Jesse photographs the man, who is scouting locations for a fashion photographer selling "jeans, models, fancy cars." Using this decaying space as backdrop positions these expensive commodities as edgy. If Jesse is rightly critiqued for commodifying poverty for the purposes of artistic expression and social commentary, he is confronted here by a growing commercial machine that uses images of poverty for the purposes of making profits for globalized fashion and cultural industries.

These conflicts consume him. He goes to the loft of a potter. Such former industrial spaces became culturally meaningful in this moment as they were turned into artist studios and then residences by upwardly mobile professionals attracted to their dramatic architecture and cultural capital.[56] While Jesse argues that art as commerce is soulless, the potter is more practical, telling him that "the aura of art is money." Revealing that she once worked as a stripper and prostitute, she refuses to be shamed by Jesse, who is disgusted by her selling her body. As they wander the open loft space, the kind that helped eradicate the Block where this woman may have worked, he yearns for a pure artistic practice and way to meaningfully connect with others. The loss of these spaces means the loss of certain communities and relationships as social relations follow spatial ones. Jesse is an accidental tourist, both a product of these urban changes and ambivalent about them.

**The Rot beneath the Glitter** | From the perspective of planners, government officials, convention promoters, and guidebooks, Baltimore experienced a renaissance in the 1980s. Film crews and location shoots brought the money Mayor Schaefer dreamed of with his nascent film commission to fruition. Tourists saw Baltimore's sights before even stepping foot on its streets when they watched *The Accidental Tourist* or *Tin Men*. For artists and writers, a more complicated story emerged. They explored the destabilization of this period through characters who were accidental tourists in the new Baltimore.

What destabilization meant varied, depending on class, gender, and race. For white men, alienation and nostalgia dominated. The alienation of Red Baker, spurred by the loss of a manufacturing economy and his inability to find common ground with women or people of color, differed from Jesse's alienation as an artist searching for authentic urban spaces and community in a city transformed by art and development. But they were both alienated. Nostalgia ranged from Levinson's and Waters's love letters to early 1960s working-class style to Yeager's affection for a bygone Block of homosocial pleasure. White women appeared in these narratives, but they played different roles—helper, supporter, and, at least in the case of Tracy Turnblad, leader. The most influential depictions of Baltimore were of its white working-class men and women as eccentrics. Although this was not the motivation of the creators of *The Accidental Tourist*, *Tin Men*, and *Hairspray*, among others, their work helped define Baltimore as Charm City.

African American men and women, however, were almost entirely absent. Aside from *Hairspray* and *Clara's Heart*, they hovered in the background or on the margins of these popular stories. Even in *Hairspray*, Motormouth Maybelle and Seaweed served primarily as supporting characters for Tracy Turnblad's bildungsroman. The texts where they starred, as in Wright's *Poor, Black and in Real Trouble*, were soon forgotten. In the next decades, though, depictions of black Baltimore, especially on television, multiplied.

# A PEOPLE'S HISTORY OF WEST BALTIMORE

## *Roc, The Wire,* and Baltimore on TV

When *Roc* premiered on the Fox television network on August 25, 1991, it opened with Charles S. Dutton as Roc Emerson, a black sanitation worker who lives with his family in Baltimore, settling on the couch to watch *The Simpsons*. His father, a retired Pullman porter called Pops, comes downstairs and asks Roc why he's watching Fox's controversial hit animated show about a white working-class family, when *The Cosby Show*, a sitcom about an upper-middle-class black family, was on at the same time. Roc responds that he's curious about *The Simpsons* because people have told him it's funny. Pops puts a hand on his shoulder and, with mock seriousness, tells him, "Son, we're black." A laugh line to be sure, but Pops expresses the assumptions of network television executives that racial solidarity would tether black viewers to *The Cosby Show*. It also suggests how cities were depicted on TV. Rarely would a sitcom locate a working-class family of any race in an urban setting. While the Huxtables lived in a beautiful Brooklyn brownstone, the Simpsons resided in small-town Springfield. *Roc*, however, made its Baltimore location a major aspect of the show.

It was not alone in using Baltimore as a setting. In fifteen of the seventeen years between 1991 and 2008, a critically acclaimed show about Baltimore aired on television. Two men were responsible for these representations. Dutton, a native Baltimorean, became an actor, director, and producer following his release from prison. *Roc*'s creator, he starred in the show from 1991 to 1994. David Simon began writing nonfiction books while a reporter for the *Baltimore Sun*. His first, *Homicide: A Year on the Killing Streets* (1991), told the story of a group of homicide detectives in Baltimore and their fruitless attempts to find reason in the city's rising murder rates. For *The Corner* (1997), an examination of the war on drugs from the perspective of drug addicts in West Baltimore, he and Ed Burns, a former Baltimore homicide cop and schoolteacher, hung out for a year on one of the city's most notorious drug corners. Both well received, *Homicide* became the basis for the acclaimed television cop show *Homicide: Life on the Street* (1993–1999). Simon adapted *The Corner* into a miniseries directed by Dutton for HBO in 2000. Simon also created the most significant representation of Baltimore and of postindustrial cities in the early twenty-first century, *The Wire* (2002–2008). Also on HBO, *The Wire* was a police procedural about drug dealers and cops. Beyond that, it examined the changing meaning of work under neoliberalism and the insufficiency of institutions from public schools to city government to contend with social problems caused by decades of inhumane public policy.

These men—and the writers, directors, actors, and others employed on their shows—created an unprecedented representation of black life in Baltimore. While critics have derided television as a vast wasteland, these shows suggest the ways that mass popular culture can encode counternarratives.[1] Each show drew from recognizable genres, like the sitcom or police procedural, but pushed generic limits through explicit engagement with politics, complicated characters, and stories without resolution. As we've seen so far, African American cultural producers and others have explored the stories of black people in Baltimore for decades, but the realities of distribution constrained the spread of those depictions. Dutton's and Simon's access to television brought their representations to broader audiences than ever before. Not just entertainment, they intended them as political interventions. They used these localized stories as windows into broader issues affecting the black community and cities everywhere.

While each of these shows has been written about separately, by examining them together, we can think about the way television countered the official and popular cultural narratives about Baltimore put forth in the 1980s and 1990s, during Baltimore's so-called renaissance. Simon and Dutton responded to the municipal hype machine that swept Baltimore's growing racial inequity beneath the rug of marketing campaigns, inoffensive art, and stories about eccentric white people. They mobilized national and local African American history and memory to promote responses to neoliberal economics and political disenfranchisement. By contrasting official histories with a people's history, they suggested the availability of multiple historical narratives and the privileging of certain stories over others.

Television, like film, in the 1990s and 2000s became a critical site where the meaning of blackness and its relationship to history was debated.[2] People learn about the past through culture, from historical fiction to documentary films to less didactic texts.[3] As media studies scholar Herman Gray argues, "Representations of blackness that are produced and circulated within commercial media and popular culture constitute strategic cultural resources and social spaces where the traces, memories, textures, definitions, and, above all, struggles for and over social and cultural life are lived and waged."[4] Although only *Roc* can be called a "black show" because its intended audience and point of view were black, all of the shows under consideration here are primarily about black characters. They drew from and shaped ideas about what blackness meant, particularly in urban locations. As public historians have pointed out, the way we narrativize the past matters because it leads to specific actions in the present. In popular historical memory, for example, the urban uprisings of the 1960s caused white people to leave cities like Baltimore, resulting in urban poverty. Although this story ignores evidence that whites were leaving long before the uprisings and that policies like urban renewal caused the impoverishment of urban neighborhoods, that it is widely believed leads policy makers to imagine that urban problems would be solved if white people could only be convinced to move back to the city.[5]

The cultural representations we looked at in the previous chapter overwhelmingly imagined Baltimore as a city of white eccentrics and the early 1960s as a golden age of community cohesion. The depiction of history in *Roc*, *The Corner*, and *The Wire* offers a very different perspective. These shows question how history is written and who is meant to consume those stories. Each show grapples with the implications of black history for the present. In *Roc* hard work and personal responsibility merge with community activism to save the neighborhood. Although Fox cited low ratings, the abruptness of *Roc*'s cancellation suggested that the network was uncomfortable with Dutton's explicit politics, which were threaded through the show in storylines about civil rights history, black nationalism, and contemporary politics.[6] *The Corner* uses the history of the Great Migration, residential segregation, and white racism as the backdrop for its examination of the lives of serious addicts. It argues, implicitly, for ending the War on Drugs and, explicitly, for a liberal response: opening more treatment centers. Finally, *The Wire* surfaced stories about the history of the black criminal underworld in Baltimore through collective memory. These stories, which rarely appear in history books, are a source of community pride, though, as we see through the ultimately tragic character Stringer Bell, they are impossible to reproduce in the neoliberal present.

These shows reached millions of people. On network TV, *Roc* and *Homicide* could be seen by any American with a television. Although *The Corner* and *The Wire* were restricted to a smaller market of cable subscribers, both are available as DVD box sets. As of 2019, *The Wire* is also available to stream on Hulu. The box set and streaming have allowed the show to attract new fans since the conclusion of its original run.

Were Dutton's and Simon's political messages received, or were they drowned out by the voyeuristic way that many white viewers watch shows about black life? Regularly cited as the best television series ever, *The Wire* has had a greater impact on how people see Baltimore than any other representation. The complexity of this series has drawn scholars to it from across many disciplines. But, for many of its fans, *The Wire* is not a crash course in urban studies but a show about quasi-mythical gangsters fighting flawed-but-brilliant cops in an urban fantasy realm. As with the circulation of rap music in the 1990s, the allure of danger drew fans. Through these narratives, Baltimore became Bodymore, a place defined by blackness, heightened experiences, and death. The pleasure of viewing comes from consuming this spectacle as an outsider.

**Dutton/Simon** | Their life stories could not have been more different, though by the early 1990s their paths converged when they worked on *The Corner* together. Dutton, a native Baltimorean and son of a truck driver, grew up in an East Baltimore housing project before being incarcerated for manslaughter. While in solitary confinement he read an anthology of black playwrights, discovering a love of theater. He began acting after his release, appearing in August Wilson's plays *Ma Rainey's Black Bottom* and *The Piano Lesson*. Simon, the child of a journalist and public relations executive and a homemaker in Washington, DC, graduated from the University of Maryland, College Park, before becoming a crime reporter for the *Baltimore Sun*. By the late 1980s, both focused their considerable talents on examining the problems plaguing Baltimore, which included record numbers of murders, high rates of HIV/AIDS and drug use, entrenched poverty, and high unemployment.

Although Dutton could have left Baltimore behind, he decided to use his influence to depict the issues affecting the urban black community on television, to reach an audience with little access to Broadway theater and hopefully inspire young people. In this, his interests intersected with the needs of Fox. An upstart competing with the big three networks, the broadcaster focused initially on appealing to African American viewers who, surveys showed, watched more network television than whites but were less represented there. In the early 1990s,

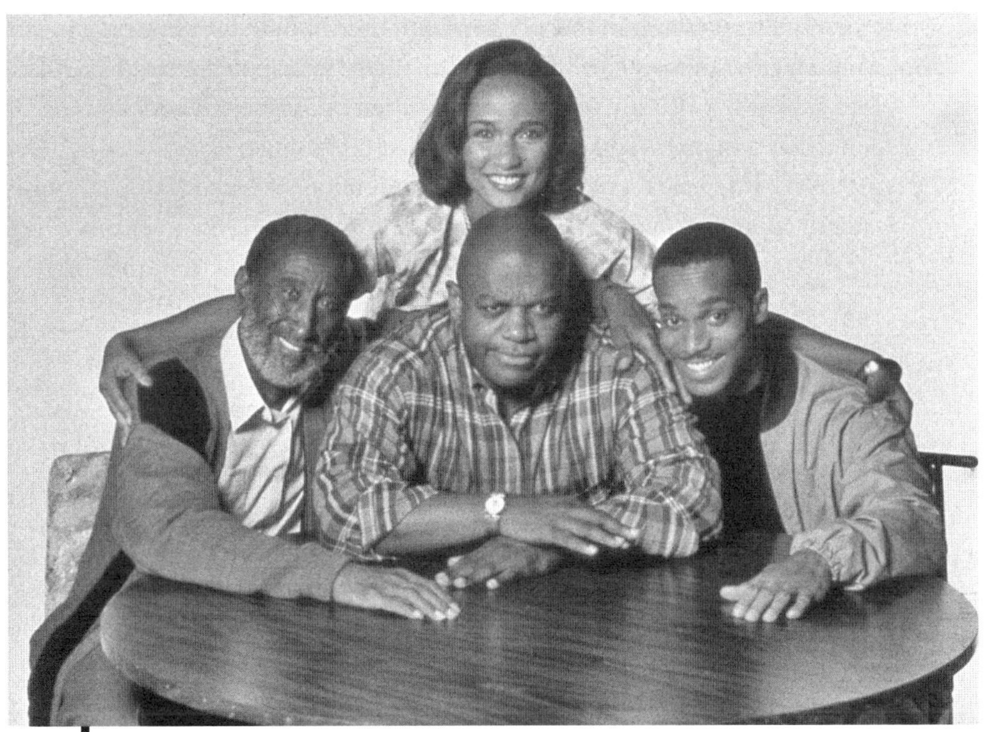

The cast of *Roc*. The short-lived show, created by Charles S. Dutton (*center*) and set in Baltimore, offered a rare image of an African American working-class family on TV. *From left*, Carl Gordon, Ella Joyce, and Rocky Carroll. Photofest

Fox's lineup included shows like *In Living Color*, a sketch comedy with an interracial group of performers; *Living Single*, a sitcom about a group of single black women starring Queen Latifah; and *New York Undercover*, a gritty cop show that cast a black and a Puerto Rican man as partners. *Roc* fit well with Fox's strategy to appeal to black viewers.

With *Roc*, Dutton depicted a loving working-class African American family in the format of the half-hour sitcom. *Roc* centered on Dutton's character Roc Emerson, a tough-looking but kindhearted sanitation worker in Baltimore, who, when overwhelmed or anxious, would sputter out his catchphrase, "I ain't got that worked out yet." The remainder of the regular cast was filled by African American actors Dutton had worked with previously on stage. Ella Joyce played his wife, Eleanor, a nurse. Carl Gordon took the role of Roc's father, Andrew "Pops" Emerson. Rocky Carroll played his mooching, jazz musician brother. Emphasizing their theatrical training, they performed the second season live, a first since the early days of television. Each of these episodes began with a cast member proving the liveness of the episode by holding up a newspaper with that day's date. In one extraordinary sequence, Joyce performed a monologue by Lady Macbeth. She growls through the fierce Shakespearean lines, eyes blazing until she suddenly shifts into African American vernacular, saying, "Don't you be messing with Lady Macbeth, child." The performance proved her acting technique with a classical, white text while her shift in voice and tone suggested that what was assumed to be natural black ways of talking were also performances, a wink at black audiences.

Behind the scenes, Dutton produced the show, maintaining creative control for its three-season run. He brought other African Americans to be part of his team, like Stan Lathan, who was one of the earliest black directors, responsible for the Baltimore film *Amazing Grace*, starring Moms Mabley. Kyle Bowser, also African American, was the executive producer. Black creative control was critical for the show to address its intended audience: urban black viewers.[7] As the first episode suggested, it was a rebuttal to the most famous black family sitcom of the 1980s and 1990s, *The Cosby Show*. While the Huxtables of *The Cosby Show* also lived in a city, the problems they faced were quite different from those of Roc and his family. Like *Roseanne* did for working-class white midwesterners, *Roc* depicted working-class black folks struggling to make ends meet and watching opportunities dry up around them.

*Roc* refused to shy away from contemporary political issues. Although many episodes follow generic sitcom formulas—Roc runs into an ex-girlfriend who tries to seduce him, Joey borrows money that he loses on a horse race—the show repeatedly commented on politics. Several episodes discuss the 1992 presidential election, culminating in one set on election day. Roc, who has not decided who to vote for, describes his choices as a "president who didn't want to sign a civil rights bill, a governor whose state doesn't have a civil rights bill and a Texas billionaire who refers to blacks as 'you people.'" Another episode features a pregnant homeless woman Roc finds going through his garbage. While the episode takes a turn toward slapstick comedy when the woman goes into labor and Eleanor, knocked out on sleeping pills, is unable to help, it ends with Roc, using President George H. W. Bush's words against him, asking, "Where is this kinder and gentler nation?" *Roc* even reached beyond the boundaries of the television screen with calls to action, as in episode 14 of season 3, which ends with Dutton out of character and in a room of young black people, talking to parents about the epidemic of drugs and violence facing their children. While espousing individual responsibility, he also gives the number for a national violence hotline.

Although dramatic shows engaged with crime and drug use, few sitcoms did. In the early 1990s moment of the crack epidemic, *Roc*, however, depicts Baltimore as a city under assault by drugs and increasing violence. Andre, a drug dealer, is introduced when he moves his criminal operation into Roc's neighborhood. The episode, emphasizing that the dealer is an unwelcome force, is titled "Nightmare on Emerson Street," to reference the popular series of *Nightmare on Elm Street* movies in which a disfigured, seemingly unstoppable monster kills people in their dreams. A figure of unfettered capitalist greed who doesn't care about the black community, Andre battles Roc, the representative of working-class respectability and community, in several episodes. Defying the sitcom formula of resolving every problem by the end of the episode, Andre appears numerous times in an unfinished storyline. While drug dealing is depicted, *Roc* never shows drug users or addicts because they might trouble the show's view of the drug trade as pitting predatory dealers who are outsiders to the neighborhood against good, drug-free citizens in the neighborhood.

***Homicide*** | Just before *Roc*'s cancellation, another TV show set in Baltimore premiered, David Simon's *Homicide*, produced by Barry Levinson. For Simon, the book on which it was based was a breakthrough into popular nonfiction. With *Homicide* becoming a TV show in 1993, Simon's career shifted from journalism to television writing and production. Most police procedurals focus on a group of police officers working together to successfully solve crimes using accepted law enforcement techniques.[8] *Homicide* tweaked the formula. Some cases were never solved. The detectives were not heroes but working men and women who talked about overtime pay and engaged in shady activities.

*Homicide*, like other detective stories, used investigating murder as a reason for its protagonists to explore the city's every corner. Novelist Laura Lippman's Tess Monaghan series worked similarly. In the pursuit of truth, Monaghan ranges over Baltimore's urban geography. Because she was raised there and, like Lippman, worked as a journalist, Monaghan understands the city's history, social hierarchies, politics, and secrets, which makes her an excellent detective. While Lippman uses Monaghan to critique many of the same issues we've been considering, including economic inequality, downtown real estate development, municipal obsession with branding, and rising crime rates in poor areas, she also brings us into lesser-known geographies, like the Orthodox Jewish community of Northwest Baltimore.[9]

While it never received high ratings, *Homicide* was critically acclaimed for its depiction of detectives with unique personalities—dyspeptic John Munch, brilliant but arrogant Frank Pembleton, tough and superstitious Kay Howard, and the haunted Tim Bayliss, among others. While the show included salacious episodes, like a crossover with the police procedural *Law & Order* where a lesbian hit woman murders a low-level government employee, it mainly examined what it means to solve homicides in a city where the number of people being killed keeps rising. A large whiteboard where the murder cases are listed became the series' key symbol of futility. In the finale, the name of the 280th victim is added in red, identifying it as an unsolved crime.

**Collaborating on *The Corner*** | Simon's and Dutton's paths crossed on *The Corner*, a six-part HBO miniseries, in 2000. Production of *The Corner* showed the racial politics at work in TV. Like Fox in the 1990s, HBO wanted shows that would set it apart from its competition. *The Corner*'s empathetic view of drug addiction gave it a political perspective appealing to HBO. Gary and Fran McCullough and their son DeAndre are the main characters in both the nonfiction book and miniseries, which follow their trajectory from economic stability through addiction, crime, and poverty. Only Fran beats her addiction. When Simon pitched the show to the studio executives, they were interested but concerned about the racial dynamics of a white man writing a show about black drug addicts, even if it was based on Simon's and his partner's ethnographic observations of a real drug corner in Baltimore. Chris Albrecht, the president for original programming for HBO, wanted a black writer and director for the series. Simon suggested David Mills for the writer, and Albrecht pushed for Charles Dutton to direct. Dutton and Simon clashed throughout the filming about racial issues. Dutton fought for more black people to be hired on the crew. He also questioned whether Simon's work exploited black people, ultimately displaying black suffering for white audiences.[10]

Each episode begins with Dutton, standing in for Simon, questioning the characters. He asks DeAndre why he sells heroin when he sees how it's destroyed his father's life and what Fran's relationship with her parents was like. With these questions and exposition around plot points like Gary stealing copper from abandoned houses to resell as scrap metal, it's clear that the intended viewer for the show is an outsider to this world. The show positions the viewers as liberal, sympathetic to the addicts who are depicted on-screen as complex human beings. Dutton's narration and the visuals show that addiction is a social and structural issue, rather than simply a personal failing. Disinvestment in neighborhoods like West Baltimore created the drug corners, while mass incarceration and the War on Drugs devastated these areas further by increasing surveillance and punishment rather than rehabilitation and health care. *The Corner* avoids simplistic sentimentality. The characters use and manipulate each other. When DeAndre's girlfriend Tyreeka finds out she's pregnant, she asks DeAndre for $200 for an abortion, even though they are free. DeAndre tells his mother he needs $400 for it, which she increases to $600 when asking another relative, each one skimming profit from the next. For Dutton, these depictions and others in the miniseries shaded into stereotypes.

***The Wire*** | If *The Corner* examined the lives of drug users and addicts, *The Wire*, which aired on HBO from 2002 to 2008, looked at drug dealers and the police who chase them. It was written by a team of writers known for nonfiction and crime fiction; Simon served as executive producer. In many ways, *The Wire* blends *Homicide: A Year on the Killing Streets* and *The Corner*, with scenes and incidents taken directly from both books. It critiques the governing institutions in a contemporary city, with each season focusing on a different one. The first, about the drug war, follows a special detail of detectives including Jimmy McNulty, a womanizing alcoholic who is driven to punish the guilty; Bunk Moreland, his tough-talking, cigar-smoking partner; the brilliant Lester Freamon; Kima Greggs, a lesbian trying to rise through the ranks of the police; tough-guy partners Thomas "Herc" Hauk and Ellis Carver; screw-up Roland "Prez" Pryzbylewski; and their no-nonsense lieutenant, Cedric Daniels. The detail gets a wire, or sets up surveillance, to take down the extensive drug operations of Avon Barksdale; his second-in-command, Stringer

Bell; and a group of drug dealers, including Avon's nephew D'Angelo Barksdale, loyal killer Wee-Bey Brice, and corner kids Poot, Bodie, and Wallace. Bubbles, a drug addict who is also a police informant, and Omar Little, a gay man who robs drug dealers, round out the major characters in the first season.

This season depicts the police and the Barksdale machine as parallel organizations struggling within their own bureaucracies to survive. Season 2 examines the loss of blue-collar work in postindustrial Baltimore by following a group of unionized dockworkers who have become involved in drug trafficking and importing illegal goods to pay lobbyists to get a bill passed to deepen the bay, allowing more ships to enter the port. Literal signs of gentrification—ads for a new upscale condo in the port area—suggest that their plans will fail in the face of the demographic and economic change of renaissance Baltimore. The third season shifts its gaze to city hall. Ambitious city councilmember Tommy Carcetti runs for mayor on a platform of crime reduction. Police officials "juke" the stats by recoding crimes to make it look like the crime rate is decreasing. Major Howard "Bunny" Colvin, a police officer on the verge of retirement, is tired of such antics and legalizes drugs in one area of the city, known as Hamsterdam. In the fourth season, we see the failure of the school system to educate and protect young black men from being sucked into the drug trade. The final season indicts the media when McNulty decides the only way to get funding to investigate a growing number of drug-related murders is to pretend that there's a serial killer at large, which an unscrupulous journalist at the city's major daily paper promotes.

**When Television Becomes Politics** | As these summaries suggest, Dutton and Simon saw their work as political commentary on social issues in order to affect public policy. National and local political figures took interest in their work, though rarely in the ways they hoped. Charles Dutton, especially as Roc, appealed to black liberal politicians, while Simon butted heads with Baltimore mayor Martin O'Malley's desire for a positive image for the city.

*Roc*'s engagement with national political and social issues and the positive image of a black working-class family it promoted led the Congressional Black Caucus to protest the show's 1994 cancellation, to no avail.[11] In Baltimore, Dutton appeared at anti-violence events with Mayor Kurt Schmoke, Baltimore's first elected African American mayor.[12] A lawyer, Rhodes scholar, and former athlete, Schmoke used a strategy of acknowledging racial difference while emphasizing shared concerns to appeal to both black and white residents of the city, which meshed with the politics of *Roc*.[13]

As mayor, he quickly distinguished himself from the larger-than-life Schaefer. He told the *New York Times* that he was "not the kind of Mayor who's going to waste the city's money painting my name all over town when Baltimore has so many other more important things to spend money on."[14] Instead, he advocated for medicalization, or treating drug abuse as a public health, rather than law enforcement issue, and increasing the number of needle exchange programs and universal drug addiction treatment centers, rather than street-level busts of dealers. Other political leaders scorned his plans. New York mayor Ed Koch called Schmoke "a brilliant spokesman for a bad idea."[15] Responding to the backlash, Schmoke retreated from medicalization and even used a 1995 episode of his monthly local television program, *The Mayor's Show*, to air footage of a drug raid by police that could have been taken from *The Wire*.[16] After his term ended, however, he used television to promote his earlier ideas about abating drug use. He played himself in *Homicide: The Movie* (2000) and the Baltimore health commissioner in season 3 of *The Wire*. In both, the legalization of drugs is a plot point, allowing a debate to occur in a way that could not have happened politically in the law-and-order years of the 1990s.

If Schmoke saw television as an opportunity to visualize and address social issues, Baltimore's next mayor, Martin O'Malley, tried to control it. O'Malley, a white lawyer originally from Washington, DC, was elected to the Baltimore City Council in 1991. Even at this early moment, he began expressing concerns about the depiction of Baltimore. When the *Washington Post* reported on the bump to tourism that the show *Homicide* had brought to Baltimore, O'Malley responded, "We've lost a heck of a lot of our population. The primary reason for that is crime and the fear of crime, and what that has done to property values and schools," suggesting that a show about murder was only adding to the problem.[17]

Surprising many, O'Malley ran for mayor in 1999 when Schmoke announced that he would not run again. With the African American vote split between two black candidates, O'Malley won on campaign promises about reducing crime through zero-tolerance policies (a trajectory followed by Carcetti in season 3 of *The Wire*). He needed to visualize these successes. While the police commissioner had removed the real department whiteboard because *Homicide* made it a prominent visual indictment of the department's inability to solve murders in the late 1990s, it returned under O'Malley to show how the solve rate was increasing.[18]

In many ways, O'Malley followed the tracks Schaefer laid, particularly by promoting large-scale public-private projects and protecting the city's image (he would also go on to be governor). If *Homicide*'s depiction of Baltimore concerned O'Malley, *The Wire* infuriated him. Infamously, at the start of the second season, the city's film office delayed routine film permits and referred all questions about the change in policy to O'Malley's office.[19] The city council passed a resolution criticizing the show and calling for new efforts to promote a more positive image of the city. O'Malley told Simon, "We want to be out of *The Wire* business." Simon threatened to move the filming to another city. Not only would Baltimore lose the influx of filming dollars into the local economy; the show would still be said to take place there.[20] O'Malley relented and filming continued, but this battle suggested how much had changed since the 1970s. With many cities competing for film money and Simon's clout, O'Malley could not win this fight. But he continued to try. One year after his election, O'Malley replaced Schmoke's city slogan, "Baltimore: The City That Reads," with the hubristic "The Greatest City in America." While he wanted to encourage pride in the city, a local man scoffed and suggested his own slogan, reflective of the high crime rate: Bodymore, Murdaland.[21]

**Yesterday Was the Bomb** | In *The Corner*, Gary and a friend score heroin. They shoot up in the Victorian house he and his family once lived in, though now it is a dilapidated shell. As they sink into their fix, Gary's friend says that the high is weak, "not like yesterday." Gary agrees. "Yesterday was the bomb." Time, particularly the relationship to the past, is a critical lens to view cultural representations about Baltimore in the 1990s and through the first decade of the twenty-first century. *Roc*, *The Corner*, and *The Wire*, and, to a lesser degree, *Homicide*, juxtapose official histories to collective memory to comment on the city. Addiction is often described as a timeless state. As William Burroughs, famed author and heroin addict, described, addiction is defined by the "algebra of need," a cyclical process of obtaining and using drugs.[22] This cycle repeats. Each day is the same as the next. However, Gary and his friend suggest that there is change over time. Because they are addicts who become increasingly tolerant of their drug of choice and are also not rich enough to ensure the quality of their purchases, yesterday is always better than today. No high can compete with the first one. In this instance, the past creates a desire for a return to a previous state of pleasure and happiness.

*The Wire* continues this theme of the persistence of the past. While gunfire punctuates many episodes, there is only one bomb in the series. In the first episode of the third season, titled "Time after Time," the Franklin Terrace housing project is demolished by implosion. Poot and Bodie, who grew up in the towers, argue about the meaning of the demolition. Poot is nostalgic, reminiscing about his first sexual experiences, which occurred there. Bodie refuses to romanticize. He rags on Poot, "You gonna cry over a housing project now?" and reminds him of the sexually transmitted infections he got from those sexual encounters. For Poot, his memories of the towers are about the people who lived there. Bodie sees no relationship between the place and the people. The city, he argues, will build "new shit" but not because there is any concern about the people.

Interspersed with their conversation are the words of Mayor Clarence Royce, who tells the enthusiastic crowd that a new day is dawning for Baltimore with the destruction of housing projects that were associated with rising levels of crime and violence. "We will learn from those mistakes," he intones. "Reform is a philosophy . . . Are you ready for a new Baltimore?" But there will be no improvement. The city's addiction to neoliberal policies that prioritize the needs of the downtown business elite over average residents ensures that. Time after time, the opening credit sequence suggests, the drug game will continue, though it will morph and adapt to changed conditions. The implosion emphasizes this point. Clouds of debris roll into the streets, choking onlookers. The demolition starts an unintended war between the Barksdale organization and Marlo Stanfield's crew as they seek new territory. In this case, nostalgia is misplaced. The past can be physically destroyed, but its traces haunt the present.

Film scholar Stanley Corkin has argued that *The Wire* shows how neoliberal institutions attempt to destroy the past in their endless quest for future development.[23] History, at best, can be mobilized to give symbolic value, but it is not truly valued. The Grain Pier, the development that Frank Sobotka fought against in season 2 in his quest to save union jobs on the waterfront, has become a condominium development. Like Harborplace, it leverages the symbolic value of its former life as industrial space to be sold to the upwardly mobile.[24] Laura Lippman explores this theme as well in *Baltimore Blues*, sardonically describing an expensive gym called the Sweat Shop opening in a former factory where women workers died in the early twentieth century, and, in *Charm City*, in a reference to *Red Baker*, a bar with "ersatz Marxist décor . . . and the real picket signs from famous Baltimore strikes," catering to college kids.[25] But as Gary and Poot suggest, people offer a counternarrative based in sources, like personal memory, that are often disregarded in the writing of official histories.[26] These memories create a different engagement with the past, one that draws critically on it not as nostalgia but as a politics for the present. As anthropologist Michel-Rolph Trouillot describes, the creation of historical narratives silences certain voices. Events happen, but, unless they are documented and archived, they cannot become part of the historical record.

Documentation, however, is always incomplete. *The Wire* raises this issue in its final season about the media. While a fake story by a lying reporter about a serial killer of homeless men ends up winning a Pulitzer Prize, the real story of Omar's death is ignored. Omar, who robbed drug dealers, helped kill Stringer Bell, and lived by a strict moral code, is legendary on the streets of West Baltimore, where children yell, "Omar's coming," as soon as they hear his trademark whistling. His life is ended, however, when he is killed by a young boy in a convenience store. The newspaper editor cuts a short article about the murder because he does not see it as real news. The murder of a black man is simply too common in Baltimore to matter. By not including it in the newspaper—the historical source of record—Omar's death and, by extension, his life, are lost to future historians who want to understand this place and time. This is the moment of "fact creation" in Trouillot's terms, when an event becomes a documented source available to historians to craft their narratives.[27] Similarly, in *The Corner* the documentary film crew capturing the stories of the McCullough family invokes fact creation as well.[28] Without Simon and Burns's ethnographic observations of this area of Baltimore, there would be no official documentation of what these lives were like.

Thus, official narratives conflict with personal ones. The official narratives of Baltimore are represented directly through murals and monuments, which are repeatedly referenced visually. Omar and Stringer Bell's parley on neutral ground in season 1 takes place downtown at the Inner Harbor. They talk near a historic fountain donated in 1906 by Charles E. Booth, a prominent businessperson.

Three episodes later, in the courthouse where several members of Barksdale's crew will be sentenced to prison, we see a large mural of the burning of the *Peggy Stewart*, a ship full of tea, which arguably started the Revolutionary War. In the next season, confused white tourists stop a young black man to ask directions to the historic home where Edgar Allan Poe died in Baltimore. The young man has no idea what they're talking about even though the house is in his neighborhood. In each case, we see the official history contrasted by the action. Omar and Bell are both successful businessmen, but neither will have his name on a piece of public sculpture. Nor will either appear in a mural. That the Poe historic house is in the same West Baltimore neighborhood where much of the show takes place demonstrates how locality is different from geography. For the white tourists, the historic house museum is the sole reason to be in this neighborhood. For the black man, it is his home and where he plies his trade. The chasm between the city's official memory and its residents is underscored at each moment.

**It Takes a Garbageman to Clean Up Our Streets |** Authoritative narratives of black history figure into these shows as well. In the acclaimed "Prison Riot" episode of *Homicide* season 5, which stars Charles S. Dutton, the police are called in when a prison riot turns deadly. In two scenes, the camera lingers on a mural that depicts black students sitting behind desks, with black men, dressed in suits and holding books, walking away from this classroom. Over it all, a black man looks down with his arms outstretched as if to protect or encircle this group. The reality of the school-to-prison pipeline, where young black men are given few opportunities to learn but many to encounter law enforcement, contradicts this vision of black education as a source of freedom. *Roc* mentions the Great Blacks in Wax Museum, a Baltimore institution that displays wax reproductions of important moments and leaders in black history, several times. Pops tells Roc, "I love it there. This month, they got a new fantasy exhibit—Rosa Parks shoving a white man off the bus." Through Pops viewers are introduced to aspects of black nationalist history. He hangs pictures of Malcolm X throughout the house. When a young man whom Roc has been working with visits wearing a Malcolm X hat, Pops criticizes him for participating in the consumer commodification of X's legacy. He tells him, "Malcolm did not die so the vultures of capitalism could feed off his legacy leaving the bones of his ideals to decay into a fashion trend." One uncomfortable laugh from the studio audience. He tells him that when they—an earlier generation—had a message, they went marching in the streets, not shopping.

*Roc* offers a vision of black politics linked to a history of grassroots organizing, direct protest, and political work grounded in black history and using black symbols and culture. The show incorporates both Baltimore's history and African American politics and life more broadly as historical memory. For the first and most of the second season, the theme song was an a cappella version of "God Bless the Child," originally written by Billie Holiday and Arthur Herzog Jr. and recorded by Holiday, who lived in Baltimore and performed in the black clubs on Pennsylvania Avenue. The song is played over a series of sepia-toned photos of contemporary Baltimore, which "gives a real sense of the city."[29] Even though most of the series takes place in Roc's house, the photos, filtered to look historic, show inner-city streets, check cashing stores, impromptu sidewalk sales, bus stops, and bars. Through this opening montage, *Roc* argues that history is essential to understanding contemporary African American life.

The family confronts poverty, homelessness, drug dealing, and gang violence over the course of the series, with grassroots organizing intended to change political priorities, symbolized most pointedly through the show's engagement with the 1992 presidential election. After a young boy named Terrence is killed in a drive-by shooting outside Roc's house, he organizes a community meeting. Employing discourses of history—this neighborhood used to be safe—Roc inspires the crowd to want change for the future. But it's clear that traditional urban machine politics won't fix this problem because their city council representative has been indicted in a kickback scandal. The crowd urges Roc to run for his seat in the upcoming special election on the slogan, "It takes a garbageman to clean up our streets." With overtones of the Memphis sanitation workers' strike of 1968, Roc agrees, meeting with Latinx and black Muslim constituents, a cross-racial and religious alliance based on a shared class position. Although Roc loses because he cannot afford to run TV ads like his opponent, we see in miniature the trajectory of Black Power politics in the late twentieth century, as cultural nationalists like Amiri Baraka went from community organizing and street-level protests to involvement in political elections.

**When Are We Going to Stop Hearing about Racism?** | While *Roc* offers hope that community organizing can address urban problems, *The Corner* confronts the continuing effects of structural racism. The first episode opens with Dutton in front of the camera, explaining how he grew up on a corner like the one he's standing on in West Baltimore. Echoing the work of sociologists and ethnographers, he explains that the corner is the neighborhood's vital center.[30] "On one hand the corner pulsates with life, the energy of human beings trying to make it to the next day. But it's also a place of death" because of addiction and violence. Acknowledging that the corner has changed since his youth, he notes that the number of penal institutions in Maryland has increased from five in the 1960s to twenty-eight today.

Following Gary as he walks into a corner store, Dutton asks him why he started shooting heroin. The real answer doesn't come from Gary's individual story, though that is the backbone of the series, but through the camera's lens. It sweeps around from the doorway of the corner store, lingering on three young black men who might be dealing drugs. They are the most proximate cause of why Gary is shooting heroin. But it continues past them, taking in the three other corners at the intersection. At each, men sit around without legal work to keep them busy in the daytime. Buildings crumble, the streets are filled with garbage. This suggests three causes: the ready supply of drugs and dealers, high rates of unemployment leading to poverty, and a built environment that is the result of decades of disinvestment, which, the series will imply, is connected to residential segregation. Although Gary mentions that the corner store he is standing in front of burned during the 1968 riots, there is no narrative time spent on that event. The problems are deeper and broader.

Racism undergirds each of these causes. During a talk radio show blaring out of Gary's father's cab, we hear a caller exclaim, "When are we going to stop hearing about racism? Slavery was like three hundred years ago." More than simply wrong about historical facts, the caller is also misguided in linking slavery's end to the end of racism. Gary's family history suggests as much. His father's family migrated to Baltimore from South Carolina, likely to escape the Jim Crow South. But he collided with Baltimore's residential segregation, becoming the first black family to move into a white neighborhood. In response, the white families moved out. The series does not connect the dots between white flight and government disinvestment in black neighborhoods, but this moment suggests the deep-seated racism of the city.

Steady employment eased some of the burden. Gary's father quickly found a job at a foundry, allowing him to send Gary to college (though he left early when his girlfriend, Fran, became pregnant). Even without a college education, Gary found work, including a job in quality control at Bethlehem Steel. But, as we see in a flashback, he chafes against the white men who control the union. When he complains to them that there are white workers who are engaging in unsafe practices, they tell him that he needs to show more loyalty to his union brothers. Even more devastating is the absence of work owing to the suburbanization of industry. Fran, during her attempt to get clean, gets a job at a factory in the suburbs, but the bus commute there is so long that it is economically unfeasible for her to keep the job.

These myriad issues come together to create the conditions for rampant drug addiction. Gary, a natural-born philosopher, goes to see *Schindler's List*, a Stephen Spielberg film about the Holocaust. He connects the dehumanization of Jewish people in Germany that preceded the Holocaust with the dehumanization of Baltimore's poor black residents. While he blames heroin addicts to a degree for their drug use, he refuses to ignore the role of racism in addiction. Even when Gary "was making money it didn't matter because I was still a nigger." The police, who are ignorant of neighborhood history, see the dealers and junkies as less than human, justifying their violent treatment. When Cardy, a "working man" who is not part of the drug trade, parks on the street to visit his mother, police officers humiliate him, making him drop his pants to frisk him, simply because they have the power to do so. Rather than nostalgia, here we see how ignorance of history by those in power is dangerous for those who are marginalized.

Unlike the solutions offered by *Roc* or *The Wire*, which are rooted in the history of black social movement organizing, *The Corner* posits a liberal response: more treatment. At the end of the last episode, Dutton interviews the real Fran, DeAndre, Tyreeka, and George "Blue" Epps, an artist and recovering addict, asking them what a happy ending would look like for the story they are telling in *The Corner*. Fran, who has successfully kicked her addiction, hopes that the series will spur the opening of more treatment centers.

**Dream with Me |** Unlike the eradication of the towers and the redevelopment of the Grain Piers into condos, which destroy the past, characters in *The Wire* exhibit a need to remember the past throughout the show. At times it is mournful, as when McNulty and his new partner Diggins are on the police boat in the first episode of season 2. In sight of the massive Bethlehem Steel plant at Sparrows Point, McNulty explains that his father was laid off from the factory in 1973; Diggins responds that his was in 1978. The death of the plant—once among the largest in the world—foreshadows the doomed struggles of the dockworkers who are the subject of this season. But because the problems discussed in *The Wire* are structural, there is no ultimate political or social action that can make meaningful change. Individuals can succeed despite their disadvantages, as with Bubbles, who, at the end of the series, is sober and living with his sister and her family. But most individuals are trapped in their circumstances.

At other times, however, memories of the past become part of a people's history of West Baltimore, a counternarrative to official histories of the city contained in murals and monuments. These memories are of hustlers and criminals, men who lived on the social margins but who were, in the context of this neighborhood, important figures. Kima is embarrassed in season 1 when Bubbles, her street informant, can't believe she doesn't know who No-Heart Anthony is—doubly so, when McNulty gives a capsule summary of his criminal career. In other episodes, black characters reference Butch Stamford, Charlie Sollors, Frank "Pee Wee" Matthews: all historical figures of the drug trade, some real, some fictional. While older figures, like Prop Joe or Butchie, Omar's blind confidante, have direct memory of many of these figures, no one plays historian more than Stringer Bell, Avon Barksdale's second-in-command. Many people writing about *The Wire* focus on Bell as a capitalist businessman but ignore his role as the show's historical consciousness. He asks ruthless up-and-coming drug kingpin Marlo Stanfield in episode 5 of season 3, "Are you a student of history?" before rattling off the names of several "smart players" from Baltimore's past: Melvin, Little Will, Peanut, and so on. His brand of black capitalism is inspired by Baltimore history and Black Power.

His mention of Little Will is pointed. In fact, he mentions him again in the next episode, telling Barksdale, "We could do like Lil Willie back in the day, all that number money. Run this goddam city." The historical figure William Lloyd "Little Willie" Adams is the fictional Bell's role model, the man whom he seeks to pattern his career upon. Born in North Carolina in 1914, Adams moved to Baltimore during the Depression. A numbers runner as a teenager, he became a multimillionaire. Because banks refused to lend to black people, Adams became a de facto lending institution to black Baltimore, investing in everything from beauty salons to taverns to Super Pride supermarkets. His most important investment was the Parks Sausage Company, the first black-owned company to trade on Wall Street. He owned Carr's Beach, a popular black amusement park in Annapolis, and Adams Realty Company.

Adams supported desegregation efforts in the late 1940s. In 1949, he moved his family into Forest Park, a white neighborhood, which was quickly followed by his sudden arrest, seen by many as retaliation for his crossing the residential color line. He never served time even though he was convicted because the Supreme Court overturned his conviction on a technicality. He testified before the Kefauver Special Committee on Organized Crime and paid hefty fines. In the early 1950s, he quit his illegal activities and became a legitimate business owner, investor, and political player, thanks, in part to his wife. In 1946, Victorine Adams started the Colored Women's Democratic Club, the first political organization for black women in the state. Victorine was elected to the Maryland state legislature and then the Baltimore City Council in 1967, the first woman of any race to do so. The Adamses helped elect William Donald Schaefer the white mayor of a black majority city, for example, and Parren Mitchell to Congress. Willie's clout was such that when the Mary land State Lottery was started in 1973—basically, the government legalized the numbers racket immortalized in *The City of Anger*—Adams was hired as a consultant.[31] Stringer Bell married Adams's business success with ideas of Black Power. As Barksdale tells Bell in season 3 as they reminisce about their childhood dreams, "You was always heavy into the black pride bullshit. Talking about how you was going to get yourself two grocery stores and make motherfuckers proud." For Bell, economic self-sufficiency for himself and for the black community defined success.

But Bell cannot accomplish his dreams of legitimacy in the political landscape of twenty-first-century Baltimore. Like Adams, he branches out into real estate, starting a development company called

B&B, to renovate West Baltimore property he bought with drug money. He is told that "with the stadium this area is like inner Harbor East ten years ago." Corrupt state senator Clay Davis thwarts Bell's plans by tricking him into unnecessarily paying him thousands of dollars for permits. Omar and Brother Mouzone, a New York hitman, murder Bell at the site of his condo development on Barksdale's orders.

Why couldn't Bell make the shift that Adams made? Politics plays an important role. In Adams's time, Baltimore was becoming a black majority city. The Democratic Party realized it needed to ensure the black vote, which it did through working with people like Adams and his wife. But by the mid-2000s when Bell is making his own aborted transition, the Democratic political machine in Baltimore was entirely controlled by black people. At a party for Democratic operatives, we see that the party's most important strategists are all African American, as are the mayor and his team. Though they are both black, Davis exploits Bell's lack of political power for his own financial gain. There is no reason for the political leaders to work with or help Bell because he represents a constituency they already have sewn up.

The past shapes the present of *The Wire*, but it teaches complicated lessons. Just before D'Angelo Barksdale is strangled in prison, he participates in a discussion of *The Great Gatsby*, by F. Scott Fitzgerald, who lived in and wrote about Baltimore. The teacher asks whether the group agrees with Fitzgerald's idea that there are no second acts in American history. D'Angelo passionately argues that Fitzgerald's message in the novel is that the "past is always with us. Where we come from, what we go through, how we go through it." Through the television representations of Baltimore in *Roc* and *The Wire*, we see two different ways the past informs the present. *Roc* presents a past of black grassroots political organizing connected to place-based multiracial communities. In *The Wire*, neoliberal government and development destroy vestiges of the past, except for those that support official historical narratives or can be commodified. But in the memories of the people of West Baltimore live the forebears who built illegal and legal empires. Stringer Bell draws from this collective memory as he strives to become a legitimate business owner. In a changed political context, however, this is impossible, and he, the historical consciousness of the series, is destroyed. While *Roc* offers hope by focusing on the struggling but stable black working class, *The Corner* and *The Wire* suggest futility. Grounded in social reality, these fictional representations of black Baltimore have the further effect of defining an imaginary version of the city that would, by the 2000s, be known as Bodymore.

**This Is a Tomb: Defining Bodymore** | Lester Freamon, *The Wire*'s Sherlock Holmes, paces through an alley lot looking for a clue that will help him figure out what has happened to the people murdered on the orders of the ruthless Marlo Stanfield. As he looks up, he sees before him several abandoned houses with boarded-up doors. Peering closer, he notices that some doors have rusted screws, but others have silvery-new ones, shot into the frame with professional skill. He realizes, suddenly, that the dead bodies have been put inside these abandoned buildings, the source of the local children's urban fables about zombies roaming West Baltimore. He turns to Bunk and explains his realization. "This is a tomb," he says. Bunk touches the screws, steps back and takes in the full picture. The implications are tremendous. Thousands of abandoned houses line the streets of Baltimore, left behind by reverse redlining, eviction, and condemnation. How many shelter bodies instead of living people? "Fuck me," Bunk mutters to himself.

Because of its complicated storytelling about urban life and support of ardent fans from journalists to academics, *The Wire* has become the most impactful representation of Baltimore in the twenty-first century. When Martin O'Malley ran for the Democratic Party nomination for president in 2016, he was dogged by questions about *The Wire*'s representation of Baltimore. It has been the subject of popular and scholarly books.[32] Several universities have offered classes on it, and it has inspired countless conferences, newspaper and magazine articles, and online discussions. Sonja Sohn, who played Kima Greggs, founded a nonprofit organization, ReWired for Change, to help at-risk families and youth in Baltimore. Wendell Pierce, who played Bunk Moreland, tweeted that his investment in the Nelson Kohl Apartments, located in Station North, created 165 construction jobs and thirty-five permanent jobs, ironically putting him in the real estate development business that the series critiques.[33] Five seasons of filming on location meant jobs for many Baltimore extras and economic benefits for the local economy. Although there are no other TV shows that have matched its unflinching examination of the tangled web that defines any contemporary city, *The Wire* helped define the real city of Baltimore, Maryland, as the imaginary city of Bodymore, Murdaland, a name that appears spray-painted on a wall in the opening credits in seasons 3 and 4. For Baltimore residents, the graffiti critiqued the city's indifference to black suffering. Ironically, *The Wire* spread this image far beyond the city's borders, making it, as Freamon suggests, a necropolis, or city of the dead.

But, of course, it is not the entire city. Bodymore is a city within a city. It is defined relationally, by contrast with the few other areas of Baltimore we see, like the Inner Harbor, the downtown, and, occasionally, the suburbs. Disregard for human life defines Bodymore. Through its tight focus on crime and drugs, *The Wire* helps define Bodymore as an African American space. Although the second season focused on white criminals and the cops and politicians in all seasons are racially diverse, the depiction of Bodymore in seasons 3–5 is primarily of a place where blackness is connected to death. Because it presents its stories as realism, highlights its use of specific local details, like dialect, and compresses its time line so that these events happen in quick sequence, viewers interpret its depiction of Bodymore as accurate.[34] But the "crime that *The Wire* can't name," as George Lipsitz explains, is what made these problems: the residential segregation that caused these neighborhoods to deteriorate into concentrated poverty.[35] We see the aftermath of these inequities, but there is no space within the narrative to explain these structural issues (unlike in *The Corner*, for example, which uses flashbacks to gesture at them).

Simon also ignores the community activism taking place in these neighborhoods in his TV shows, even when he has written about it. In the book version of *The Corner*, he profiles Ella Thompson, who runs a recreation center for children. In the real Baltimore, the Community Building in Partnership project in Sandtown-Winchester and community-based organizations in East Baltimore have tried to make positive change for people living in these neighborhoods.[36] While Simon and the other writers should be celebrated for refusing simplistic liberal solutions to difficult urban problems, it is appropriate to critique the choices they made to ignore these efforts at community uplift.

**Consuming Bodymore** | While many fans enjoy the show's complexity, understanding it as a critique of institutional inertia, deindustrialization, and the war on drugs, for others, *The Wire* offers the titillation of slumming. As historian Robin Kelley noted of gangsta rap in the 1990s, many listeners assumed that lyrics describing crime and violence were reportage rather than fiction. These songs appeal to "listeners for whom the 'ghetto' is a place of adventure, unbridled violence, erotic fantasy, and/or an imaginary alternative to suburban boredom."[37] For many viewers, Bodymore is an unfamiliar, dangerous space where quasi-mythical gangster characters live and die by a code. Sociologist Sudhir Venkatesh watched episodes of *The Wire* with several "thugs" who had sold drugs and wrote about it in a series of blog posts for the popular Freakonomics website. Assured that Freakonomics readers would be both fans of *The Wire* and have no connection to the drug trade, the "thugs" proceeded to validate and critique the show's authenticity.[38]

Because it includes detailed local references and location shooting, *The Wire* even draws people to visit Baltimore to experience where it took place. From minibus to self-guided tours through the city, viewers see for themselves the devastation and poverty centered in the show while also reliving important scenes where they were filmed.[39] With admonitions to "prepare to feel extremely visible, stared at, and uncomfortably out of place!" the tours position the participants as outsiders who are there to gaze at others, rather than to be gazed at (even as it chastises people for doing so).[40] Novelist Gary Shteyngart parodies this dynamic in *Lake Success* when his hedge-fund manager main character encounters German tourists on a *Wire* tour enthusiastically taking photos of weeds and discarded cigarette packs imbued with meaning because they are in a West Baltimore neighborhood.[41] As John Urry has argued, tourists travel to other people's home to watch their daily lives. By doing so, tourists see their difference from these other people, defining themselves in contrast with them.[42] *The Wire* tours use the thrill of tourism to allow people to view poverty without living it themselves.

For some young people who move to Baltimore, part of the thrill of living there is knowing that it is a dangerous city. That Guy's on Heroin, a now-defunct website based in Baltimore, posted photos of drug users, referred to in dehumanizing terms as zombies, nodding out in public places, "to rate some of the better (and worse) junkies we see on a day to day basis."[43] The captions positioned the photographers as edgy urban dwellers, unafraid in these environments. The site's tagline was "living in Baltimore, fighting zombies," and it offered T-shirts that say "Your city is fucking hardcore." Commenters criticized the site for its lack of empathy for drug users.

Fan obsession with the character of Omar Little suggests how even shows that tell politically complicated stories can be reduced to generic tropes. When journalist Bill Simmons interviewed President Barack Obama, an avowed fan of the show, he asked him to settle an "office debate" about who was the best character on *The Wire*.[44] When Obama met with David Simon three years later to talk about mandatory sentencing reform, much of their conversation revolved around *The Wire*.[45] In both instances, Obama referred to the same character as his favorite: Omar Little, the gay man with a scar who made his living robbing drug dealers with a shotgun. In a world defined by the rules of the "Game," Omar lived by a code of honor that saw the killing of citizens, people not in the drug world, as out of bounds. Yet he was ultimately a victim of the growing injustice in his world, gunned down not by a true adversary but by a child in a corner store. Omar, played by Michael K. Williams, was legendary for countless viewers, journalists, and critics. Articles like "10 Reasons Omar from *The Wire* Was the Ultimate Badass" and "Why Omar Is the Greatest Character on *The Wire*, No Doubt" exemplified the exaltation of this antihero.[46] One fan even posted a series of videos on YouTube creating an avatar that looks like Omar to play the violent video game *Grand Theft Auto 5*, in which players commit crimes to complete missions.[47] Through manipulating his character's looks, he literally embodied Omar in the game.

To be sure, Omar is a compelling character, a gay African American man whose emotional and moral complexity is rare on television. But he is also the character least connected to the systems and institutions that come under critique throughout the show. Smart, tough, vicious, and self-made, Omar incorporated aspects of several African American literary, film, and music traditions, including the "bad man," blaxploitation heroes, and gangsta rap personas. He, as his whistled anthem "The Farmer in the Dell" suggests, stands alone. While he has friends and partners, his criminal enterprise is a sole proprietorship. He engages with the police and with the dealers on his own terms. If the show's genius is to use the theme of surveillance to depict the interconnectedness of seemingly diametrically opposed institutions, Omar exists outside of this view. Simon himself has critiqued this veneration. Agreeing that Omar is a great character, he believes that focusing on "things like who's cooler, Omar or Stringer, at this late date . . . gives short shrift" to "the ideas of the show."[48]

**Ain't Never Gonna Be What It Was** | The imaginary Bodymore is mapped onto the real Baltimore. Although *Roc* attempted to use TV to depict a respectable black working-class family, it was superseded by other shows that gazed more intently at black criminality and violence. While *The Corner* and *The Wire* offered a people's history of the black neighborhoods of Baltimore, many viewers preferred to focus on the vicarious thrill of inner-city violence. This Wild West of male freedom exists next door to other Baltimores, ones that are defined through white eccentricity and femininity. We now turn to the closing chapter to consider the racial implications of defining the city's identity as Bodymore or Charm City in the early twenty-first century through an analysis of Baltimore club music and the Hon, an icon of white working-class femininity.

# WELCOME TO BALTIMORE, HON!

## Race, Gender, and Urban Branding at the End of the Century

As we have seen, writers and artists joined city planners and other officials in envisioning Baltimore's past and future. While many of the cultural producers discussed so far used Baltimore expansively, as a case study of issues affecting many cities, city officials searched for and promoted cultural representations of what made Baltimore unique to draw visitors and upwardly mobile residents. By the early twenty-first century, they were fighting to attract what Richard Florida, urban development theorist, calls the "creative class." He argues that the rise of a class of workers in creative industries like design, education, and technology are the key to economic growth for cities who know how to attract these high-income, high-status people. According to Florida, they want "vibrant urban districts, abundant natural amenities and comfortable urban 'nerdistans' for techies so inclined."[1] Tolerance attracts LGBTQ communities as well as immigrants.

Florida's ideas became policy in Baltimore through the 2005 Baltimore City Economic Growth Strategy, released by Mayor Martin O'Malley's office. It envisions Baltimore as a growing, successful place, if it can leverage its "harbor, historic architecture, and tight knit neighborhoods." These assets give the city "a special character, that creatively utilized, can shape the world's view of Baltimore and its competitiveness."[2] While the inclusion of LGBTQ communities and tech industry workers was new, Florida's advice was an extension of what Baltimore officials had been hyping since Schaefer was mayor. Baltimore built on its earlier renaissance narrative by marrying its economic development to quality of life, defined not as residents' access to health care or the proportion of longtime residents able to afford staying in their neighborhoods, but as reducing crime, supporting job creation and training in the education and medical sectors, and access to arts and cultural amenities. Echoing Schaefer's language of entrepreneurship, the report warned that "the greatest risk of all is being too cautious" (12). Rather than proceed from the deficit model of the Schmoke administration, which focused government resources on areas of need, Mayor O'Malley identified sources of strength. Building on them, it was assumed, would trickle benefits down to other areas.

Unfortunately for Baltimore, by 2005 many cities boasted waterfront developments, historic architecture, and tight-knit neighborhoods. Since the 1970s, containerized shipping and transcontinental air travel put cities into greater competition with each other. To be a great city in the era of globalization is "to recognize the increasingly global competition to retain and attract residents, jobs, and capital, and the necessity to make decisions and investments that advance the city's prospects for success" (43). While large-scale development is central, the "vitality of more informal amenities, such as restaurants, cafes, bookstores and outdoor festivals [are all] tangible assets that play a role in fostering creativity and innovation" (40). Cities copied each other's strategies, building stadiums, cultural districts, and bike paths, making them more alike than ever.

Heritage became a central tool for cities like Baltimore to define their uniqueness. As feminist geographer Doreen Massey has argued, globalization and gentrification threaten to wipe out differences between places, leading to a "search after the 'real' meanings of places, the unearthing of heritages and so forth."[3] Heritage, as this suggests, is never solely about the past. Instead, it is a way to talk about the problems of the present. Heritage is more than its common sense definition as tangible places and things would have it. It is better understood as "a discourse concerned with the negotiation and regulation of social meanings and practices associated with the creation and recreation of 'identity.'"[4] This discourse passes "on exclusive myths of origin and continuance, endowing a select group with prestige and common purpose."[5] Heritage creates a usable past, one that often downplays relations of power and conflict between communities. The National Trust for Historic Preservation defines "heritage tourism" as "traveling to experience the places, artifacts and activities that authentically represent the stories and people of the past and present."[6] In drawing visitors as well as residents, cities brand themselves with coherent, easily identifiable images drawn from the past that are both distinctive enough to be unique and familiar enough to appeal. These efforts, "intentionally . . . blur the lines between museums, classrooms, tourism, art, festivals, and other local celebrations, recreation, economic development, and the cityscape itself."[7]

Baltimore argued that, in addition to its cultural amenities and comparatively low housing costs, its working-class, white ethnic, southern heritage gave it the unique, intangible quality of charm. As professionals and, later, real estate developers moved into formerly white blue-collar neighborhoods like Fells Point, starting in the 1970s, and, later, Highlandtown and Hampden, new businesses like tattoo shops, yoga studios, and comic-book stores opened to serve them. Communities of lifestyle rather than ethnicity defined these neighborhoods as rising rents and property taxes pushed out older, poorer residents. While gentrification changed some neighborhoods, others deteriorated, forgotten because officials didn't see their heritage as useful in drawing the creative class.

The concept of heritage shines a light on the circulation of two very different representations of working-class Baltimore from the 1990s through the first decade of the twenty-first century: the Hon and club music. "Hon" was simply a term of endearment used in white working-class neighborhoods until Denise Whiting, a local business owner, turned it into an icon of the white working-class woman from the 1960s, through her café, its annual heritage festival, and souvenirs and other products emblazoned with a white woman wearing a beehive hairdo and cat-eye glasses. Whiting successfully made the Hon a symbol of Hampden, the gentrifying neighborhood where her café was located. While Baltimore debated whether an image of a white working-class woman could represent a working-class majority African American city, she attempted to control the use of the Hon, embroiling her in controversy over who owned local heritage.

A different kind of heritage defined Baltimore club music. One of Baltimore's most influential cultural exports, it was developed by local black DJs as dance music for working-class black communities. Deeply connected to Baltimore, club music incorporated the history of black cultural production into its beats and lyrics. While it circulated locally at first through radio, nightclubs, and record labels, it spread globally in the twenty-first century, repackaged by producers like Aaron LaCrate as gutter music or club crack. LaCrate sold Baltimore club music by reducing Baltimore to the stereotype of Bodymore, a paradigmatic ghetto space. In this form, it became popular outside the city, helping to distribute an image of Baltimore within hip music and club circuits that emphasized the danger of black urban spaces. Like the go-go music of Washington, DC, Baltimore club music "serves as a metaphor for the black urban experience in the second half of the twentieth century" of creative cultural innovation, appropriation, and displacement.[8]

Arising at nearly the same time but separated by race and geography, the gender and racial politics of urban branding are evident in the trajectories of the Hon and Baltimore club music. The Hon became Baltimore's usable past because it fit the city's strategy to define itself as unique through quirky cultural practices rooted in local heritage to appeal to the creative class. The sassy but feminine Hon positioned the city as friendly and open to strangers, countering the other major image of Baltimore as crime-ridden and dangerous. Club music, which was raunchy, sexually explicit, and produced within local black contexts, did not appeal to the same markets, even though it had a better claim as heritage because it truly was a unique outgrowth of the city's African American culture. Club music gave Baltimore an internationally recognized identity for fans of dance music, but these people were not the city's target audience.

Placing these stories in relationship to each other raises several key questions. Why are certain cultural heritages used to represent a city instead of others with equal claim? Who decides what is an authentic heritage and what is cultural appropriation? What happens to the places forgotten by globalization and gentrification? Implicit in these questions is a counterfactual one: What would it have looked like if club music had been adopted as Baltimore's usable past? How would that have changed the flow of dollars from city hall or the relationship between West Baltimore and downtown? But these questions can only ever be hypothetical. As the 2005 economic development report made clear, there is no space in the neoliberal Baltimore of the twenty-first century for that image.

**Birth of the Hon** | To a student of semiotics a sign is a floating reference, a signifier whose meaning is arbitrary and mutable. To Baltimore city officials, the Welcome to Baltimore sign on Interstate 295 is very real. The dull brown wooden panels tell commuters from DC when they have crossed the border into their home city, hopefully giving them enough warning to make their exit. While the freeway winds promiscuously through city after city, the sign marks a point where this specific place begins.

In 1991, someone spray-painted the word "HON" at the end to make it read, "Welcome to Baltimore, HON." This mysterious culture jammer moved from merely demarcating Baltimore's political borders to setting its racial, gender, and historical boundaries. White working-class communities in Baltimore have used "hon," the shortened form of "honey," as a term of endearment for decades. Michael Olesker, a well-known local writer, argued that "'Hon' is the verbal emotional center of Baltimore . . . Even in a time of great social transition and political upheaval—where many of us are first learning to eat quiche, even though we're still mispronouncing it—'hon' is still the common denominator of the mother tongue, a word that embraces all of us into the same community without asking first of name, rank, and zip code."[9] Uninterested in sociolinguistics, the highway patrol saw the addition as simple vandalism and removed it.

Undaunted and perhaps inspired, a couple of years later, the "Hon Man," as he was dubbed by local *Baltimore Sun* columnist Dan Rodricks, put up a laminated piece of office paper that read "HON" on the sign. When the highway patrol removed it again, he replaced it. Without Rodricks's intervention, the Hon Man would have likely remained a small-time nuisance to police and source of amusement to commuters. But Rodricks published a column championing the Hon Man as a "secret civic sprite" involved in a battle against "government dragoons" and "chowderheaded bureaucrats who did not respect or understand . . . [an] act of honorable vandalism."[10] More than "honorable vandalism," "hon" in the 1990s began to be used aggressively to promote a particular heritage for the city and one of its quickly changing neighborhoods, Hampden, located several miles north of downtown. As globalization and gentrification seemed to threaten unique local cultures, "hon" was meant to serve as an anchor, a sign, and a rallying point.

Not everyone appreciated these changes, understanding them as part of larger debates about the racial identity of the city. In response to Olesker, Wiley A. Hall, another *Baltimore Sun* columnist, wrote about growing up in Baltimore's African American community in a pointed piece that exclaimed, "My Baltimore may use double negatives, but it don't never say 'hon.'" The Hon did not encapsulate his Baltimore heritage, which included a different set of cultural references and geographies, from snowballs (shaved ice flavored with syrup) sold on city street corners to historically black Morgan State University. While Olesker and Rodricks elided racism in their embrace of the Hon, Hall centered it, arguing that Baltimore's slogan must encompass the "totality of the city—one that calls to mind the crab cakes and the lake trout. One that embraces the warmth of those waitresses who greet their customers as 'hon' and the pain of those who weren't allowed to eat there; the nostalgia for the old Baltimore and the hope that the new one will be ever better."[11] The Hon tied Baltimore's heritage to whiteness or, at best, a multiculturalism that saw ethnicity and race as simply cultural expressions divorced from political reality.

The war of words shifted into a policy debate in 1994. Thanks to Rodricks's columns, attention grew. With growing public support for the Hon Man, state senator Barbara Hoffman proposed an amendment to the state budget in March 1994 to withhold $1 million in highway funding from the city unless it permanently altered the sign to read "Welcome to Baltimore—Hon!" Now referred to as Hon-gate, Mayor Schmoke responded that the Hon was inappropriate as a representation of the city. Echoing Hall, he said that the Hon had little or no meaning to the African American majority of Baltimore and was both a sexist and racist term. The debate became part of the long-standing power struggle over resource allocation between the city and the suburbs. While the five surrounding counties have a relatively strong economy, "the problem of the region as a whole is the city."[12] If the branding efforts of the past had been done under the auspices of city government, then Hon-gate suggested that state government was stepping in where it hadn't been involved before. Arguments over resources, however, served as the public expression of a deeper debate over community memory, race, and the politics of heritage in a postindustrial city. While the Hon may be an appropriate way for one community to remember itself, Schmoke offered, it was inappropriate for the city as a whole because it misrepresented the city in the past, present, and future. Which community represents the true Baltimore? Who gets to decide?

Like many cities, Baltimore contended with deep economic and social problems in the 1990s. The crack epidemic decimated neighborhoods with increased drug abuse, homicide rates, and illness. In this context, the Hon was an attempt at finding the "security of identity" that Massey identified through a term that nostalgically referenced an earlier, seemingly more quiescent time. To justify making the Hon sign permanent, supporters tried to prove the term's historic connection to Baltimore, making it meaningful to the city as a whole. But no one could show definitively that "hon" is a specifically Baltimorean term. Linguists note that the Baltimore accent stretches into Philadelphia and that "hon" is used in many places. When archivists at the Maryland Historical Society searched its holdings, which date back to the nineteenth century, they found no reference to "hon." Nonetheless, many white Baltimoreans were undeterred. As Olesker argued in the *Baltimore Sun*, "For generations around here, 'hon' has been an unselfconscious term of casual affection. If that's not ownership of a term, it's at least a long-term lease."[13] Even if people in other parts of the country used "hon," certain residents considered its connection to Baltimore's dialect and social history uniquely representative of the city. Emotion, rather than historical evidence, drove the debate.

Two days after Senator Hoffman's proposal, African American state senator Larry Young made a counterproposal designed to bring to light the racial issues surrounding the Hon and heritage. If black residents roundly denied that "hon" was a term with any meaning to their community, then it could not be a viable representation of the demographic reality of the city or the heritage of its majority. His suggestion? Change the Welcome to Baltimore sign to read "Welcome to Baltimore Bro," using a black colloquial expression to let nonblack residents experience the feeling of exclusion. However, others argued that while "bro" may have roots in African American culture, it had been broadly adopted. As Olesker wrote to Young in the *Baltimore Sun*, "You've got to start spending more time around white teen-agers for whom 'bro' is both a standard greeting and an unspoken acknowledgement that the street parlance of black teens has become standard usage."[14]

Understood everywhere, "bro" has little perceived emotional or historic connection with Baltimore. Most importantly, though, "bro" could never be put on the official Welcome to Baltimore sign because it would not do the cultural work necessary to prepare the city for tourists and new residents. Instead of positioning Baltimore as hospitable and welcoming, "bro" would masculinize the city by associating it directly with African American men. In contemporary American culture, black masculinity, especially *youthful* black masculinity, is defined as dangerous. While the specter of danger is a major selling point for record companies marketing gangsta rappers or, as we will see later, in the popularization of Baltimore club music outside the city, it is not the image that Baltimore is likely to embrace to draw vacationers or day trippers. By controlling the words on the welcome sign, government power is being used to literally write specific representations of race and gender into the spaces of the city for the purposes of selling it. As one letter to the editor of the *Baltimore Sun* advocated, "If certain people really feel the need to have 'Hon' publicly displayed in association with this city, let's put it where it belongs: on the Highlandtown bridge over Eastern Avenue," connecting it to one of the white ethnic communities it sprang from.[15]

But instead of Highlandtown claiming the Hon, another neighborhood did: Hampden. A former mill village that was once the largest producer of cotton duck fabric in the country, Hampden was known for its insularity, a product of its geographical location (bounded by Druid Hill Park on one side, Johns Hopkins University on another, and the wealthy neighborhood of Roland Park on the other) and its population, which was overwhelmingly white. As Hampden resident Margaret Doyle noted in an oral history taken in 1979, "Hampden . . . was pretty much a closed community for many years."[16] According to the 1980 Census, the vacancy rate for housing in Hampden was only 4 percent, demonstrating the stability of the population, which has allowed its residents to see themselves as a community distinct from the rest of Baltimore.[17]

Through the viewpoint of people of color, Hampden's isolation and homogeneity are the result of racist attitudes, practices, and outright violence that ensured white dominance. From the perspective of city officials, Hampden was the perfect example of the "tight knit neighborhoods" heralded in the Economic Growth Strategy. Because of its low housing costs and reputation for neighborhood cohesion, Hampden began to gentrify in the 1990s, as artists and young professionals moved into the neighborhood. New stores opened, like Atomic Books, a hip bookstore and comic-book shop where John Waters picked up his mail. An active merchants association argued that shopping locally was critical to the continued liveliness of the neighborhood and preservation of local identity. No business epitomized this more than the Cafe Hon, a retro diner that capitalized on the word "hon" by turning it into a person—a caricature of a 1960s diner waitress, a "middle-aged woman with her hair done up in a teased beehive, wearing cat's-eye glasses, leopard-print stretch pants and high-heeled sandals, accompanied by the ever-present scent of Aqua Net hairspray."[18]

Opened in 1992 by Denise Whiting, in 1994 the café sponsored the first HonFest, a celebration of working-class women that included a quasi–beauty contest to crown the Best Hon among entrants who dressed up as extreme versions of the Hon and spoke with an exaggerated Baltimore accent. The winners were given such déclassé prizes as a leopard-print toilet seat cover and a case of Aqua Net hair spray. Whiting smartly drew from the public controversy spurred by the Welcome to Baltimore sign and localized it even further, claiming Hampden as Hon territory. Hampden's own homogeneity and its history of excluding African Americans further consolidated the idea of the Hon as white. As Janine Bradley, the head of the Hampden Village Main Street Association, told me when I asked her in 2002 whether the Hon still existed, "Baltimore is 60 percent black and they're not Hons."[19]

Within weeks, the State Senate dropped the amendment, effectively ending the public debate, though the Hon Man continued his grassroots activities. The creation of Cafe Hon and, especially, HonFest meant that Hon culture was assuming a greater significance in branding Hampden and Baltimore. Whiting, as a small business

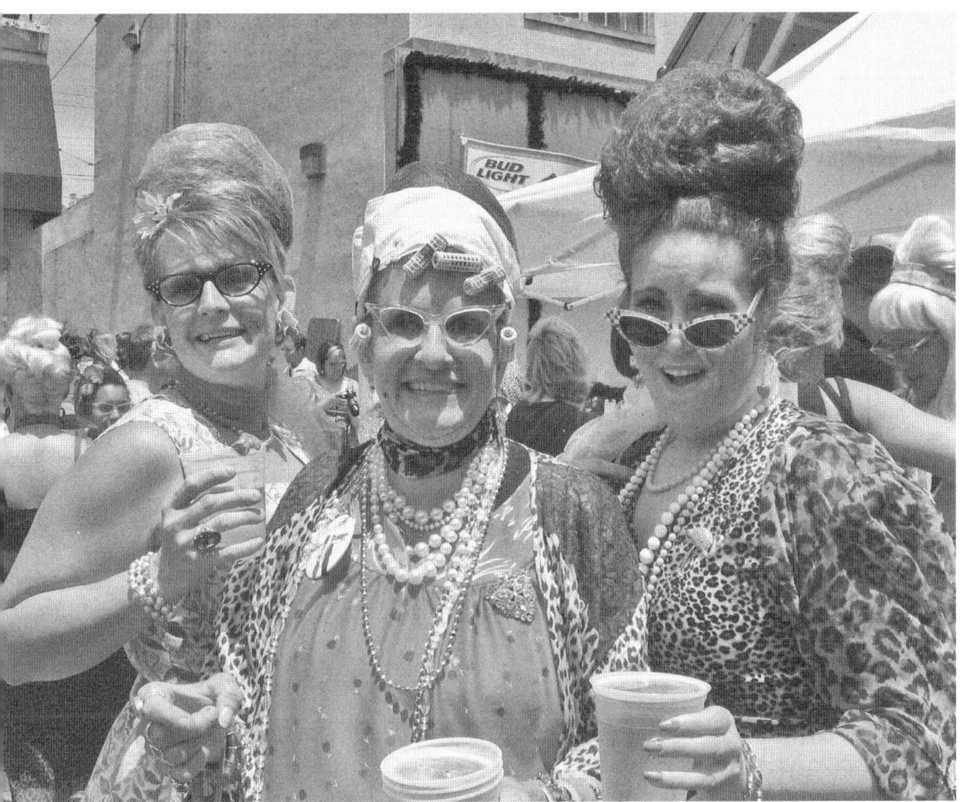


Women dressed as the Baltimore icon the Hon for neighborhood festival HonFest in 2006.
Mary Rizzo

owner, worked tirelessly to promote her enterprises. She turned "hon" from a word to a cultural image recognizable enough to sell as souvenirs symbolic of Baltimore's unique heritage. Her efforts succeeded for two reasons. First, they merged perfectly with the need to differentiate places through reference to local heritage. As we have seen, various representatives of Baltimore spoke passionately about the linguistic roots of Hon. Whiting's vision of the Hon as a person, which borrowed heavily from John Waters's representations of working-class women in *Hairspray*, defined Baltimore as friendly, quirky, charming, and sassy. No city sells itself solely through its services. Visitors must feel comfortable, safe, and secure if they are to be expected to spend any time or money there. The Hon creates this sense by associating Baltimore with a friendly greeting that is connected to white working-class southern femininity. From Scarlett O'Hara to *Steel Magnolias*, the southern woman is a nationally recognizable type, constructed repeatedly through popular culture and through public performances of femininity such as the beauty pageant and sorority rush. The southern lady, that "imaginative construct of white, slaveholding southern men, who looked to her to rationalize their peculiar race/gender system," is defined through her charm, beauty, and grace, virtues accompanied by a strong will and sense of right and wrong.[20]

Baltimore's paradigmatic version of white working-class southern femininity, the Hon, is a waitress who brings a layer of personal connection to an essentially commercial transaction. Permanently affixing "HON" to the Welcome to Baltimore sign positioned the city in the feminized role of hospitality: the Hon embraces visitors and makes them part of the community. The power of this image is clearly seen in the way visitors consistently conflate the image of the Hon with reality in their descriptions of the city. A journalist writing about traveling to Baltimore for the New Orleans *Times-Picayune* described how "we were sitting in Café Hon, a faux 1950s diner near the Johns Hopkins main campus. 'You decided what you want, hon?' the waitress asked, breathing life into the appellation."[21] The waitress's "emotional labor" consisted of fulfilling stereotypical notions about the Hon as an exemplar of southern charm and hospitality, showing that "the *emotional style of offering the service is part of the service itself.*"[22] Instead of assuming the waitress was simply calling her "hon" because she was made to do so by her employer, the journalist sees it as proof of an essential aspect of Baltimore's unique culture. Image and reality, Hon and real waitress, collapse into each other—and into a service-oriented economy—and become the basis for understanding the city as a whole.

The feminine, friendly Hon turns Hampden from a neighborhood in a dangerous city into a quirky small town perfect for tourists or new residents. Like the "Keep Austin Weird" campaign that capitalized on the attitude of residents as well as its noncorporate stores to distinguish that city, Cafe Hon and HonFest fused with Hampden's buy-local efforts to define the neighborhood as different from the rest of Baltimore and from competitor cities, like Washington, DC.[23] The placement of the sign on the Baltimore–Washington Parkway is particularly important in this regard. New residents, many of whom work in Washington, DC, were drawn by Baltimore's cheaper real estate as well as the city's character, which is constructed through cultural representations that use the Hon. Souvenir shops sell numerous Hon products, including T-shirts, local beer, and tchotchkes. From café to festival to souvenir, the Hon and her language became Baltimore's heritage, one that defines the city in a way that other large cities cannot. As one *Washington Post* journalist opined in 1997, "Baltimore is where Regular Joes live and make something other than money, offering the visiting Washingtonian a glimpse of what America must be like."[24]

**In the Club** | At nearly the same time that Denise Whiting, the Hon Man, and a state senator battled to raise the Hon as the quintessential image of Baltimore, black cultural producers created a new sound that depicted their experience of life in a place more likely to be called Bodymore, Murdaland, than Charm City. Within a few years, Baltimore club music would circulate outside the city, to places like New York and Philadelphia, where it would morph into the sonic representation of black Baltimore.

The roots of Baltimore club music go back to the era of disco. America ached in the 1970s, "a nation increasingly riven by race, ethnicity, age, region, ideology and style."[25] Between economic stagnation (giving rise to the word "stagflation" to describe rising inflation in a moment of slow growth), a foreign war we were clearly losing that had been delegitimized by massive public protests, and a president resigning from office because of corruption and scandal, the country turned to new cultural expressions to make sense of the world. Disco music, designed for dancing, played in massive nightclubs. Merging with the increasing visibility of the gay community, disco became a key aspect of urban gay culture as well as African American culture. In fact, African American musicians propelled the format. Black singers like Sylvester and Donna Summer cooed their innuendo-filled lyrics over a fast-paced beat, topping the charts throughout the mid- to late 1970s, becoming superstars and icons.

Ironically, Chicago became the site of both the mainstream death of disco and its rebirth as house music. By the late 1970s, white backlash to the racial and sexual openness of disco rose to a pitch—a baseball pitch, in fact. In 1979, DJ Steve Dahl invited fans and the members of an anti-disco army to Comiskey Park in Chicago for a ballgame that included blowing up a crate of disco records.[26] An ill-fated idea: after the explosion, fans ran out of the stands, damaging the field.

While disco's mainstream popularity faltered, local music producers in Chicago tweaked the disco sound by adding more electronic elements, developing what came to be called house music in the 1980s. In this pre-digital era, producers created their own records using samples from records they owned. They were distributed primarily through record stores specializing in dance music, patronized mostly by DJs. Because of this relatively limited circulation, dance music genres came to be deeply related to particular places. If house was created in Chicago, then techno, which was more synthesized, became Detroit's signature sound.[27] But, as these musical genres began to circulate beyond the boundaries of particular neighborhoods or cities, their meaning in relation to place and race changed.

Black dance music developed alongside hip hop. Coming out of New York City in the late 1970s, hip hop was a syncretic cultural form that included rapping, DJing, break dancing, and graffiti. Sampling defined its music. *Billboard* magazine even published a story in 1979 on "disco rappers," describing the genre as encompassing "a spinner who talks in a lyrical, rapid fire, streetwise dialogue over the pulsating rhythm track" originating "in the black discos of New York."[28] Hip hop spoke specifically to its social context. Created by working-class African American and Latinx youth, hip hop responded to their economic and social marginalization. In its early days as a localized subculture, hip hop created community, through parties in public parks or through the explicitly political activities of a DJ like Afrika Bambaataa, who positioned his Zulu Nation as a hip hop alternative to gang activity. Songs like "The Message" by Grandmaster Flash and the Furious Five expressed despair about the danger and economic disparities working-class communities faced. In the late 1970s, hip hop spread beyond its geographic origins, including to Baltimore.[29] In the mid-1980s, teen rapper Tupac Shakur, long before his meteoric rise and sudden death, and his friend, Dana Smith, won a contest sponsored by the Enoch Pratt Free Library. Their song "Library Rap," performed with their East Side Crew, is now held in the library's Special Collections, becoming part of the official heritage of the city.[30] While rap would also take root in Baltimore, the city's music producers made club music Baltimore's unique contribution to black popular music.

Baltimore producers and DJs like Frank Ski, Scottie B, DJ Technics, Shawn Caesar, and DJ Booman experimented with merging hip hop and house to create a unique sound. Essentially, Baltimore club music is "the simple repetition of kick drums on top of ancient beats on top of yet another layer of bass-heavy drums on top of a single phrase or exhortation repeated vocally ad nauseum," with occasional horn blasts or shouts as punctuation.[31] In Scottie B's 1991 song "I Got the Rhythm," he whispers, "I got the rhythm, you got the rhythm," over a multilayered drum beat. There are no other words, which is the case in most Baltimore club music tracks. Sampling was key to club music's sound. By using samples, producers positioned their songs within a sonic heritage, a lineage that leads to the present performance. The samples used in Baltimore club music came from a wide variety of sources. "Mr. Postman" sampled the chorus of African American girl group the Marvelettes' early 1960s hit "Please Mr. Postman." Using the alias 2 Hyped Brothers and a Dog, in 1991–1992 Frank Ski's "Doo Doo Brown" borrowed controversial rap group 2 Live Crew's "C'mon Babe," with the title chanted over it, creating another early Baltimore club hit.[32] In these ways, the Baltimore club producer acknowledged a web of influences that extended beyond the city. Unlike other popular music like rock, these songs do not build up to a crescendo. Instead, there is a "a relentless 'here/here/here/here' as persistent as the kick drum" created through the song's repetition of simple phrases.[33] Catharsis is everywhere and nowhere.

Baltimore club music both shaped its urban context and was shaped by it. As Murray Forman argues, the South Bronx determined hip hop's development, as black and Latinx, especially Puerto Rican, youth shared their musical traditions to create a new sound relevant to a postindustrial city that had carved out few spaces for them. Instead, they reinscribed public places through break dancing on street corners, DJing parties in parks, and tagging subway trains that traveled through the city. Recorded hip hop music circulated through local means, like cassette tapes sold out of cars or in small record stores, in these early days before rising to national interest. And, of course, rappers spoke urgently and often eloquently about the city where they lived in their songs, proving that "the spatial complexities of hip hop, far from being incidental or insignificant, are central to all that emerges from it."[34]

Place determined the development of club music in Baltimore in its origination moments in three ways. First, the music circulated through a geographically bounded chain of local music labels, record stores, and radio stations. Club music records were not primarily intended for purchase by individual consumers to listen to in their homes; the music was created for DJs to play in clubs or on local radio stations. Between 1993 and 1997, Baltimore label Unruly Records released forty 12-inch club music singles. Unruly cornered the market because its producers were also club and radio DJs, so they played the label incessantly.[35] Once Unruly paused its production schedule, Rod Lee stepped in with his label Club Kingz. Producers and consumers all lived in Baltimore.

Second, certain nightclubs became known for playing Baltimore club music, which produced a particular social space. The Paradox, a South Baltimore club that opened in 1991 in a thirteen-thousand-square-foot former warehouse, became one of the most important homes for club music. Serving no alcohol, the venue did not have to abide by the laws that other clubs did, so its legendary parties, DJed by the biggest names in club music like Rod Lee, could extend past sunrise. In this space, crowds of locals from around the city came together to dance, creating an imagined Baltimore community that transcended lines of neighborhood though, overwhelmingly, not crossing lines of color. If HonFest called to mind a homogenously white Hampden of the early 1960s, Paradox eliminated the boundaries between the neighborhoods where Baltimore's black residents lived in the present. While these divisions would reassert themselves outside the club, within that magic circle, a different image of Baltimore ascended to prominence, one that was unapologetically black.[36]

Place also structured the songs themselves. The lyrics, referred to as "hood tracks" by club music scholar Andrew Devereaux, referenced specific places within Baltimore.[37] Miss Tony, the stage name of Anthony Boston, a black DJ who performed in drag, used this pattern repeatedly in his songs. In "Living in the Alley," Tony's crackly voice places the listener with him in an alley with nowhere to turn. Speaking to the economic destitution that stalks Baltimore's communities of color, the song intersperses this line with shout-outs to places like Park Heights and Cherry Hill, and a call for help. Tony's geographic scale shifts through the song from microlocal references to specific housing projects to a street, like Harford Road, that passes through several neighborhoods. Designed to make dancers or partygoers shout loudly to represent their local area, these songs allowed people to express geographical loyalty while locating them within Baltimore. Like many rap songs that use telephone exchanges or street names, hood tracks show a sense of place in this music. Baltimore club music is of and from a specific city. These references may make little to no sense outside of this context or to listeners who are not deeply familiar with the area, but this hardly matters when the context is local, when the floor that is vibrating with bass is in the same place that is being sung about.

**Miss Tony, the Black Divine** | Urban branding attempts to define cities as unique spaces. Interestingly, these discourses often utilize gendered imagery that carries messages about class, race, and power. In the late nineteenth century, writers described the annexation of an area by a nearby city as a marriage in which the larger city was always the groom.[38] Since the 1970s, however, city officials, concerned that pervasive media images of urban crime made cities seem unsafe and inhospitable, switched the gendering. As media studies scholar Steve Macek shows, the consistent depiction of cities in 1970s and 1980s movies as places where women were threatened with violence defined these places as male and, increasingly, nonwhite.[39] For Baltimore officials looking to attract upwardly mobile new residents and tourists, a feminized, welcoming image was critical to counter this perception. The Hon, friendly but sassy and defined as part of a uniquely local heritage, fit their needs. Club music, which had a stronger heritage claim, however, was raunchy, sexually explicit, and both too masculine and too queer. Songs suggesting that "this pussy drive you crazy" or asking "where the hoes at" would be accompanied by grinding on the dance floor. And although the dance floor was dominated by women, the production, DJing, and record labels were generally controlled by men.[40]

These seemingly rigid lines of who made music and who danced to it were troubled by people like DJ K-Swift, one of the most successful women in club music, whose career was cut short by her accidental death. Miss Tony's cross-dressing persona similarly crossed boundaries around gender performance and sexuality in ways that are reminiscent of Divine. Unlike Divine, Miss Tony never became an internationally known queer icon because of his born-again Christianity, early death, and lack of access to the queer arts scene that embraced Divine. Instead, Tony came to represent Baltimore within the black communities where club music blared from speakers, while Divine has become a representative of white Baltimore arts and eccentricity.

Famous as an originator of the club music scene, Tony sang some of its most well-remembered songs, like "Whatzup? Whatzup?," while DJing and hosting the *Big Fat Morning Show*. Like Divine, Tony was tall and heavyset, described as over six feet and three hundred pounds. Both dressed in extravagant drag. Kevin Brown, a former reporter, described Tony as "a club figure because he brought the gayness and he was flamboyant. I mean, the wig, the nails, the makeup, the hair. And he brazenly did it. It wasn't like *Ima be a drag queen*, it was *Ima be a draaaaag queen*."[41] Like Divine, Tony's performances included aggressive interactions with fans. Tony would point to men in the audience when he was DJing and flirt with them or suggest that he had already had sex with them. Because of his persona, he could get away with it.

Clubgoers knew Tony starting from the late 1980s into the late 1990s. From 1994 to 1999, he appeared regularly on radio station 92Q in drag, until his conversion in 1998. By the time that club music would become known outside the city in the middle of the first decade of the twenty-first century, discussed in more detail later, Tony was dead. Miss Tony died as a local celebrity, one who turned away from the club for religion, but whose memory is invoked in all discussions of the early years of Baltimore club music.

In death, too, the lives of Miss Tony and Divine diverged. Divine, a model for Baltimore's Hon iconography, has been embraced as a symbol of the city's eccentric whiteness. The American Visionary Art Museum in Baltimore, dedicated to collecting and displaying work by self-taught artists that reflects their uniquely individual vision, includes a larger-than-life rotating statue of Divine in the ruby fishtail gown and bleached-blonde hairdo made famous in

*Pink Flamingos*. A group of organizers is advocating for the creation of a monument to Divine, featuring a close-up photo of her face, on the location where she ate dog feces in the final scene of *Pink Flamingos*. As the *Baltimore Sun* explains, "Nothing bespeaks Baltimore's love for the quirky more than the city's embrace of Divine."[42] However, Miss Tony who, unlike Divine, was actually from Baltimore city, is not eligible to play the role on the same scale, even though he was equally a queer iconoclast and culture worker who, it can be argued, helped create what has been called "one of [Baltimore's] foremost cultural exports."[43]

Miss Tony, however, has become a touchstone for black Baltimoreans. When Black Lives Matter activist DeRay Mckesson announced that he would run for mayor of Baltimore in 2016, he proved his local credibility by referencing Baltimore club music and mentioning Miss Tony specifically.[44] As journalist Brandon Soderberg has explored, the memory of Miss Tony lives on through cultural production by African American Baltimoreans. Tony's famous early 1990s song "How You Wanna Carry It (What's Up What's Up)," which includes shout-outs to specific locations in Baltimore, is often referenced by rappers, while a poster of Tony with two speech bubbles repeating the name of the song created by artist Sorta appeared around the city, to "put Tony's subversive career in people's faces as a wave of gentrification moved through the city."[45] In addition to helping create Baltimore club music, Miss Tony's legacy respatializes Baltimore to proudly and loudly emphasize the diversity of its black neighborhoods, a project continued by black cultural producers today.

**Charm City versus Bodymore |** In the 1990s, both Hon culture and Baltimore club music became known within a local geographical context. Both employ heritage in making claims to be representative of certain neighborhoods and, for the Hon, Baltimore as a whole. By 2005, however, both began circulating far beyond the city's borders. In these wider geographies, the meaning of these cultural texts shifted, as did the relationships between their promoters and fans. Whiting's failed efforts to control the meaning and use of the Hon relied on discourses of heritage that created powerful emotional connections around the Hon but gave other people claim to her as well. As club music circulated globally, it came to define Baltimore. Music producer Aaron LaCrate helped bring Baltimore club music to the notice of a globalized club music culture, but only by tying it to simplistic images of the Baltimore ghetto as Bodymore that ignored the music's original meaning to the working-class communities who created and consumed it.

**Baltimore Club Goes Global** | Mainstream newspapers like the *Washington Post* and the *New York Times* published articles about Baltimore club music, giving it a level of fame that was a far cry from its roots in all-night parties in neighborhoods very different from those touted by these publications in their travel and tourism sections.[46] As this music circulated outside the local area, how it represented the city changed as well. Thanks to producers like Diplo and Low Budget (collaborating as Hollertronix) and Baltimore-born LaCrate, the sound began to be categorized as its own subgenre of dance music by "cleverly relying on the image of the Baltimore 'hyperghetto.'"[47] Following a trajectory similar to that of gangsta rap music, associated with excessively violent imagery in the 1990s that was seen as specific to places like South Central Los Angeles, Baltimore club moved from a sound created by and meaningful to working-class African Americans to a commodity version of cartoonish blackness that enticed and fascinated white producers and dancers.[48]

Aaron LaCrate's story is exemplary. LaCrate, who is white, grew up in Highlandtown, a white working-class area of Baltimore much like Hampden. LaCrate got involved in hip hop culture as a teen, dabbling in fashion design before DJing, promoting parties, and producing. He differentiated himself from his competitors by successfully defining Baltimore club music as its own genre through tropes of ghetto authenticity. The cover of his mixtape *Bmore Gutter Music*, volume 1, depicts signs of Baltimore—the white marble steps, a sticker reading "BELIEVE," one of O'Malley's city slogans. But the rowhouses have boarded-up windows, surveillance cameras monitor the street, and a sign proclaims it a "school free drug zone." While there are no people shown, it is clearly a black ghetto. Gunshots punctuate songs to make clear that danger and violence shape the spaces where the music was made. Unlike the artwork or poetry in *Chicory*, which this image resembles, it is designed to use Baltimore's black neighborhoods to sell music outside of the city to people looking for authentic black music, defined since the popularity of gangsta rap in the 1990s as deriving from black poverty and crime. The release of *Bmore Club Crack*—which could be bought online or in big box stores, unlike early club music records that were sold in local record stores—strengthened the association between the genre, city, and criminality for people outside of it. When K-Swift DJed a party in a Baltimore warehouse, she was surprised to find the attendees were white youth, often from places as far away as Philadelphia or Connecticut. They were attracted to the "raw and heavy" sound, which Jason Urick, the party's organizer, described as "primitive," trading on assumptions dating back to early scientific racism that black culture is uncivilized.[49]

Other hip hop and urban fiction similarly positioned Baltimore as Bodymore, the emblematic space of black destitution. On 50 Cent's album *The Massacre*, his song "A Baltimore Love Thing" uses heroin as a metaphor for obsessive love. Urban fiction novels told stories of drugs and crime set in Baltimore. Treasure Hernandez's series the Baltimore Chronicles barely acknowledges the city it's supposedly set in while telling a twisting, almost Dickensian tale of twin brothers (one with a deformed face), foster families, betrayal, and corruption. Shannon Holmes wrote his first novel, *B-more Careful*, while in prison. He mentions Baltimore intersections and nightclubs, as well as neighborhoods, in his fantasy version of gang life, where a drug kingpin amuses himself by having his white chauffeur drive him up to other cars to ask whether they have Grey Poupon mustard. Holmes's success, which relied on positioning Baltimore as an iconic ghetto defined by drug dealing and gangsters, earned him a publishing contract with Simon & Schuster. The successful film commission brought numerous film and TV productions to Baltimore.[50] In the dance movie *Step Up* (2006), actor Channing Tatum plays a white kid growing up in foster care in Baltimore. While he finds opportunity through admission to a prestigious dance school, his best friends, who are black, contend with tragedy that they can't escape.

LaCrate's profiting from hyperaggressive images of black Baltimore criminality earned him scorn from many locals for capitalizing on black music, divorcing a cultural expression from its local context, and enriching himself through association with stereotypical images of black authenticity. As Andrew Devereaux notes, LaCrate emphasized the authenticity of these subgenres by saying in interviews, "This is no white boy shit," and distinguishing between club and dance music, which he called "gay."[51] Baltimore music journalist and blogger Al Shipley complained in 2007 that "it kinda bummed me out that his [LaCrate's] version of Bmore club was the version that a lot of people out of town, in New York and other countries, got exposed to first, and identified primarily with the scene," rather than versions of others who had been producing longer.[52] Music writer Tom Breihan, originally from Baltimore, called this version "a collection of fake club music from out-of-town DJs and producers who pretty much just imitated a local phenomenon and changed it enough so they could sell it without getting sued."[53]

LaCrate used his cultural capital to frame club music to appeal to white audiences attuned to a global music culture but who were also searching for the latest "authentic" subgenre. While white appropriation of black cultural expression is hardly new, Labtekwon, a Baltimore indie rapper, condemned LaCrate and others involved in spreading club music through the discourse of heritage. "We use this music as a point of refuge and cleansing," he explained.

> This is the same purpose for music and dance in Traditional African culture . . . Baltimore has a legacy in music because we were one of the main stops on the "Chitlin" circuit. Bmore has turned out great Soul Music since Billie Holliday [*sic*] to Doc Soul Stirrer to Club Music. Pennsylvania Avenue was once a Mecca for Black entertainment for many years. This is our legacy. The northernmost city of the south and the southernmost city of the north. We are the city of slick.[54]

If LaCrate flattened the image of Baltimore into an overdetermined ghetto, Labtekwon connected club music to black cultural producers across the globe. Rather than being framed for the consumption of white club kids, in this version, club music speaks to a history of black artistic production under constraint, a history that creates a lineage between the trials of generations ago and those experienced today. Club music has always been influenced by these global circuits and relations, but its meaning is also deeply localized.

**Hon-Gate |** Throughout the 1990s, HonFest and Hampden grew together. If Hampden had once been the conservative white southern mill village in the metropolis, the 1990s saw its meaning within and outside the city shift dramatically to become a hip, charming, tolerant neighborhood. It drew visitors and new residents with its real estate prices, low crime rates, and heritage of working-class quirkiness. Soon after O'Malley launched the BELIEVE campaign in 2002, Hampden was plastered with stickers reading BEEHIVE placing kitsch and white working-class femininity at the center of the discourse about the city. While the homicide rate in the city increased more than 5 percent between 1990 and 1998, on Hampden's main drag, Thirty-Sixth Street, pawn shops and luncheonettes closed to make way for boutiques selling specialty goods.[55] Between 1999 and 2004, the average sale price of a Hampden rowhouse more than doubled.[56] HonFest pushed these changes and capitalized on them. While a few hundred people attended the first several HonFests, by 2004 an estimated twenty thousand donned beehive wigs. Just four years later, approximately fifty thousand Hons filled several blocks along Thirty-Sixth Street for what had become a two-day event and arguably the largest heritage festival held in a city that hosted many such festivals.[57]

Hampden's rise occurred, in part, thanks to media attention and marketing strategies that defined the neighborhood as quirky, kitschy, fun, and welcoming, with an authentic working-class heritage in distinction to the larger city, which was marked as dangerous. Although not part of official city marketing, John Waters's *Pecker*, filmed in Hampden, added to the discourse on white working-class quirkiness. The film follows a young photographer nicknamed Pecker, whose photos of his strange neighbors and family dazzle the New York City art world. The big-city art glitterati see his work as outsider art, sincerely capturing the strange place he comes from. They swarm Baltimore searching for the authenticity that they can never have because their social sphere is defined by ironic detachment and privilege. Article after article repeated these tropes of Hampden and Baltimore as a place without pretension because of its authentic working-class roots. The *New Yorker* covered the city's efforts to turn Waters's Baltimore into a tourist destination with the remaking of two of his films, *Hairspray* and *Cry-Baby*, as musical theater. Tom Noonan, president of the Baltimore Area Convention and Visitors Association, positioned Waters's version of the city against preconceived notions of it as industrial or crime-ridden, arguing that Waters, for all of his outrageousness, "encapsulates what Baltimore is all about . . . [It] has a quirkiness to it."[58] Frank Deford, sportswriter, NPR commentator, and Baltimore native, saw the city's relationship to neighboring DC change over his lifetime. While for generations Baltimore played second fiddle, now "even those fancy-schmancy citizens of the capital have come to admire Baltimore for its quirkiness. Hey, there's this place that's actually real only 40 miles away. You better bleeve it, hon."[59] And when the *Baltimore City Paper*, the local alt-weekly, sought to define kitsch, it went first to the antique store named Fat Elvis in Hampden, where a local argued that "everyone is friendly and the people are not pretentious at all."[60] As these examples suggest, Hampden defined itself through whiteness, femininity, and working-class kitsch, which competed with other, less positive images of Baltimore as a whole. City leaders and representatives resorted to tropes identified most specifically with Hampden and the white working-class neighborhoods to brand the city.

These images made sense only through difference—Hampden was not like the rest of Baltimore because of its white working-class heritage, so Baltimore was not like other cities because it embraced this cultural heritage rather than that of its majority black population. Such ideas showed that Hampden's supposed isolation was a lie. This space was clearly connected to the rest of the city. Perhaps harder to see, it was also connected to global flows of capital and people, which impacted its development and set the stage for serious conflicts in the twenty-first century. This could be seen through changes at HonFest itself. Early HonFests included space for locals to hold garage sales. A decade later, professional vendors had taken their place. With thousands of people attending, Denise Whiting convinced global corporations like Bacardi and Heineken to sponsor the event.

It also gave her political clout that allowed her to negotiate with the city. When the city assessed a fine for the giant pink flamingo that hung on the front of Cafe Hon, Whiting complained, creating a cause célèbre. She claimed the flamingo was public art, not subject to a fine. When authorities disagreed, she removed the bird and held a rally at Baltimore City Hall where hundreds of pink flamingo lawn ornaments were staked into the ground. Former Best Hon winners attended. Mayor Sheila Dixon acknowledged that her employees would likely be upset but wondered why the city "didn't reach out to the flamingo and work with" Whiting to resolve the issue. Even though another business owner in Hamden had called the city to complain about the flamingo, Whiting positioned the flamingo dispute as "a symbol of the small businesses that are the backbone of the current economy and its crisis."[61] The city renegotiated the fee, halving it, and added an exit sign for Hampden to the Jones Falls Expressway, making it even easier for tourists and travelers to get to Hampden.

Whiting understood that the audience for her café and festival shifted over time from residents to tourists from the region and much farther away. The Hon's high profile ensured a market for her products (the comfort food sold at the Cafe Hon as well as branded souvenirs at her geographically named shop, Hontown), unlike the other small retailers that had opened in Hampden over this period. Without the marketing machine that kept Whiting's businesses in the public eye, these shop owners needed to protect themselves from corporate competition. When Walmart proposed building a superstore in a former automotive showroom in Remington, just south of Hampden, the merchants association, city council representative, and a newly created smart growth organization, Bmore Local, fought it. Benn Ray, head of the association, argued that the "clustering of these businesses suggests to large, out-of-state corporate interests that there are established markets here that they can exploit and dominate—at the expense of the small business retail that has worked hard here for years—in some cases, for generations."[62] Small businesses, like hardware stores or corner grocers, could lose enough business to Walmart to cause them to close and give Walmart even greater market share. Mary Pat Clarke, city council representative from the neighborhood, put forward living wage legislation to deter the store opening.[63] But one local business owner vocally defended Walmart: Denise Whiting. In a letter to the *Baltimore Sun*, Whiting located her Baltimore as the city "before blockbusting, steering, riots and urban sprawl," where department stores anchored the downtown, creating memories in the minds of little girls who were taken to (segregated) lunch counters for egg salad and ice cream floats.

Walmart, in Whiting's mid-twentieth-century fantasy, would revive the department store while also fighting e-commerce. Even if Walmart workers are the "working poor," she asked whether they would have jobs at all without the global retail giant, ending with a simple statement in support of "development in the city of Baltimore. It's smart business."[64] While Bmore Local and the merchants association feared Walmart's encroachment on their profits, Whiting understood that it was not competition for her business, with its aggressive branding and public relations notoriety. In fact, if Walmart drew more shoppers to the area, she could potentially profit. If in the early 1990s Whiting saw herself as part of a buy-local movement in Hampden, by the early 2000s, her geographic radius had shifted to such a degree that her businesses existed beyond the local area as much as in it.

While community members rallied around Whiting during flamingogate (as it came to be called), Whiting's Walmart stance annoyed her small-business neighbors, as did the growth of HonFest, which, they argued, negatively affected their businesses. Some, too, took issue with the Best Hon contest, which, they believed, mocked rather than honored working-class women.[65] But not even a giant flamingo could cause a bigger flap than the revelation in late 2010 that Whiting owned several trademarks associated with the word "hon."[66] The trademark covered the use of the word on items like bumper stickers and mugs. Locals saw Whiting capitalizing on a cultural heritage that belonged to everyone (at least every white person) in Baltimore. She argued that she was simply protecting her intellectual property, that the Hon had become her brand, rather than Hampden's or the city's. When the Maryland Transit Administration wanted to use the phrase "Get yours, hon," to promote its new mass transportation pass, Whiting asserted her right to approve the promotions and publicity using the phrase. The owner of a gift shop in Towson received a cease and desist letter from Whiting's attorney. When these incidents and the trademark became public knowledge, it unleashed a firestorm of controversy.

Protests were held outside Cafe Hon, and a local man vowed to test the trademark by selling coffee mugs with the word "hon" on them. Merging two representations of the city, a protestor referenced one of David Simon's police procedurals to express his displeasure in a sign that read, "Honicide: Life on 36th St.," suggesting that Whiting committed a crime in claiming the word "hon." The Facebook page No One Owns Hon, Hon, created a virtual space for protest. NPR covered the story nationally.[67] Local zine *Smile, Hon, You're in Baltimore* devoted an issue to it, with writers condemning Whiting for the "Disney-ification of white trash to sell overpriced diner food."[68] Native son and writer Rafael Alvarez lobbed the ultimate Baltimore insult at Whiting, calling her "Robert Irsay in a dress," a reference to the despised owner of the Colts who snuck the football team out of the city to move them to Indianapolis.[69]

The flames diminished only after temperamental chef Gordon Ramsay featured Cafe Hon on his reality TV show *Kitchen Nightmares* in 2012. Although the show generally focuses on restaurants struggling because of bad food or poor front of house staff, in this case, the fix was more public relations oriented (though the food and decor needed some help, too). As the promo voice-over asks, can Ramsay "save this restaurant from a city that would prefer it didn't exist?"[70] The episode begins with a shot of the Welcome to Baltimore sign, introducing Hampden as a "proud community located just outside of Baltimore," suggested how thoroughly the neighborhood had developed an identity separate from its city. Following the redemption narrative of reality TV, Whiting agreed, at Ramsay's urging, to return the word "hon" to the people by giving up her trademarks. The episode closes with an obligatory final shot of a full dining room humming with murmurs of contentment.

As of 2019, the café still exists, as does HonFest. By using the discourse of heritage in creating her mini-empire, Whiting cohered an image of the neighborhood located in the 1960s, a time of supposed safety, simplicity, and good neighborliness that ignored the racism that kept the area homogenously white. Indeed, Whiting promoted an online poll at HonFest to "change Baltimore's official slogan to, 'Welcome to Baltimore, HON!'" to "highlight the kind and generous spirit" of the city.[71] In a city grappling with economic and social problems, this vision appealed to business and civic leaders who saw it as a usable past that could draw young, upwardly mobile residents and tourists. While the Hon derives from a white ethnic working-class past, African American women have begun to embrace the term, and several have competed in the Best Hon competition. In 2018, Whiting crowned the first black Best Hon, Amber Nelson.[72] It remains to be seen whether the Hon image will shift as women of color take it on or whether they will simply adopt the style in toto. However, Whiting did not recognize that by encouraging white Baltimoreans to emotionally connect with the Hon, they would also feel ownership over the word and image. When she used these images to appeal to audiences far outside of Hampden and Baltimore in ways that threatened other small businesses in the neighborhood and asserted control over the use of the term as her intellectual property, they criticized her for trying to own a piece of Baltimore's history. Her success in defining the Hon as the heritage of Hampden and Baltimore ironically led to her reduced control over it.

**Baltimore, Branded** | The last decade of the twentieth century saw the creation of two distinct cultural forms in Baltimore based in aspects of the city's history. As gentrification displaced many working-class people, Hon culture assembled a supposedly local white working-class women's heritage from various cultural texts, like John Waters's films, style, and memory, seasoned with a large dash of kitsch. Popularized through HonFest, Hon culture came to be centered in Hampden. Various people, from political figures to local business owners, situated the image of the Hon as the representation of Baltimore.

Although Baltimore club music developed alongside Hon culture, it came out of the black working-class experience located primarily in the black neighborhoods of West and East Baltimore. Drawing from the heritage of black popular music from the 1960s through rap, Baltimore club was sexually explicit and aggressive in its sound. While this made it incompatible with Baltimore's efforts to draw the creative class, it was packaged by entrepreneurial music producers for consumption outside the city by people of different class and racial backgrounds than it was originally intended for. But although Whiting could negotiate a freeway exit ramp sign to promote her neighborhood, the city was not offering Baltimore club producers any help in promoting their culture.

Gender played a role, with race, in determining which of these heritages would be given official approval. Although the Hon image is derived from the drag performance of Glenn Milstead as Divine, she has come to stand for Baltimore's version of white southern femininity, friendly but with just enough attitude to make her interesting. She is Charm City embodied. Miss Tony, who dressed in drag, is honored in black Baltimore neighborhoods but has not broken through into wider recognition. As we've seen throughout this book, Charm City was built by transforming Waters's white queer antisociality into eccentricity and combining it with other invocations of white working-class quirkiness, from Anne Tyler's novels to Barry Levinson's films. Bodymore, however, is defined through a one-dimensional notion of blackness as representing danger, crime, and death. A figure like Miss Tony has no place in it, even if the later imagining of Baltimore club music added to the discourse of Bodymore. By the early twenty-first century, these cultural representations firmly established the boundaries of Charm City and Bodymore.

# EPILOGUE

Geographer David Harvey, who was teaching at Johns Hopkins University at the time, once called Baltimore "a mess. Not the kind of enchanting mess that makes cities interesting places to explore, but an awful mess."[1] Because of the neoliberal policies instituted by Mayor William Donald Schaefer, businesspeople, and other leaders in response to the traumatic shift to a postindustrial economy, Baltimore became his case study of civic deterioration. Sadly, on an official level, little has changed. The death of Freddie Gray while in police custody in 2015 revealed the racial and economic inequality that defined the city. Since then, journalists have proven what black Baltimoreans already knew: the Baltimore police have terrorized black communities for years.[2] Two mayors, Sheila Dixon and Catherine Pugh, resigned because of corruption scandals.

Even while the city rocks from these upheavals, its artists continue their work. Writers, filmmakers, musicians, and poets make art about Baltimore, from indie rockers like Wye Oak to rapper Young Moose, from poet Kenneth Morrison to writers Ta-Nehisi Coates, D. Watkins, and Rafael Alvarez. Filmmakers Matthew Porterfield and Lotfy Nathan make nuanced movies about regular people living in the city, while even more underground filmmakers simply put their films on YouTube. One of the most widely regarded documentaries of 2017, the impressionistic *Rat Film* (2017), by Theo Anthony, uses the history of rat eradication in Baltimore as a metaphor for urban planners' projects to manage populations through segregation laws, redlining, and public housing projects. After scenes of Baltimore residents who keep pet rats interspersed with scenes of official and unofficial city exterminators, the film ends speculatively. Over a shot of people sitting on Federal Hill watching the July 4th fireworks display over the city, the inflectionless female narrator tells us that Baltimore has been abandoned. The explosions are not fireworks but massive demolition. The crowds are cheering as the city is destroyed because it is a chance to start over, to imagine a new world. But the film offers this option slyly. Isn't displacing all the people and razing the buildings just a variation of the slum clearance of the 1950s? Who makes the decisions about what the new city will look like? In a city with a history of racism and injustice as long as Baltimore's, can we ever really start over? As a city exterminator states, "There's never been a rat problem in Baltimore. It's always been a people problem." Rather than offer an answer, *Rat Film* raises some of the key questions of this book. What is the relationship between films, TV shows, plays, poems, and songs to the place they are about? How do these representations shape those places? Can art be a space for resistance, especially to urban policies that hurt working people and people of color?

Yes and no. There are several takeaways from this book. First, representation matters. People develop ideas about places they have never visited based on how they are portrayed in culture. Artists have always created stories about places. Those texts, whether John Waters's *Mondo Trasho* or *Female Trouble* or Anne Tyler's *The Accidental Tourist*, are always in conversation with the city of fact to express their visions of the city's problems and possibilities. But such representations of Baltimore, which often used realism to prove their authenticity, tended to follow the segregation of the real city. Because Baltimore is hypersegregated, a story about a particular neighborhood is likely to be a story about black or white Baltimoreans but not both (and not about other racial and ethnic groups that also live in the city). Looked at over time, the stories told about white neighborhoods shifted from portraying white innocence in the face of segregation to white deviance marked as queer radicalism to white eccentricity.

The stories about the places where African Americans lived were different. These stories focused on danger, crime, and death. At times, the producers of these stories intended them to promote segregation, as with *The Buddy Deane Show*. Others, like William Manchester's *The City of Anger*, offered a liberal vision of racism in the city that replicated stereotypes of African Americans while attempting to critique contemporary social issues. Civil rights activists identified this bifurcation and fought for spaces where they could make their own representations of the city in response. *Chicory* and club music are among the results.

This trend toward cultural segregation merged with the shift to a postindustrial economy, which gave these images even more power as they were mobilized by a municipal image-making machine. As cities like Baltimore contended with the shift to a postindustrial economy in the 1970s, municipal leaders attempted to shape positive images of the city through culture to draw visitors, creating an entrepreneurial, neoliberal government. Under Mayor William Donald Schaefer, the city created new departments and commissions for arts and supported arts activities to animate city streets in safe, contained ways. While Schaefer used federal and other funds to pump money into small arts organizations, the overwhelming goal was to draw the middle class back to the city. This meant competing with cities like Pittsburgh or Cleveland by creating large-scale projects like Harborplace and activities like Artscape.

While I am a cultural historian, not a policy analyst, cities that continue to pursue arts and culture as replacements for a lost industrial economy should do so with caution. Although government can shape the city's image, promote work that fits its vision, and even co-opt work where possible, it can't control everything. Regarded as a failure at the time, the Charm City branding campaign ultimately created Baltimore's most long-lasting nickname, while the otherwise anodyne slogan promoted by Mayor Schmoke in the late 1980s, "The City That Reads," was mercilessly parodied as "The City That Breeds" and the "The City That Bleeds." When the city constantly trumpets the importance of culture, activists, critics, and concerned citizens can leverage that culture to make their own claims on the people in charge.

The real question, however, is: What is the role of art in a democratic society? For urban leaders in Baltimore and elsewhere, arts add value by drawing upwardly mobile professionals, convention- and conference-goers, and tourists to the city. Arts and culture, as sociologist Sharon Zukin and Harvey suggest, have become part of a symbolic economy that gives an area or city a certain caché that makes it attractive to predominately upper-middle-class or wealthy and overwhelmingly white people. Downtown, or the neighborhood designated as the arts district, draws investment, pulling resources from residential areas that might need more financial support. Gentrification occurs and, along with it, displacement of the working class. While the city promotes location filming by Hollywood production companies through tax breaks and grants support established arts organizations, writers, filmmakers, musicians, and artists outside of these structures struggle to get by.

But art can be more than this. Cities that see themselves as true centers of arts and culture should support local artists (defined broadly), neighborhoods outside the downtown, and art that represents place in nuanced ways. Arts funding today is hard to come by, but we only need to look back at the War on Poverty to see how federal funding spurred a massive wave of artistic output in visual arts, theater, literature, and so on. As we saw in chapter 3, the War on Poverty supported the creation of a black poetry magazine called *Chicory* in whose pages regular Baltimore residents expressed their anger at the very government funding the publication. These poems are now an archive that otherwise would be lost that helps us understand what people in Baltimore thought. As historian Devin Fergus argues, artists find "operational space" even in programs that are not intended for that purpose, though this comes at some cost to their ability to critique the system.[3] Thanks to the Comprehensive Employment and Training Act, arts leaders like Philip Arnoult of the Baltimore Theater Project and public historians like Ted Durr of the Baltimore Neighborhood Heritage Project funded their community-based projects by successfully making the claim that they were training people in marketable skills.

Looking back, the grassroots cultural productions I have uncovered were supported through clever uses of public funding. These resources allowed working-class people to explore the role of the arts as a public sphere, to make art, and to learn skills in communities that had few resources. When those funds dried up, much of that work did as well, though there are artists like self-trained photographer Devin Allen, who has raised money to give Baltimore youth cameras so they can capture their view of their city. *Chicory*'s work is continued by organizations like Writers in Baltimore Schools and Dew More Baltimore, which both work with teen poets. Artpartheid, a project of United Diverse Artists, works to end racial disparities in arts funding in Baltimore. To put it bluntly, John Waters or David Simon don't need federal or state funds to make their art. As white middle-class professionals, they have access to other kinds of funding (even if Waters had to hustle as a young man) for their work. What we need is a resurgent investment in the arts at the grassroots level to spur the making and circulation of new representations. While the internet has democratized the distribution of artistic work, it has not helped pay artists livable wages. It's only by distributing funds broadly that we will see new kinds of stories being told. Then the democratic potential of art will be fulfilled.

There is one final question that haunts me. Can representations of cities create more just and equitable cities? I think so. To achieve this, we must examine how power structures the production and circulation of cultural representations. Who gets to make art? Whose work is circulated, by whom and to whom? Who profits? This book offers a model for this kind of analysis. Second, influential cultural producers should refuse to continue to segregate the two Baltimores into Charm City and Bodymore. While the cultural representations I have examined here mostly see those places as separate, the reality is that their fates are intertwined. Although David Simon's television show *The Wire* does this better than almost any other representation, it relies on tropes of the ghetto as a space for self-made men to prove themselves, undercutting its structural analysis. It also ignores the work that community organizations have done to better the city. Of course, no one cultural text can cover every topic or place, or else it will end up like Borges's map replicating the city. But with more funding, more representations will become available from a broader section of the population. In the aggregate, there will also be a greater diversity of perspectives, perhaps making it harder for politicians and tourism agencies to elevate simplistic visions of the city over all others. This is critical because popular culture is more than escapism. It helps us make sense of the world around us. It can also help us to imagine, together, what the future of Baltimore and other cities looks like.

# NOTES

## Introduction

1. Catherine E. Pugh, "Baltimore Can Do Better: Here's How," *Washington Post*, January 12, 2018.

2. Farah Stockman, "Baltimore's Mayor, Catherine Pugh, Resigns amid Children's Book Scandal," *New York Times*, May 2, 2019.

3. David Harvey, *Spaces of Capital: Towards a Critical Geography* (New York: Routledge, 2001).

4. Mike Rowe, "Rewiring *The Wire*," Mike Rowe (blog), November 6, 2014. http://mikerowe.com/2014/11/rewiring-the-wire/.

5. David Simon, "*The Wire* and Baltimore," David Simon (blog), November 11, 2014. http://davidsimon.com/the-wire-and-baltimore/.

6. Sherry H. Olson, *Baltimore: The Building of an American City* (Baltimore: Johns Hopkins University Press, 1980).

7. John David Rhodes and Elena Gorfinkel, eds., *Taking Place: Location and the Moving Image* (Minneapolis: University of Minnesota Press, 2011); Eric Avila, *Popular Culture in the Age of White Flight: Fear and Fantasy in Suburban Los Angeles* (Berkeley: University of California Press, 2004); Paula J. Massood, *Black City Cinema: African American Urban Experiences in Film* (Philadelphia: Temple University Press, 2006); and Murray Forman, *The 'Hood Comes First: Race, Space, and Place in Rap and Hip-Hop* (Middletown, CT: Wesleyan University Press, 2002).

8. Carlo Rotella, *October Cities: The Redevelopment of Urban Literature* (Los Angeles: University of California Press, 1998), 3.

9. Aaron Cowan, *A Nice Place to Visit: Tourism and Urban Revitalization in the Postwar Rustbelt* (Philadelphia: Temple University Press, 2016).

10. Sharon Zukin, *Loft Living: Culture and Capital in Urban Change* (Baltimore: Johns Hopkins University Press, 1982); and David Harvey, *The Condition of Postmodernity: An Enquiry into the Origins of Cultural Change* (Oxford: Blackwell, 1990).

11. Miriam Greenberg, *Branding New York: How a City in Crisis Was Sold to the World* (New York: Routledge, 2008), 9.

12. Jon C. Teaford, *The Rough Road to Renaissance: Urban Revitalization in America, 1940–1985* (Baltimore: Johns Hopkins University Press, 1990).

13. Suleiman Osman, *The Invention of Brownstone Brooklyn: Gentrification and the Search for Authenticity in Postwar New York* (New York: Oxford University Press, 2012).

14. Sharon Zukin, *Landscapes of Power: From Detroit to Disney World* (Berkeley: University of California Press, 1991), 22.

15. Richard Ben Cramer, "Can the Best Mayor Win?," *Esquire*, October 1984, 57–72; Roberto Brambilla and Gianni Longo, *Learning from Baltimore: What Makes Cities Liveable?* (New York: Institute for Environmental Action, 1979). National publications from the *New York Times* to *Smithsonian* magazine have covered Baltimore as a tourist destination. See, for example, "52 Places to Go in 2018," *New York Times*, February 12, 2018; Frank Deford, "My Kind of Town: Baltimore, Maryland," *Smithsonian*, January 2007, 18, 20, 22.

16. Teaford, *The Rough Road to Renaissance*, 299.

17. Henri Lefebvre, *The Production of Space* (Cambridge, MA: Blackwell, 1991), 26.

18. Frank Budgen, *James Joyce and the Making of Ulysses and Other Writings* (New York: Oxford University Press, 1972), 69.

19. Kevin Lynch, *The Image of the City* (Cambridge, MA: MIT Press, 1960), 2.

20. William H. Whyte, *The Social Life of Small Urban Spaces* (New York: Project for Public Spaces, 1980), 69–71.

21. Marshall Berman, *All That Is Solid Melts into Air: The Experience of Modernity* (New York: Penguin Books, 1988), 302.

22. Tim Reardon, "Neighborhood Guide: Spending Time in the Eraserhood," *Philadelphia Inquirer*, May 29, 2016, http://www.philly.com/philly/blogs/things_to_do/Neighborhood-guide-Spending-time-in-the-Eraserhood.html.

23. Caitlin Blanchfield, "Urban Industry Redefined: The Brooklyn Navy Yard," *Urban Omnibus* (blog), September 19, 2012, http://urbanomnibus.net/2012/09/urban-industry-redefined-the-brooklyn-navy-yard/.

24. Richard Harrington, "Welcome to Baltimore, Hon," *Washington Post*, July 8, 2005.

25. Christopher Mathias, "How One Man's Death Shows the Chasm between Black and White Baltimore," *Huffington Post* (blog), January 6, 2016, https://www.huffingtonpost.com/entry/adam-marton-thelonius-monk-baltimore_us_568d4d03e4b0a2b6fb6e38c5; "A Tale of Two Baltimores," *All In with Chris Hayes*, MSNBC, May 5, 2015, http://www.msnbc.com/all-in/watch/a-tale-of-two

-baltimores-440375875556; Jennifer S. Vey and Alan Berube, "Yes, There Are Two Baltimores," *The Avenue* (blog), May 15, 2015, https://www.brookings.edu/blog/the-avenue/2015/05/15/yes-there-are-two-baltimores/; and Lawrence Brown, "Two Baltimores: The White L vs. the Black Butterfly," *City Paper*, June 28, 2016.

26. Douglas S. Massey and Nancy A. Denton, *American Apartheid: Segregation and the Making of the Underclass* (Cambridge, MA: Harvard University Press, 1998), 75.

27. US Census Bureau, "QuickFacts: Baltimore City, Maryland; United States," https://www.census.gov/quickfacts/fact/table/baltimorecitymaryland,US/PST045217.

28. US Census Bureau, "QuickFacts: Philadelphia County, Pennsylvania," https://www.census.gov/quickfacts/fact/table/philadelphiacountypennsylvania/PST045217.

29. Jefferson Cowie, *Stayin' Alive: The 1970s and the Last Days of the Working Class* (New York: The New Press, 2010).

30. Randi Henderson, "Randy Newman Ready to Take Knocks Here," *Baltimore Sun*, February 3, 1978.

31. Dylan Jones, "Nina Simone Didn't Enjoy Recording 'Baltimore' but It Was One of Her Strongest Albums," *Independent*, April 2, 2011, https://www.independent.co.uk/voices/columnists/dylan-jones/dylan-jones-nina-simone-didnt-enjoy-recording-baltimore-but-it-was-one-of-her-strongest-albums-2257480.html.

32. Ruth Feldstein, *How It Feels to Be Free: Black Women Entertainers and the Civil Rights Movement* (New York: Oxford University Press, 2013).

33. Avila, *Popular Culture in the Age of White Flight*, xiii.

34. D. Watkins, "Stoop Stories," in *The Beast Side: Living and Dying while Black in America* (New York: Hot Books, 2015), 3–16.

35. Laura Lippman, *No Good Deeds* (New York: William Morrow, 2006), 189.

36. Mary Rizzo, "The Café Hon: Working-Class White Femininity and Commodified Nostalgia in Postindustrial Baltimore," in *Dixie Emporium: Tourism, Foodways, and Consumer Culture in the American South*, ed. Anthony J. Stanonis (Athens: University of Georgia Press, 2008), 264–85.

37. Steve Macek, *Urban Nightmares: The Media, the Right, and the Moral Panic over the City* (Minneapolis: University of Minnesota Press, 2006), xii.

38. Stacy M. Brown, "Ashley Minner Sheds Light on Baltimore's Lumbee Community," *Baltimore Sun*, March 16, 2018.

39. Harold McDougall, *Black Baltimore: A New Theory of Community* (Philadelphia: Temple University Press, 1993); Antero Pietila, *Not in My Neighborhood: How Bigotry Shaped a Great American City* (Chicago: Ivan R. Dee, 2012); Howell S. Baum, *Brown in Baltimore: School Desegregation and the Limits of Liberal-*

*ism* (Ithaca, NY: Cornell University Press, 2010); Robert R. Gioielli, *Environmental Activism and the Urban Crisis: Baltimore, St. Louis, Chicago* (Philadelphia: Temple University Press, 2015); Elizabeth Fee, Linda Shopes, and Linda Zeidman, *The Baltimore Book: New Views of Local History* (Philadelphia: Temple University Press, 1991); and Emily Lieb, "'White Man's Lane': Hollowing Out the Highway Ghetto in Baltimore," in *Baltimore '68: Riots and Rebirth in an American City* (Philadelphia: Temple University Press, 2011), 51–69.

40. George Lipsitz, *Time Passages: Collective Memory and American Popular Culture* (Minneapolis: University of Minnesota Press, 1990), 16.

41. Rhonda Y. Williams, *The Politics of Public Housing: Black Women's Struggles against Urban Inequality* (New York: Oxford University Press, 2004).

42. Thomas J. Sugrue, *The Origins of the Urban Crisis: Race and Inequality in Postwar Detroit* (Princeton, NJ: Princeton University Press, 2005); and Matthew F. Delmont, *Nicest Kids in Town: American Bandstand, Rock 'n' Roll, and the Struggle for Civil Rights in 1950s Philadelphia* (Berkeley: University of California Press, 2012).

43. Jim Wheeler, "Why Is Baltimore so Wired to 'The Wire'?," *Baltimore Sun*, April 6, 2016, http://www.baltimoresun.com/news/opinion/oped/bs-ed-light-city-20160406-story.html.

## 1 | The City of Anger

1. Antero Pietila, *Not in My Neighborhood: How Bigotry Shaped a Great American City* (Chicago: Ivan R. Dee, 2012), 89–92.

2. Beryl Satter, *Family Properties: Race, Real Estate, and the Exploitation of Black Urban America* (New York: Henry Holt, 2013).

3. Kenneth Durr, *Behind the Backlash: White Working-Class Politics in Baltimore, 1940–1980* (Chapel Hill: University of North Carolina Press, 2003), 99.

4. W. Edward Orser, *Blockbusting in Baltimore: The Edmondson Village Story* (Lexington: University Press of Kentucky, 1994), 135.

5. David Freund, *Colored Properties: State Policy and White Racial Politics in Suburban America* (Chicago: University of Chicago Press, 2007), 12.

6. Richard Rothstein, *The Color of Law: A Forgotten History of How Our Government Segregated America* (New York: Liveright, 2018); and Kevin Kruse, *White Flight: Atlanta and the Making of Modern Conservatism* (Princeton, NJ: Princeton University Press, 2005).

7. Laurajane Smith, *Uses of Heritage* (New York: Routledge, 2010), 106–13.

8. Jeff Wiltse, *Contested Waters: A Social History of Swimming Pools in America* (Chapel Hill: University of North Carolina Press, 2007).

9. Lisa Wade, "The Manly Origins of Cheerleading," *Sociological Images*

(blog), December 28, 2012, https://thesocietypages.org/socimages/2012/12/28/the-manly-origins-of-cheerleading/.

10. danah boyd, "White Flight in Networked Publics: How Race and Class Shaped American Teen Engagement with MySpace and Facebook," in *Race After the Internet*, ed. Lisa Nakamura and Peter A. Chow-White (New York: Routledge, 2012), 203–22.

11. James Baldwin, *The Fire Next Time* (New York: Vintage International, 1993), 5–6.

12. Matthew F. Delmont, *Nicest Kids in Town: American Bandstand, Rock 'n' Roll, and the Struggle for Civil Rights in 1950s Philadelphia* (Berkeley: University of California Press, 2012).

13. Excellent work on Baltimore civil rights activism can be found in C. Fraser Smith, *Here Lies Jim Crow: Civil Rights in Maryland* (Baltimore: Johns Hopkins University Press, 2012); Lee Sartain, *Borders of Equality: The NAACP and the Baltimore Civil Rights Struggle, 1914–1970* (Jackson: University Press of Mississippi, 2013); Robert J. Brugger, ed., "Civil Rights and Race Relations in Maryland," special issue, *Maryland Historical Magazine* 89, no. 3 (1994); Robert M. Palumbos, "Student Involvement in the Baltimore Civil Rights Movement, 1953–1963," *Maryland Historical Magazine* 94, no. 4 (1999): 449–92; and August Meier, *A White Scholar and the Black Community, 1945–1965: Essays and Reflections* (Amherst: University of Massachusetts Press, 1992).

14. Garrett Power, "Apartheid Baltimore Style: The Residential Segregation Ordinances of 1910–1913," *Maryland Law Review* 42, no. 2 (1983): 289–328.

15. Satter, *Family Properties*, 45.

16. "Housing," William Manchester Papers, Wesleyan University Special Collections, Middletown, CT, Box 35, Folder 11.

17. William Manchester Papers, Wesleyan University Special Collections, Box 35, Folder 12, n.d.

18. William Manchester, "The Life and Times of a Slum Landlord," *Reporter*, November 15, 1956, 26.

19. John Dos Passos to Stanley Kauffman, June 21, 1953, William Manchester Papers, Wesleyan University Special Collections, Box 35, Folder 3.

20. Carlo Rotella, *October Cities: The Redevelopment of Urban Literature* (Los Angeles: University of California Press, 1998).

21. Letter from William Manchester, May 16, 1967, William Manchester Papers, Wesleyan University Special Collections, Box 37, Folder 2.

22. William Manchester, *The City of Anger* (Boston: Little, Brown, 1981), 68. Hereafter parenthetical.

23. Bradford Jacobs, "Novel about the Numbers," unidentified paper, n.d., William Manchester Papers, Wesleyan University Special Collections, Box 37, Folder 1.

24. William Manchester Papers, Wesleyan University Special Collections, Box 35, Folder 12.

25. Kruse, *White Flight*, 9.

26. Andrea Friedman, "Sadists and Sissies: Anti-pornography Campaigns in Cold War America," *Gender and History* 15, no. 2 (2003): 201–27.

27. Ruth Feldstein, *Motherhood in Black and White: Race and Sex in American Liberalism, 1930–1965* (Ithaca, NY: Cornell University Press, 2000), 61.

28. Donald Bogle, *Toms, Coons, Mulattoes, Mammies, and Bucks: An Interpretive History of Blacks in American Films* (New York: Viking Press, 1973).

29. John Goodspeed, "A New Dance Craze for the Nation: The 'Madison,'" *Baltimore Sun*, May 8, 1960.

30. *Shake, Rattle and Roll: The Buddy Deane Scrapbook*, Maryland Public Television, 2003.

31. Kirstine Taylor, "Untimely Subjects: White Trash and the Making of Racial Innocence in the Postwar South," *American Quarterly* 67, no. 1 (March 2015): 55–79.

32. John Waters, "Ladies and Gentlemen . . . the Nicest Kids in Town!," in *Crackpot: The Obsessions of John Waters* (New York: Scribner, 2003), 97–110.

33. Karal Ann Marling, *As Seen on TV: The Visual Culture of Everyday Life in the 1950s* (Cambridge, MA: Harvard University Press, 1996), 5.

34. Waters, "Ladies and Gentlemen," 97.

35. *Shake, Rattle and Roll.*

36. Bill Osgerby, "'A Caste, A Culture, A Market': Youth, Marketing, and Lifestyle in Postwar America," in *Growing Up Postmodern: Neoliberalism and the War on the Young*, ed. Ronald Strickland (Lanham, MD: Rowman and Littlefield, 2002), 24.

37. Delmont, *Nicest Kids in Town*, 2.

38. Durr, *Behind the Backlash*, 103.

39. Grace Elizabeth Hale, *A Nation of Outsiders: How the Middle Class Fell in Love with Rebellion in Postwar America* (New York: Oxford University Press, 2011).

40. Mary Rizzo, *Class Acts: Young Men and the Rise of Lifestyle* (Reno: University of Nevada Press, 2015).

41. Michael Olesker, *Journeys to the Heart of Baltimore* (Baltimore: Johns Hopkins University Press, 2015): 226.

42. Laura Wexler, "The Last Dance," *Baltimore Style*, September/October 2003.

43. "What Is the Civic Interest Group," August Meier Papers, Schomburg

Center, New York Public Library, Box 64, Folder 11, Civil Rights Movement Baltimore 1962–1967.

44. Meier, *A White Scholar and the Black Community*, 137–47.

45. "The Price of a Ticket," *Time*, March 1, 1963, 20.

46. "Theater Slump Laid to Protests in Baltimore," *Washington Post*, July 9, 1963.

47. Meier, *A White Scholar and the Black Community*, 140.

48. Lizabeth Cohen, *A Consumers' Republic: The Politics of Mass Consumption in Postwar America* (New York: Vintage Books, 2004).

49. Joseph Turow, *Breaking Up America: Advertisers and the New Media World* (Chicago: University of Chicago Press, 1997).

50. John A. Jackson, *American Bandstand: Dick Clark and the Making of a Rock 'n' Roll Empire* (New York: Oxford University Press, 1997), 231.

51. Meier, *A White Scholar and the Black Community*, 162.

52. "Northern Student Movement of Baltimore," Summer 1963, August Meier Papers, Schomburg Center, Box 66, Folder 6.

53. Todd Gitlin, *The Sixties: Years of Hope, Days of Rage* (New York: Bantam Books, 1993), 132.

54. Tony Warner, *Buddy's Top 20: Baltimore's Hottest TV Show of the 50's and 60's and the Story of the Guy Who Brought It to Us, Buddy Deane!* (Malvern, AR: Warner Marketing, 2003), 219.

55. Warner, *Buddy's Top 20*, 222.

56. "Buddy Deane Show Picketed by CIG," *Cumberland News* (Cumberland, MD), June 29, 1962.

57. *Shake, Rattle and Roll.*

58. Quoted in Wexler, "The Last Dance," 134.

59. Danny Schechter, *The More You Watch, the Less You Know* (New York: Seven Stories Press, 1997), 77–78.

60. Wexler, "The Last Dance," 166.

61. John Baker, unpublished manuscript, in possession of the author.

62. Schechter, *The More You Watch*, 78.

63. "Teens Integrate, Rap Dance Show," *Afro-American*, August 17, 1963.

64. Schechter, *The More You Watch*, 78.

65. Wexler, "The Last Dance," 168.

66. "Deane Says Integration Problems Ended TV Show," *Baltimore Sun*, December 14, 1963.

67. "Balto Disk Jock Sez He Was Fired Because of an 'Integration Battle,'" *Variety*, December 18, 1963, 24.

68. Louis R. Cedrone Jr., "Buddy Deane Show Leaves WJZ-TV," *Evening Sun* (Baltimore), January 7, 1964.

69. Thomas J. Sugrue, *The Origins of the Urban Crisis: Race and Inequality in Postwar Detroit* (Princeton, NJ: Princeton University Press, 2005), 255.

70. Manchester, *The City of Anger*, x.

## 2 | From Blight to Filth

1. John Waters, *Shock Value* (New York: Thunder's Mouth Press, 1995), 59.

2. Richard Dyer, *Now You See It: Studies on Lesbian and Gay Films* (London: Routledge, 2003); Dana Heller, *Hairspray* (New York: John Wiley & Sons, 2011); Chris Holmlund, *Female Trouble: A Queer Film Classic* (Vancouver: Arsenal Pulp Press, 2017); Michael Moon and Eve Kosofsky Sedgwick, "Divinity: A Dossier, a Performance Piece, a Little Understood Emotion," *Discourse* 13, no. 1 (1990–91): 12–39; Karl Schoonover, "Divine: Towards an Imperfect Stardom," in *Hollywood Reborn: Movie Stars of the 1970s*, ed. James Morrison (New Brunswick, NJ: Rutgers University Press, 2010); and Matthew Tinkcom, *Working like a Homosexual: Camp, Capital, and Cinema* (Durham, NC: Duke University Press, 2002).

3. Larry Grobel, "John Waters: I Don't Want to Go to Jail for Making a Movie," *Los Angeles Free Press*, August 22–28, 1975.

4. Robert M. Fogelson, *Downtown: Its Rise and Fall, 1800–1950* (New Haven, CT: Yale University Press, 2001); Benjamin Looker, *A Nation of Neighborhoods: Imagining Cities, Communities, and Democracy in Postwar America* (Chicago: University of Chicago Press, 2015); Jon C. Teaford, *The Rough Road to Renaissance: Urban Revitalization in America, 1940–1985* (Baltimore: Johns Hopkins University Press, 1990); Samuel Zipp, *Manhattan Projects: The Rise and Fall of Urban Renewal in Cold War New York* (New York: Oxford University Press, 2010).

5. Eric Avila, *Popular Culture in the Age of White Flight: Fear and Fantasy in Suburban Los Angeles* (Berkeley: University of California Press, 2004), ch. 3.

6. C. Fraser Smith, *William Donald Schaefer: A Political Biography* (Baltimore: Johns Hopkins University Press, 1999), 148.

7. Anna Breckon, "The Erotic Politics of Disgust: *Pink Flamingos* as Queer Political Cinema," *Screen* 54, no. 4 (Winter 2013): 515.

8. Rhonda Y. Williams, *The Politics of Public Housing: Black Women's Struggles against Urban Inequality* (New York: Oxford University Press, 2004), 42.

9. Teaford, *The Rough Road to Renaissance*, 19.

10. Samuel Zipp, "The Roots and Routes of Urban Renewal," *Journal of Urban History* 39, no. 3 (2012): 368.

11. Wendell E. Pritchett, "The 'Public Menace' of Blight: Urban Renewal and the Private Uses of Eminent Domain," *Yale Law and Policy Review* 21, no. 1 (2003): 1–52.

12. Beryl Satter, *Family Properties: Race, Real Estate, and the Exploitation of Black Urban America* (New York: Henry Holt, 2013), 61; and Arnold Hirsch, *Making the Second Ghetto: Race and Housing in Chicago, 1940–1960* (Chicago: University of Chicago Press, 1998), 34.

13. Emily Lieb, "Row House City: Unbuilding Residential Baltimore, 1940–1980" (PhD diss., Columbia University, 2010), 79.

14. Martin Millspaugh and Gurney Breckenfeld, *The Human Side of Urban Renewal* (New York: Ives Washburn, 1960), 59.

15. *Progress Report Relating to Activities of the Greater Baltimore Committee*, January 5 through July 31, 1955, University of Baltimore, 7, http://archives.ubalt.edu/gbc/pdfs/R0054_GBC_S01_B01_F004_P1.pdf.

16. Maryland State Archives, Annapolis, Department of Business and Economic Development, Division of Tourism and Promotion, 1960–1975, Box 3.

17. Brandi Lynette Blessett, "Dispersion or Re-segregation: A Spatial and Temporal Analysis of Public Policies and their Impact on Urban African American Mobility" (PhD diss., Old Dominion University, 2011), 113.

18. *Outline of Urban Renewal*, 1964, Baltimore Urban Renewal and Housing Authority, Pamphlet Collection, Urban Archives, Temple University, Philadelphia, PA.

19. James F. Waesche, "Should We Raze or Restore Them?," *Baltimore Sun*, June 5, 1966; "$2.5 Million Program to Fight Housing Blight," *Afro-American*, September 21, 1968; "New Post Office in Renewal Area," *Afro-American*, December 14, 1968; and J. Anthony Lukas, "'The Block' Seat of Old Baltimore's Libido Awaits Bulldozers," *New York Times*, April 13, 1970.

20. Pritchett, "The 'Public Menace' of Blight," 3.

21. *Dear Sir*, Housing Authority of Baltimore, 1949, Pamphlet Collection, Urban Archives, Temple University, Philadelphia, PA.

22. "200 at Office Site Hearing," *Baltimore Sun*, November 6, 1953.

23. *The Dollars and Sense of Urban Renewal*, BURHA, Pamphlet Collection, Urban Archives, Temple University, n.p.

24. *No, Yes*, Baltimore Housing Authority, Pamphlet Collection, Urban Archives, Temple University, n.p.

25. Avila, *Popular Culture in the Age of White Flight*, 75.

26. Looker, A *Nation of Neighborhoods*, 95–96.

27. "The Baltimore Plan Is Ready for Appraisal," *Baltimore Sun*, January 31, 1953.

28. Alexander Von Hoffman, "The Lost History of Urban Renewal," *Journal of Urbanism: International Research on Placemaking and Urban Sustainability* 1, no. 3 (November 2008): 286–87.

29. *Lead the Way to a Baltimore Plan for Your Community: An Outline Guide for Use in Presenting "The Baltimore Plan" Film*, 1953, Pamphlet Collection, Urban Archives, Temple University.

30. Theodore William Durr, "The Conscience of a City: A History of the Citizens' Planning and Housing Association and Efforts to Improve Housing for the Poor in Baltimore, Maryland, 1937–1954" (PhD diss., Johns Hopkins University, 1972), 429–30.

31. Homer Hoyt, quoted in Pritchett, "The 'Public Menace' of Blight," 17.

32. *Harlem Park: Its People and Their Homes*, 1959, BURHA, Pamphlet Collection, Urban Archives, Temple University, 6.

33. Looker, *A Nation of Neighborhoods*, 70.

34. Louise Parker Kelley, *LGBT Baltimore* (Mt. Pleasant, SC: Arcadia, 2015).

35. John Waters, *Role Models* (New York: Farrar, Straus and Giroux, 2010), 130–31.

36. Waters, *Shock Value*, 62.

37. James Miller, ed., *Democracy Is in the Streets: From Port Huron to the Siege of Chicago* (Cambridge, MA: Harvard University Press, 2004), 285–86.

38. Waters, *Shock Value*, 80.

39. On male hustlers in Mt. Vernon, see Waters, *Shock Value*, 83. "Mt. Vernon Urban Renewal Plan," 1960, Maryland Historical Society, Baltimore.

40. Chloé Griffin, *Edgewise: A Picture of Cookie Mueller* (Berlin: BBooks, 2015), 23.

41. Waters, *Role Models*, 60.

42. Earl Arnett, "Filmmaking Efforts Are Increasing Here," *Baltimore Sun*, February 11, 1974.

43. JoAnn Harris, "Baltimore Film Fete Planned for Saturday," *Baltimore Sun*, April 12, 1970.

44. Robert G. Maier, *Low Budget Hell: Making Underground Movies with John Waters* (Davidson, NC: Full Page, 2011), 12.

45. Waters, *Shock Value*, 77–78.

46. Robert Maier, *Notes on Location Scouting and Management Handbook* (Boston: Focal Press, 1994).

47. Kenneth Turan, "Baltimore's King of Repulsion," *Washington Post*, April 20, 1975.

48. C. Catharsis, review of *Multiple Maniacs*, *Harry*, April 17, 1970.

49. Breckon, "The Erotic Politics of Disgust," 515.

50. *Pink Flamingos*, DVD, Dreamland Studios, 1972.

51. Danny Fields and Fran Lebowitz, "*Pink Flamingos* and the Filthiest Peo-

ple," *Interview*, May 1973, reprinted in *John Waters Interviews*, ed. James Egan (Jackson: University Press of Mississippi, 2012), 29.

52. R. H. Gardner, "John Waters' Latest Reinforces the Cult," *Baltimore Sun*, June 3, 1977.

53. "Female Trouble," *Variety*, February 5, 1975.

54. Dyer, *Now You See It*, 170

55. Martha Shelley, "Gay Is Good," *Rat*, February 24, 1970, reprinted in Karla Jay and Allen Young, *Out of the Closets: Voices of Gay Liberation* (New York: New York University Press, 1992), 31.

56. Richard Meyer, "Gay Power Circa 1970: Visual Strategies for Sexual Revolution," *GLQ* 12, no. 3 (2006): 441–64.

57. Betty Luther Hillman, "'The Most Profoundly Radical Act a Homosexual Can Engage In': Drag and the Politics of Gender Presentation in the San Francisco Gay Liberation Movement, 1964–1972," *Journal of the History of Sexuality* 20, no. 1 (January 2011): 153–81.

58. Waters, *Shock Value*, 15.

59. "Combahee River Collective: A Black Feminist Statement," *Off Our Backs*, no. 6 (1979): 6.

60. Leerom Medovoi, "A Yippie-Panther Pipe Dream: Rethinking Sex, Race, and the Sexual Revolution," in *Swinging Single: Representing Sexuality in the 1960s*, ed. Hilary Radner and Moya Luckett (Minneapolis: University of Minnesota Press, 1999), 135.

61. E. Patrick Johnson, ed., *Black Queer Studies: A Critical Anthology* (Durham, NC: Duke University Press, 2005).

62. Maier, *Low Budget Hell*, 28.

63. Schoonover, "Divine," 171.

64. Waters, *Shock Value*, 102.

65. Waters, *Role Models*, 131.

66. Julia Foulkes, "Seeing the City: The Filming of *West Side Story*," *Journal of Urban History* 41, no. 6 (2015): 1045.

67. Joseph S. Wiles to the City Council of Baltimore, January 24, 1972, University of Baltimore, Special Collections, digitized.

68. Elizabeth M. Nix and Deborah R. Weiner, "Pivot in Perception: The Impact of the 1968 Riots on Three Baltimore Business Districts," in *Baltimore '68: Riots and Rebirth in an American City*, ed. Jessica I. Elfenbein, Thomas L. Hollowak, and Elizabeth M. Nix (Philadelphia: Temple University Press, 2011), 185.

69. Martin Millspaugh, *Baltimore's Charles Center: A Case Study of Downtown Renewal* (Washington, DC: Urban Land Institute, 1964).

70. For more information on locations in Waters's films, I have created an interactive digital map that can be accessed at https://bit.ly/2u9ok7D.

71. Griffin, *Edgewise*, 33.

72. Maier, *Low Budget Hell*, 54.

73. Linda Shopes, "Fells Point: Community and Conflict in a Working-Class Neighborhood," in *The Baltimore Book: New Views of Local History*, ed. Elizabeth Fee, Linda Shopes and Linda Zeidman (Philadelphia: Temple University Press, 1991), 137.

74. Waters, *Shock Value*, 15–16.

75. Paula Massood, *Black City Cinema: African American Urban Experiences in Film* (Philadelphia: Temple University Press, 2003), 110.

76. Waters, *Shock Value*, 56.

77. Waters, *Shock Value*, 58.

78. Waters, *Shock Value*, 59.

79. Hirsch, *Making the Second Ghetto*, ch. 5.

80. Eric Avila, *Folklore of the Freeway: Race and Revolt in the Modernist City* (Minneapolis: University of Minnesota Press, 2014).

81. R. H. Gardner, "'Grace' Maligns City and Is Lousy," *Baltimore Sun*, September 23, 1974.

82. "Irreverent Look at Politics & People," *Baltimore Afro-American*, September 28, 1974; Ida Peters, "What's Happening," *Baltimore Afro-American*, October 12, 1974.

83. Waters, *Shock Value*, 53.

84. Aaron Cowan, *A Nice Place to Visit: Tourism and Urban Revitalization in the Postwar Rustbelt* (Philadelphia: Temple University Press, 2016), 134.

## 3 | "The Most Authentic Microphone of Black Folks Talking Ever Devised"

1. Carol Calloway, "About the Riot," *Chicory* 18 (September 1969).

2. J. Allen Jones, "The Mourning Before" and "The Mourning After," *Chicory* 12 (June 1968).

3. "Black Stands for Me," *Baltimore Afro-American*, December 6, 1969.

4. Daniel Widener, *Black Arts West: Culture and Struggle in Postwar Los Angeles* (Durham, NC: Duke University Press, 2010), 91.

5. Karen Ferguson, *Top Down: The Ford Foundation, Black Power, and the Reinvention of Racial Liberalism* (Philadelphia: University of Pennsylvania Press, 2013).

6. Devin Fergus, *Liberalism, Black Power, and the Making of American Politics, 1965–1980* (University of Georgia Press, 2009).

7. James Smethurst, *The Black Arts Movement: Literary Nationalism in the 1960s and 1970s* (Chapel Hill: University of North Carolina Press, 2005), 378–79.

8. *Chicory* digital archive, Digital Maryland, http://collections.digitalmaryland.org/cdm/landingpage/collection/mdcy.

9. Joanna Dee Das, "Between the 'Culture of Poverty' and the Cultural Revolution: Katherine Dunham's Performing Arts Training Center in East St. Louis, 1965–1973," *Journal of Urban History* 41, no. 6 (2015): 981–98.

10. Sam Cornish and Lucian W. Dixon, *Chicory: Young Voices from the Black Ghetto* (New York: Association Press, 1969), 10.

11. Harry S. Smith, "Baltimore—Exposure of Concentrated Employment Program (C.E.P.)," *Black Panther* 5, no. 6 (August 8, 1970): 6.

12. Kevin Mumford, *Newark: A History of Race, Rights, and Riots in America* (New York: New York University Press, 2008), 32–35.

13. Gwendolyn D. Pough, *Check It While I Wreck It: Black Womanhood, Hip-Hop Culture, and the Public Sphere* (Boston: Northeastern University Press, 2004), 16–17.

14. Martin Millspaugh and Gurney Breckenfeld, *The Human Side of Urban Renewal* (New York: Ives Washburn, 1960), 7.

15. Health and Welfare Council of the Baltimore Area, *A Letter to Ourselves: A Proposal for a Master Plan for Human Redevelopment* (Baltimore, 1962), 1–2.

16. *A Plan for Action on the Problems of Baltimore's Disadvantaged People* (Baltimore: Health and Welfare Council of the Baltimore Area, 1964), 1.

17. Economic Opportunity Act of 1964, Pub. L. 88-452, 78 Stat. 508.

18. Garth Mangum and Stephen Mangum, "Human Renewal in the Revitalization of the Industrial City," *Annals of the American Academy of Political and Social Science* 488 (November 1986): 157–76; Community Progress, Inc., *The Human Story* (New Haven, CT: Community Progress, 1966).

19. Health and Welfare Council, *Letter*, 15–16.

20. Health and Welfare Council, *Letter*, 5.

21. Michel Foucault, *Technologies of the Self: A Seminar with Michel Foucault* (Amherst: University of Massachusetts Press, 1988), 158.

22. "Goucher Slates Seminars in 10 Cities," *Baltimore Evening Sun*, April 15, 1960; "The Man From Nowhere," *Baltimore Sun*, April 2, 1962.

23. *Plan for Action*, 20–21.

24. *Plan for Action*, 43.

25. *Plan for Action*, 46.

26. *Plan for Action*, 99.

27. *Plan for Action*, 46.

28. "Pratt's Community Action Program," *Staff Reporter* 33, no. 6 (March 15, 1966): 4.

29. Marcia Sanders, "Resolving Racial Tensions," *Staff Reporter* 31, no. 1 (January 2, 1964).

30. "Problem of Negro Identity," *Staff Reporter* 35, no. 6 (March 15, 1968): 1–2.

31. Carl Schoettler, "Negro Poet Issues 2nd Book," *Baltimore Evening Sun*, March 8, 1965.

32. Sam Cornish in discussion with the author, telephone, November 6, 2014.

33. Scot Brown, *Fighting for US: Maulana Karenga, the US Organization and Black Cultural Nationalism* (New York: New York University Press, 2005), 6.

34. Smethurst, *The Black Arts Movement*, 14.

35. John Edgar Wideman, *Brothers and Keepers* (New York: Penguin Books, 1984), 111.

36. James D. Sullivan, *On the Walls and in the Streets: American Poetry Broadsides from the 1960s* (Urbana: University of Illinois Press, 1997).

37. Smethurst, *The Black Arts Movement*, 77.

38. Evelyn Levy, "Library Service in the Inner City," *Wilson Library Bulletin*, 1967, 476.

39. Inside cover, *Chicory* (January 1968).

40. Sam Cornish in discussion with the author, telephone, November 6, 2014.

41. "Dropouts Contributing to *Chicory*, Poverty Program Verse Magazine," *Baltimore Evening Sun*, November 29, 1966.

42. Theodore R. McKeldin, *No Mean City, an Inquiry into Civic Greatness* (Baltimore: Published by the author in cooperation with the Maryland Historical Society, 1964).

43. Brown, *Fighting for US*, 40, 83–87.

44. Earl Caldwell, "Black Panthers Serving Youngsters a Diet of Food and Politics," *New York Times*, June 15, 1969; David McClintock, "Negro Militants Use Free Food, Medical Aid to Promote Revolution," *Wall Street Journal*, August 29, 1969; and Roy Haynes, "Hate-Police Indoctrination Told at Trial," *Los Angeles Times*, July 28, 1971.

45. Cornish and Dixon, *Chicory*, 8.

46. Paul H. Stacy, "A Bitter Beauty," *Hartford Courant*, April 19, 1970.

47. Sam Cornish, "Turk," in *Black Fire: An Anthology of Afro-American Writing*, ed. Amiri Baraka and Larry Neal (Baltimore: Black Classic Press, 2007), 399.

48. Carl Schoettler, "Dropouts Contributing to Chicory, Poverty Program Verse Magazine," *Baltimore Evening Sun*, November 29, 1966.

49. Marion Reid, *Chicory* 12 (June 1968).

50. As of January 2020, all *Chicory* issues, except from 1970-71, are available at https://collections.digitalmaryland.org/digital/collection/mdcy.

51. Carl Schoettler, "10th Anniversary Party to Mark The Flavor of Chicory," *Baltimore Evening Sun*, November 18, 1976.

52. Dellyse Maxine Harris and Jannis R. Rhodes, "A Message from the Ghetto," *Chicory* 13 (July 1968).

53. Rhonda Y. Williams, "'To Challenge the Status Quo by Any Means': Community Action and Representational Politics in 1960s Baltimore," in *The War on Poverty: A New Grassroots History*, ed. Annelise Orleck and Lisa Gayle Hazirjian (Athens: University of Georgia Press, 2011), 71.

54. Charles V. Flowers, "Council Rejects Mayor's Choice," *Baltimore Sun*, February 16, 1965, vertical files, Enoch Pratt Free Library, Baltimore, MD; James Griffith, chairman of CORE, to Mayor Theodore R. McKeldin, January 4, 1965, BCA BRG9-25-21 Box 377, folder 3, Baltimore City Archives, Baltimore, MD.

55. Charles V. Flowers, "Dr. Humphrey Quits," Sunday, June 30, 1965, vertical files, Enoch Pratt Free Library.

56. Bernice Burton, "Parren Mitchell," *Chicory* 30 (December 1966).

57. Peter Bachrach, "A Power Analysis: The Shaping of Antipoverty Policy in Baltimore," *Public Policy* (Winter 1970): 177.

58. Quoted in Rhonda Y. Williams, "The Pursuit of Audacious Power: Rebel Reformers and Neighborhood Politics in Baltimore, 1966–1968," in *Neighborhood Rebels: Black Power at the Local Level*, ed. Peniel E. Joseph (New York: Palgrave Macmillan, 2010), 234.

59. David Runkel, "If Mayor Has Way," *Evening Sun*, June 26, 1968.

60. Robin Frames, "Walter Carter Gets Nomination," *Evening Sun*, August 20, 1968, vertical files, Enoch Pratt Free Library. See also Aiden James Faust, "Neighborhood Matters: What Baltimore Learned from the War on Poverty" (master's thesis, University of Maryland, Baltimore County, 2015).

61. "Carter Is 'Discouraged': Cites 'High Casualty' Rate," *Baltimore Afro-American*, June 29, 1968.

62. Donald Grafton Gwynn, "White Liberals (Most of Them or All of Them, I Think Sometimes)," *Chicory* 12 (June 1968).

63. Frances Fox Piven and Richard A. Cloward, *Regulating the Poor: The Functions of Public Welfare* (New York: Pantheon Books, 1971).

64. June Booth, "What Welfare Does to You," *Chicory* 14 (September 1968).

65. *Chicory* 7 (July 1967).

66. *Plan for Action*, 175.

67. Stephen Henderson, *Understanding the New Black Poetry: Black Speech and Black Music as Poetic References* (New York: Morrow Quill Paperbacks, 1980), 32–33.

68. Jennifer Frost, *"An Interracial Movement of the Poor": Community Organizing and the New Left in the 1960s* (New York: New York University Press, 2005).

69. "On Being a Neighborhood Assist," *Chicory* 5 (April 1967).

70. "Community Notebook: Life with Community Action," *Chicory* 19 (November 1969).

71. Daniel Johnson, untitled, *Chicory* 15 (December 1968).

72. Bernadette Hall, "Thugs United," *Chicory* 13 (July 1968).

73. Fergus, *Liberalism*, 9.

74. Floyd Miller, "How Baltimore Fends Off Riots," *Reader's Digest*, March 1968, 109–13.

75. Turk, "Going Home," *Chicory* 1 (November 1966).

76. "Prison Camp," *Chicory* 17 (June 1969).

77. Simba, "Helmeted Policeman," *Chicory* 9 (October 1967).

78. Brown, *Fighting for US*.

79. Tina Bracken, "Troubled Sleep (Night in the City)," *Chicory* 9 (October 1967).

80. "When I Came Out," *Chicory* 5 (April 1967).

81. Peniel E. Joseph, "The Black Power Movement: A State of the Field," *Journal of American History* (December 2009): 755.

82. Judson L. Jeffries, "Black Radicalism and Political Repression in Baltimore: The Case of the Black Panther Party," *Ethnic and Racial Studies* 25, no. 1 (2002): 64–98.

83. Rhonda Y. Williams, "Black Women, Urban Politics, and Engendering Black Power," in *The Black Power Movement*, ed. Peniel E. Joseph (New York: Routledge, 2006), 84.

84. Rhonda Y. Williams, *The Politics of Public Housing: Black Women's Struggles against Urban Inequality* (New York: Oxford University Press, 2004).

85. Nancy B. Gabler, "Who Are These Black Panthers and What Do They Really Want?," *Baltimore Magazine*, 1970.

86. Jeffries, "Black Radicalism," 71.

87. Harold McDougall, *Black Baltimore: A New Theory of Community* (Philadelphia: Temple University Press, 1993), 57–58.

88. Judson L. Jeffries, "Revising Panther History in Baltimore," in *Comrades: A Local History of the Black Panther Party*, ed. Judson L. Jeffries, (Bloomington: Indiana University Press, 2007), 13–46.

89. Rhonda Y. Williams, "'We're Tired of Being Treated Like Dogs': Poor Women and Power Politics in Baltimore," *Black Scholar* 31, nos. 3/4 (Fall/Winter 2001): 36.

90. "What the SOUL School Is About," *Chicory* 14 (September 1968).

91. Beverly Havard, "Slave Woman," *Chicory* 14 (September 1968).

92. Joyce P. Williams, "The Difference," *Chicory* 32 (February 1973).

93. Vincent A. Johnson, "Chains, Chance, Change, Challenge," *Chicory* 39 (November 1973).

94. Smethurst, *The Black Arts Movement*, 15.

95. "____ on white people looking at the poor," *Chicory* 6 (May 1967).

96. Ronald Hassell, "The Soul Fish," *Chicory* 22 (February 1972).

97. bell hooks, *Yearning: Race, Gender, and Cultural Politics* (New York: Routledge, 2015).

98. Jewell Johnson, "The Man I Love," *Chicory* 40 (December 1973); David Hyman Taylor, "You," *Chicory* 40 (December 1973).

99. Lucille Clifton, *Chicory* 56 (June/July 1975).

100. Phyllis Jones, "Africa at the Park: July 23, 1972," *Chicory* 29 (November 1972).

101. Jon C. Teaford, *The Rough Road to Renaissance: Urban Revitalization in America, 1940–1985* (Baltimore: Johns Hopkins University Press, 1990), 168–69.

102. Osman, *Brownstone Brooklyn*, 245.

103. Joyce P. Williams, "A Visit to Johannesburg, South Africa," *Chicory* 66 (June/July 1976), http://collections.digitalmaryland.org/cdm/compoundobject/collection/mdcy/id/1780/rec/1.

104. Daki Napata, untitled, *Chicory* 75 (May 1977), http://collections.digitalmaryland.org/cdm/compoundobject/collection/mdcy/id/1912/rec/1.

105. Peter Harris, "In a Name (for Ketema Jawara Keita),"*Chicory* 91 (January 1979), http://collections.digitalmaryland.org/cdm/compoundobject/collection/mdcy/id/2284/rec/1.

106. Jonathan Fenderson, *Building the Black Arts Movement: Hoyt Fuller and the Cultural Politics of the 1960s* (Urbana: University of Illinois Press, 2019), 120.

## 4 | Hollywood East

1. John Waters, *Role Models* (New York: Farrar, Straus and Giroux, 2010), 62.

2. John Waters, *Shock Value* (New York: Thunder's Mouth Press, 1995), 88–89.

3. Sharon Zukin, *Loft Living: Culture and Capital in Urban Change* (Baltimore: Johns Hopkins University Press, 1982); and Miriam Greenberg, *Branding New York: How a City in Crisis Was Sold to the World* (New York: Routledge, 2008).

4. David Harvey, "From Managerialism to Entrepreneurialism: The Transformation in Urban Governance in Late Capitalism," *Geografiska Annaler: Series B, Human Geography* 71, no. 1 (1989): 3–17.

5. Alison Isenberg, *Downtown America: A History of the Place and the People Who Made It* (Chicago: University of Chicago Press, 2009), 283–92.

6. James Sanders, "Adventure Playground," in *America's Mayor: John V. Lindsay and the Reinvention of New York*, ed. Sam Roberts (New York: Columbia University Press, 2010), 84–101.

7. J. Mark Souther, *Believing in Cleveland: Managing Decline in "The Best Location in the Nation"* (Philadelphia: Temple University Press, 2017), 123–37.

8. C. Fraser Smith, "Here Is a List of City-Backed Corporations," *Baltimore Sun*, April 19, 1980.

9. Jane Jacobs, *The Death and Life of Great American Cities* (New York: Knopf Doubleday, 2016).

10. Greenberg, *Branding New York*, 10.

11. Jack Rosenthal, "For 2 Cities: New Political Eras," *New York Times*, May 1, 1971.

12. Jon C. Teaford, *The Rough Road to Renaissance: Urban Revitalization in America, 1940–1985* (Baltimore, MD: Johns Hopkins University Press, 1990), 213.

13. C. Fraser Smith, *William Donald Schaefer: A Political Biography* (Baltimore: Johns Hopkins University Press, 1999), 143.

14. "Tourism Fund Bills Readied in Maryland," *Washington Post*, September 5, 1963; and "Md Tourism Post Filled," *Washington Post*, September 9, 1965.

15. Speech of Eric I. Weile, chair, Legislative Council Committee on Tourism to the Maryland Hotel & Motor Inn Association, Linden Hill Hotel, Bethesda, MD, July 24, 1970, Department of Business and Economic Development, Division of Tourism and Promotion, 1960–1975, Box 2, Maryland State Archives, Annapolis, MD.

16. Victor Block, "Baltimore Harbor Boat Tour a Star-Spangled Attraction," *New York Times*, August 17, 1969.

17. "A Marketing Plan for Greater Baltimore," section "The Survey in Baltimore: Summary of Principal Findings," Hill and Knowlton, 1973, 9, William Donald Schaefer Papers, Box 108, Baltimore Promotion Council—Advertising Committee, Baltimore City Archives, Baltimore, MD.

18. "A Marketing Plan for Greater Baltimore," 4.

19. Sandra Hillman, "Baltimore's Promotion," in *The City as a Stage: Strategies for the Arts in Urban Economics*, ed. Kevin W. Green (Washington, DC: Partners for Livable Places, 1983), 98.

20. Kelly Baum, *New Jersey as Non-site* (New Haven, CT: Yale University Press, 2013), 19–22.

21. Hillman, "Baltimore's Promotion," 98.

22. Erika Doss, *Benton, Pollock and the Politics of Modernism: From Regionalism to Abstract Expressionism* (Chicago: University of Chicago Press, 1991).

23. Harvey S. Perloff, "Using the Arts to Improve Life in the City," *Journal of Cultural Economics* 3, no. 2 (1979): 5.

24. "Baltimore Flower, Art Festival Marred by Fistfights, Arrests," *Baltimore Sun*, May 14, 1970.

25. Hillman, "Baltimore's Promotion," 99.

26. Baltimore City Fair Booth, Baltimore Regional Studies Archives, https://archivesspace.ubalt.edu/repositories/2/digital_objects/5150.

27. James D. Dilts, "Greater Baltimore Committee Urges Visitors Council Be Replaced," *Baltimore Sun*, January 18, 1972.

28. Aaron Cowan, *A Nice Place to Visit: Tourism and Urban Revitalization in the Postwar Rustbelt* (Philadelphia: Temple University Press, 2016), 131.

29. "Dr. Max," Baltimore Promotion Council 1972–1974 folder, William Donald Schaefer papers, Baltimore City Archives, Baltimore, MD, 4.

30. Joan Bereska to Sandy Hillman, "CBS Pilot Film (Dr. Max)," memo, January 21, 1974, Baltimore Promotion Council 1972–1974 folder, William Donald Schaefer papers, Baltimore City Archives, Baltimore, MD.

31. Amazingly, John Waters thought that Baltimore police didn't bother his actors while filming *Female Trouble* because they thought that they were part of "that Dr. Max thing that CBS filmed here a while back." Chris Holmlund, *Female Trouble: A Queer Film Classic* (Vancouver: Arsenal Pulp Press, 2017), 63.

32. Clive Barnes, "Lanford Wilson's Hot L Baltimore," *New York Times*, March 24, 1973.

33. "Hot L: Banned in Baltimore," *Washington Post*, January 25, 1975.

34. Greenberg, *Branding New York*, 21.

35. Baltimore, Merchants and Manufacturers Association of Baltimore, *Monthly Report*, vol. 8, no. 6, March 1915, 13.

36. "Charm City, USA," *New York Times*, August 4, 1974.

37. City of Baltimore, *Annual Report 1976*, William Donald Schaefer Papers, Box 886, Baltimore City Archives, Baltimore, MD.

38. Elaine Eff, *The Painted Screens of Baltimore: An Urban Folk Art Revealed* (Jackson: University Press of Mississippi, 2013).

39. Press release, March 2, 1974, Formation of MACAC Folder, Box 886, William Donald Schaefer Papers, Baltimore City Archive, Baltimore, MD.

40. C. Fraser Smith, "For Some the City's Interest Rate Is No Break," *Baltimore Sun*, April 18, 1980.

41. John Strasbaugh, "Working Class Heroes," *City Paper* (Baltimore), December 14, 1979, 26.

42. Smith, *William Donald Schaefer*, 167–68.

43. Philip Arnoult, interview by Mary Rizzo, Baltimore, MD, July 18, 2014.

44. R. H. Gardner, "John Waters' Latest Reinforces the Cult," *Baltimore Sun*, June 3, 1977.

45. Mission of the Commission on Motion Picture and Videotape Productions, Box 387, Film Commission Folder, Baltimore City Archives, Baltimore, MD.

46. Paula J. Massood, *Black City Cinema: African American Urban Experiences in Film* (Philadelphia: Temple University Press, 2006).

47. C. Fraser Smith, "City-Made Quasi-public Corporations Produce New Category of Public Official," *Baltimore Sun*, April 19, 1980.

48. Harvey, "From Managerialism to Entrepreneurialism," 7.

49. C. Fraser Smith, "Two Trustees and a $100 Million Bank Skirt the Restrictions of City Government," *Baltimore Sun*, April 13, 1980.

50. C. Fraser Smith, "Schaefer Defends Use of the Trustee System," *Baltimore Sun*, April 20, 1980.

51. "Presenting Baltimore," William Donald Schaefer Papers, Box 387, Film Commission Folder, Baltimore City Archives, Baltimore, MD.

52. Lucien Rhodes, "Bar with Atmosphere Exhales on Screen," *Baltimore Sun*, February 9, 1977.

53. C. Fraser Smith, "The Story of the Credit Union Building: How Public, Private Roles were Mixed," *Baltimore Sun*, April 17, 1980.

54. Sewell Watts III to W. D. Schaefer, February 23, 1979, William Donald Schaefer Papers, Box 387, Film Commission Folder, Baltimore City Archives, Baltimore, MD.

55. Letter to Gary Stromberg, William Donald Schaefer Papers, Box 387, Film Commission 1978–1979 folder, Baltimore City Archives, Baltimore, MD.

56. Memo to Joan Bereska, William Donald Schaefer Papers, Baltimore City Archives, Box 387, Film Commission 1978–1979 folder, Baltimore City Archives, Baltimore, MD.

57. Lou Panos, "Q and A: From Hollywood East," *Evening Sun*, November 14, 1978, William Donald Schaefer Papers, Box 387, Film Commission 1978–1979 folder, Baltimore City Archives, Baltimore, MD.

58. Don materials, William Donald Schaefer Papers, Box 387, Folder, Film Commission, 1978–1979, Baltimore City Archives, Baltimore, MD.

59. Minutes of meeting, November 17, 1978, William Donald Schaefer Papers, Box 387, Film Commission 1978–1979 folder, Baltimore City Archives, Baltimore, MD.

60. "Sylvia's Scene," *Baltimore News-American*, October 29, 1978, William Donald Schaefer Papers, Baltimore City Archives, Box 387, Film Commission 1978–1979 Folder, Baltimore City Archives, Baltimore, MD.

61. William Donald Schaefer Papers, Baltimore City Archives, Box 387, Film Commission 1978–1979 folder, Baltimore City Archives, Baltimore, MD.

62. Minutes, November 17, 1978, William Donald Schaefer Papers, Baltimore City Archives, Box 387, Film Commission 1978–1979 folder, Baltimore City Archives, Baltimore, MD.

63. "Pacino Movie about No Justice in B-More," *Afro American*, n.d., William Donald Schaefer Papers, Box 387, Film Commission 1978–1979 folder, Baltimore City Archives, Baltimore, MD.

64. C. Fraser Smith, "Schaefer Defends Use of the Trustee System," *Baltimore Sun*, April 20, 1980.

65. David Harvey, "A View from Federal Hill," *The New Baltimore Book: New Views on Local History*, ed. Elizabeth Fee, Linda Shopes, and Linda Zeidman (Philadelphia: Temple University Press, 1991), 239.

66. Helen Winternitz, "15,000 Lack Hot Water as City Workers Strike," *Baltimore Sun*, July 2, 1980.

67. Martin Millspaugh, "The Inner Harbor Story," *Urban Land*, April 2003, 38; Frank P. L. Somerville, "Vote Studied on Renewal," *Baltimore Sun*, November 5, 1964.

68. Cowan, *A Nice Place to Visit*, 136.

69. Isenberg, *Downtown America*, 291.

70. Calvin Trillin, *Tummy Trilogy* (New York: Farrar, Straus and Giroux, 2000), 322.

71. Michael Demarest, "He Digs Downtown," *Time*, August 24, 1981.

72. Cowan, *A Nice Place to Visit*, 145–47.

73. Teaford, *The Rough Road to Renaissance*, 273.

74. Paul Goldberger, "Baltimore Marketplace: An Urban Success," *New York Times*, February 18, 1981.

75. "Neighborhood Album," *Baltimore Sun*, September 26, 1980.

76. "Rats, Voices and Vision: An Interview with Philip Arnoult," *NAPNOC Notes*, August 1980.

77. Baltimore Promenade, NEA grant, MS 2875, Box 2, Maryland Historical Society, Baltimore, MD. See also the Harrisons' website, http://theharrisonstudio.net/baltimore-promenade-1981.

78. Baltimore Promenade, NEA grant.

79. Baltimore Promenade pamphlet, MICA archives, Baltimore, MD.

80. Baltimore Promenade, NEA grant.

81. Carleton Jones, "Downtown 'Promenade' Focuses on City's Laid-Back Urban Delights," *Baltimore Sun*, December 13, 1981.

82. Gail A. Campbell. "Artists Lead Walk to Tie City Together," *Baltimore Sun*, December 14, 1981.

83. Isenberg, *Downtown America*, 4–5.

## 5 | Accidental Tourists

1. Jerry H. Bryant, *Born in a Mighty Bad Land* (Bloomington: Indiana University Press, 2003), 119.

2. Jerome Dyson Wright, *Poor, Black and in Real Trouble* (Los Angeles: Holloway House, 1992), 95.

3. *Bawlamer: An Informal Guide to a Livelier Baltimore* (Baltimore: Citizens Planning and Housing Association, 1981), 3.

4. "Maryland Ranks Ninth in Nation in Film, TV Production Revenues," *Baltimore Sun*, January 5, 1988.

5. Henry Scarupa, "Made in Baltimore Film to Be Screened at Cannes," *Baltimore Sun*, March 27, 1988; Henry Scarupa, "Baltimore to Berlin," *Baltimore Sun*, February 7, 1988.

6. "Godard in the Nineties: An Interview, Argument, and Scrapbook (Part I)," March 9, 2018, http://www.jonathanrosenbaum.net/2018/03/godard-in-the-nineties-an-interview-argument-and-scrapbook-part-1/.

7. John Urry, *The Tourist Gaze* (London: Sage, 2005), 3.

8. Dale Salwak, ed., *Anne Tyler as Novelist* (Iowa City: University of Iowa Press, 1994), 4.

9. "In Search of Anne Tyler in Baltimore," http://www.independent.co.uk/travel/americas/in-search-of-anne-tyler-in-baltimore-602287.html.

10. Anne Tyler, *The Accidental Tourist* (New York: Ballantine Books, 2002), 106. Hereafter parenthetical.

11. "Brief Reviews," *Atlantic*, October 1988, 106.

12. Desson Howe, "'Tourist,' Check Your Emotional Baggage," *Washington Post*, January 6, 1989.

13. Salwak, *Anne Tyler as Novelist*, 73.

14. Anna Shannon Elfenbein, "Living Lessons: The Evolving Racial Norm in the Novels of Anne Tyler," *Southern Quarterly* 43, no. 1 (2005): 64.

15. Doreen Massey, "A Global Sense of Place." In *Space, Place and Gender* (Minneapolis: University of Minnesota Press, 1994), 146–56.

16. John Updike, "Leaving Home," *New Yorker*, October 28, 1985, 106.

17. "Picks and Pans," *People*, December 1988, 24–25.

18. Wallace Stegner, "Breathing Lessons," *Washington Post*, September 4, 1988.

19. Robert Ward, *Red Baker* (Blue Ash, OH: Tyrus Books, 1985), 9. Hereafter parenthetical.

20. Kenneth Durr, *Behind the Backlash* (Chapel Hill: University of North Carolina Press, 2003), 141.

21. Jefferson Cowie, *Stayin' Alive: The 1970s and the Last Days of the Working Class* (New York: The New Press, 2010), 323.

22. Cowie, *Stayin' Alive*, 362.

23. Stephen Farber, "He Drew from His Boyhood to Make 'Diner,'" *New York Times*, April 18, 1982.

24. Antero Pietila, *Not in My Neighborhood: How Bigotry Shaped a Great American City* (Chicago: Ivan R. Dee, 2012).

25. "The 1950s . . . Really Not That Great!," *Afro-American*, March 13, 1982.

26. Ida Peters, "*The Diner* Has World Premiere," *Afro-American*, March 13, 1982.

27. Chapin Wright, "Lights! Camera! Action! Hollywood Producers Bring Money, Jobs to Maryland," *Washington Post*, April 16, 1982.

28. Memo to Mayor William Donald Schaefer, April 6, 1981, Baltimore City Archives, William Donald Schaefer Papers.

29. Sherry Olson, *Baltimore: The Building of an American City* (Baltimore: Johns Hopkins University Press, 1980), 368.

30. "Schaefer Says He Won't Allow City Diner to Get the Knife," *Washington Post*, April 27, 1986.

31. Michael Olesker, "'Tin Men' Shine as Knights in Tarnished Armor," *Baltimore Sun*, February 24, 1987.

32. Steven Rea, "A Director Comes Home Again with 'Tin Men,'" *Philadelphia Inquirer*, March 16, 1987.

33. George F. Will, "*Tin Men* Celebrates a Time and a Place," *Courier-News* (Bridgewater, NJ), March 26, 1987.

34. Olesker, "'Tin Men.'"

35. Dana Heller, *Hairspray* (Oxford: Wiley-Blackwell, 2011), 49–78.

36. Ragan Rhyne, "Racializing White Drag," *Journal of Homosexuality* 46, nos. 3/4 (2004): 181–94; and Caetlin Benson-Allott, "Camp Integration: The Use and Misuse of Nostalgia in John Waters' Hairspray," *Quarterly Review of Film and Video* 26, no. 2 (2009): 143–54.

37. John Waters, *Crackpot: The Obsessions of John Waters* (New York: Scribner, 2003), 97.

38. bell hooks, *Yearning: Race, Gender, and Cultural Politics* (New York: Routledge, 2015), 42.

39. Benson-Allott, "Camp Integration," 147.

40. Heller, *Hairspray*, 54.

41. Alisa Samuels, "Ruth Brown Is Back in Town," *Afro American*, February 27, 1988; Robert G. Maier, *Low Budget Hell: Making Underground Movies with John Waters* (Davidson, NC: Full Page, 2011), 285.

42. Patrick Goldstein, "John Waters—Hairspray Impresario," *Los Angeles Times*, February 25, 1988.

43. Richard Corliss, "Buxom Belles in Baltimore Hairspray," *Time*, February 29, 1988.

44. Janet Maslin, "Hairspray: Comedy from John Waters," *New York Times*, February 26, 1988.

45. Henry Scarupa, "John Waters Teasing Up the Town," *Baltimore Sun*, July 9, 1987.

46. Michael Olive, "It's John Waters Day Somewhere," *Baltimore Sun*, February 7, 2004.

47. Stephen Hull, "Baltimore's Bawdy Block," in *America's Cities of Sin*, transcribed on http://www.baltimoreorless.com/2010/08/baltimores-bawdy-block.

48. Gilbert Sandler, *Small Town Baltimore: An Album of Memories* (Baltimore: Johns Hopkins University Press, 2002), 112–19.

49. C. Fraser Smith, *William Donald Schaefer: A Political Biography* (Baltimore: Johns Hopkins University Press, 1999), 30–31.

50. Theodore McKeldin Papers, 2nd Term, Box 364, Folder "The Block," Baltimore City Archives, Baltimore, MD.

51. "Lots of Noise, Few Acts in the State Legislature," *News* (Frederick, MD), December 28, 1966.

52. Jefferson Price III, "Council Contains 'the Block,' and Sets Area Building Height," *Baltimore Sun*, February 1, 1977.

53. Lindsey Gruson, "Red Lights Are Fading on Baltimore's Downtown Strip," *New York Times*, May 4, 1986.

54. William Hughes, *Baltimore Iconoclast* (Writer's Showcase, 2002), 140–41.

55. Henry Scarupa, "Local Street Musician Appears in New Movie," *Baltimore Sun*, November 15, 1987.

56. Sharon Zukin, *Loft Living: Culture and Capital in Urban Change* (Baltimore: Johns Hopkins University Press, 1982); and Gabrielle Wise, "Harbor Loft

Dwellers—Downtown Pioneers in High-Ceiling Living," *Baltimore Sun*, November 7, 1979.

## 6 | A People's History of West Baltimore

1. Godfrey Hodgson, *America in Our Time: From World War II to Nixon—What Happened and Why* (Princeton, NJ: Princeton University Press, 2005), 143.

2. Paula J. Massood, *Black City Cinema: African American Urban Experiences in Film* (Philadelphia: Temple University Press, 2006).

3. Susan Porter Benson, Stephen Brier, and Roy Rosenzweig, eds., *Presenting the Past: Essays on History and the Public* (Philadelphia: Temple University Press, 1986); and Roy Rosenzweig and David Thelen, *The Presence of the Past: Popular Uses of History in American Life* (New York: Columbia University Press, 1998).

4. Herman Gray, *Watching Race: Television and the Struggle for Blackness* (Minneapolis: University of Minnesota Press, 1995), 55.

5. Thomas J. Sugrue, *The Origins of the Urban Crisis: Race and Inequality in Postwar Detroit* (Princeton, NJ: Princeton University Press, 2005); and Jon C. Teaford, *The Rough Road to Renaissance: Urban Revitalization in America, 1940–1985* (Baltimore: Johns Hopkins University Press, 1990).

6. "'Roc' Faces Cancellation," *Oshkosh Northwestern*, May 21, 1994.

7. Kristal Brent Zook, *Color by Fox: The FOX Network and the Revolution in Black Television* (New York: Oxford University Press, 1999), 78.

8. George N. Dove, *The Police Procedural* (Bowling Green, OH: Bowling Green University Popular Press, 1982).

9. Laura Lippman, *By a Spider's Thread* (New York: Avon Books, 2004). Although not writing detective fiction, Rafael Alvarez, another former reporter, uses his fiction and nonfiction writing to tell stories of often-forgotten communities. See, e.g., Rafael Alvarez, *Hometown Boy: The Hoodle Patrol and Other Curiosities of Baltimore* (Baltimore: Baltimore Sun, 1999).

10. Janny Scott, "Who Gets to Tell a Black Story?," *New York Times*, June 11, 2000.

11. Donald Bogle, *Prime Time Blues: African Americans on Network Television* (New York: Farrar, Straus and Giroux, 2001), 412.

12. Gary Gately, "TV's Charles 'Roc' Dutton Calls on Baltimore Students to Reject Violence," *Baltimore Sun*, February 15, 1994.

13. Lenneal J. Henderson Jr., "The Governance of Kurt Schmoke as Mayor of Baltimore," in *Race, Politics, and Governance in the United States*, ed. Huey L. Perry (Gainesville: University Press of Florida, 1997), 165–75.

14. B. Drummond Ayres Jr., "In Baltimore, a New Style at City Hall: The Mayor Isn't Painting His Name All Over Town," *New York Times*, April 14, 1988.

15. "Baltimore Mayor Supports Legalization of Illicit Drugs," *New York Times*, September 30, 1988.

16. David Zurawik, "Schmoke, WNUV join forces to create 'The Mayor's Show,'" *Baltimore Sun*, November 16, 1989.

17. Dana Hull, "In Baltimore, a Show to Die For," *Washington Post*, April 25, 1997.

18. "Detectives Make Gains against City Killings," *Baltimore Sun*, December 30, 2000.

19. Rafael Alvarez, *The Wire: Truth Be Told* (New York: Grove Press, 2009), 213–14.

20. "Down to the Wire," *Baltimore Magazine*, February 1, 2008, https://www.baltimoremagazine.com/2008/2/1/down-to-the-wire.

21. Gerard Shields, "'City That Reads' Makes Way for Slogan with Greatest Goal," *Baltimore Sun*, November 11, 2000.

22. William Burroughs, *Naked Lunch* (New York: Grove Press, 2009).

23. Stanley Corkin, *Connecting the Wire: Race, Space and Postindustrial Baltimore* (Austin: University of Texas Press, 2017).

24. Sharon Zukin, *Loft Living: Culture and Capital in Urban Change* (Baltimore: Johns Hopkins University Press, 1982).

25. Laura Lippman, *Baltimore Blues* (New York: Harper, 1997), 40; and Lippman, *Charm City* (New York: Harper, 1997), 299.

26. David Lowenthal, *The Past Is a Foreign Country* (New York: Cambridge University Press, 1985).

27. Michel-Rolph Trouillot, *Silencing the Past: Power and the Production of History* (Boston: Beacon Press, 1995), 26.

28. As well as the elisions of reality and representation. While *The Corner* takes place in West Baltimore, it was filmed in East Baltimore.

29. David Zurawik, "A Lot of Dutton—and Baltimore—Go into 'Roc,'" *Baltimore Sun*, July 19, 1991.

30. Elijah Anderson, *A Place on the Corner* (Chicago: University Of Chicago Press, 1978); and Elliot Liebow, *Tally's Corner: A Study of Negro Streetcorner Men* (Lanham, MD: Rowman & Littlefield, 2003).

31. Antero Pietila, *Not in My Neighborhood* (Chicago: Ivan R. Dee, 2012), 116–27; Shernay Williams, "The Legendary 'Little Willie' Adams, Dead at 97," *Baltimore Afro-American*, June 30, 2011; Frederick N. Rasmussen, "William Lloyd 'Little Willie' Adams, Prominent Venture Capitalist," *Baltimore Sun*, June 28, 2011.

32. Jonathan Abrams, ed., *All the Pieces Matter: The Inside Story of "The Wire"* (New York: Crown Archetype, 2018); Alvarez, *The Wire*; Peter L. Beilenson and Patrick A. McGuire, *Tapping into "The Wire": The Real Urban Crisis* (Baltimore: Johns Hopkins University Press, 2012); Robert Levertis Bell and Paul Farber, eds., "The Wire," special issue, *Criticism* 52, nos. 3/4 (2010); Stanley Corkin, *Connecting "The Wire": Race, Space and Postindustrial Baltimore* (Austin: University of Texas Press, 2017); Liam Kennedy and Stephen Shapiro, eds., *"The Wire": Race, Class and Genre* (Ann Arbor: University of Michigan Press, 2012); George Lipsitz, "The Crime *The Wire* Couldn't Name: Social Decay and Cynical Detachment in Baltimore," in *How Racism Takes Place* (Philadelphia: Temple University Press, 2011), 95–114; Linda Williams, *On "The Wire"* (Durham, NC: Duke University Press, 2014); and Felicia "Snoop" Pearson, *Grace after Midnight: A Memoir* (New York: Hachette Book Group, 2007).

33. Wendell Pierce (@wendellpierce), Twitter post, May 28, 2017, 8:34 a.m., https://twitter.com/wendellpierce/status/868807585272655873?lang=en.

34. David Lerner, "Way Down in the Hole: Baltimore as Location and Representation in *The Wire*," *Quarterly Review of Film and Video* 29, no. 3 (2012): 213–24.

35. Lipsitz, "The Crime *The Wire* Couldn't Name," 95–114.

36. Marisela B. Gomez, *Race, Class, Power, and Organizing in East Baltimore* (Plymouth, UK: Lexington Books, 2015); and Joan Walsh, "Community Building in Theory and Practice: Three Case Studies," *National Civic Review* 86, no. 4 (1997): 291–314.

37. Robin D. G. Kelley, *Yo' Mama's Dysfunktional! Fighting the Culture Wars in Urban America* (Boston: Beacon Press, 1997), 39.

38. Sudhir Venkatesh, "What Do Real Thugs Think of *The Wire* Part Nine," *Freakonomics* (blog), March 10, 2008, http://freakonomics.com/2008/03/10/what-do-real-thugs-think-of-the-wire-part-nine/.

39. "*The Wire* Tour," *Charm City Tour* (blog), April 24, 2016. http://www.charmcitytour.com/?page_id=15.

40. "*The Wire* Tour," Wiki, *Wikitravel* (blog), https://wikitravel.org/en/The_Wire_Tour#b.

41. Gary Shteyngart, *Lake Success* (New York: Random House, 2018), 71.

42. John Urry, *The Tourist Gaze* (London: Sage, 2005).

43. "About," *That Guy's on Heroin*, March 18, 2015, https://web.archive.org/web/20150318033408/http://thatguysonheroin.com:80/about.

44. "President Obama: Omar Little Was the Best Character on 'The Wire,'" *CBS News*, https://www.cbsnews.com/news/president-obama-omar-little-was-the-best-character-on-the-wire/.

45. Gregory Korte, "Obama and 'The Wire' Creator Talk Drugs, Crime and Omar," *USA TODAY*, https://www.usatoday.com/story/theoval/2015/03/27/obama-the-wire-david-simon-drugs-crime-omar/70539736/.

46. Jensen, K. Thor, "10 Reasons Omar from *The Wire* Was the Ultimate Badass," *IFC* (blog), July 2, 2015, https://www.ifc.com/shows/the-spoils-before-dying/blog/2015/07/10-reasons-omar-from-the-wire-was-the-ultimate-badass; Mike Sager, "Why Omar Is the Greatest Character on *The Wire*, No Doubt," *Esquire*, June 10, 2015, https://www.esquire.com/entertainment/tv/a35617/omar-little-best-wire-character-appreciation/.

47. "GTA 5 Online: Adventures of Omar Little (Episode 1)," YouTube video, posted by Popular Stranger, October 8, 2013, https://www.youtube.com/watch?v=IVHB_QQpdEs.

48. Jeremy Egner, "David Simon Clarifies His Comments about 'The Wire,'" *New York Times Blog* (blog), April 6, 2012, https://artsbeat.blogs.nytimes.com/2012/04/06/david-simon-clarifies-his-comments-about-the-wire/.

## 7 | Welcome to Baltimore, Hon!

1. Richard Florida, *The Rise of the Creative Class and How It's Transforming Work, Leisure, Community and Everyday Life* (New York: Basic Books, 2004), 11.

2. "Baltimore City Economic Growth Strategy" (Baltimore: Baltimore City Department of Planning, 2005), 12. Hereafter parenthetical.

3. Doreen Massey, "A Global Sense of Place," In *Space, Place and Gender* (Minneapolis: University of Minnesota Press, 1994), 151.

4. Laurajane Smith, *Uses of Heritage* (New York: Routledge, 2006), 5.

5. David Lowenthal, *Heritage Crusade and the Spoils of History* (Cambridge: Cambridge University Press, 2003), 128.

6. National Trust for Historic Preservation, "Heritage Tourism," August 9, 2007, https://savingplaces.org/stories/preservation-glossary-todays-word-heritage-tourism#.XV7BUnspDb0.

7. Cathy Stanton, *The Lowell Experiment: Public History in a Postindustrial City* (Amherst: University of Massachusetts Press, 2006), 5.

8. Natalie Hopkinson, *Go-Go Live: The Musical Life and Death of a Chocolate City* (Durham, NC: Duke University Press, 2012), xii.

9. Michael Olesker, "Onna Streets of Bawlamer, 'Hon' Is Where Heart Is At," *Baltimore Sun*, April 25, 1991.

10. Dan Rodricks, "We All Love You Hon," *Baltimore Sun*, November 29, 1993.

11. Wiley A. Hall III, "Let Me Tell You about MY City," *Baltimore Sun*, April 30, 1991.

12. Peter Szanton, *Baltimore 2000: A Choice of Futures* (Baltimore: Morris Goldseker Foundation, 1986), 26.

13. Michael Olesker, "Unseriously, Now, Let's Put the Smile Back in 'Hon,'" *Baltimore Sun*, March 27, 1994, 1B.

14. Olesker, "Unseriously," 1B.

15. Letter to the editor, *Baltimore Sun*, March 25, 1994.

16. Margaret Cunningham Doyle, interview by Susan Hawes, August 16, 1979, transcript, Baltimore Neighborhood Heritage Project, Langsdale Library, University of Baltimore, Baltimore, MD.

17. Lisa Leff, "Melee Bares Race Unrest in Baltimore Area," *Washington Post*, June 1, 1987, A1.

18. Jeff Brown, "Hiya Hon," *AAA World*, May/June 2005, 16.

19. Janine Bradley, interview by the author, phone conversation, Baltimore, MD, June 14, 2002.

20. Elizabeth B. Boyd, "Southern Beauty: Performing Femininity in an American Region" (PhD diss., University of Texas at Austin, 2000), 2.

21. Mary Foster, "Hi Hon! Want a Crab Cake?," *Times-Picayune*, April 10, 2005, Travel Section.

22. Arlie Russell Hochschild, *The Managed Heart: Commercialization of Human Feeling* (Berkeley: University of California Press, 2003), 5 (italics in original).

23. Joshua Long, *Weird City: Sense of Place and Creative Resistance in Austin, Texas* (Austin: University of Texas Press, 2010).

24. Steve Twomey, "Love Ya, Baltimore, but Let's Get Real," *Washington Post*, October 23, 1997, D1.

25. Bruce J. Schulman, *The Seventies: The Great Shift in American Culture, Society and Politics* (Cambridge, MA: Da Capo Press, 2002), 151.

26. Alice Echols, *Hot Stuff: Disco and the Remaking of American Culture* (New York: W. W. Norton, 2010), 206.

27. Sarah Thornton, *Club Cultures: Music, Media and Subcultural Capital* (Oxford: Polity Press, 1995), 74–75.

28. Nelson George, *Buppies, B-Boys and Bohos: Notes on Post-Soul Black Culture* (Cambridge, MA: Da Capo Press, 2001),17.

29. Radcliffe Joe and Nelson George, "Rapping DJs Set a Trend," *Billboard*, November 1979, 4.

30. John Lewis, "Tupac Was Here," *Baltimore Magazine*, September 2016, http://www.baltimoremagazine.net/2016/9/6/legendary-rapper-tupac-shakur-spent-his-formative-years-in-baltimore.

31. Scott Seward, "Why Baltimore House Music Is the New Dylan," *Post*

*Road Magazine*, Fall/Winter 2001, http://www.postroadmag.com/Issue_3/Criticism 3/SewardCritic.htm.

32. S. H. Fernando Jr., "Dance the Pain Away," *Spin*, December 2005, 80–84.

33. Andrew Devereaux, "'What Chew Know about Down the Hill?': Baltimore Club Music, Subgenre Crossover, and the New Subcultural Capital of Race and Space," *Journal of Popular Music Studies* 19, no 4 (December 2007): 319.

34. Murray Forman, *The Hood Comes First: Race, Space and Place in Rap and Hip-Hop* (Middletown, CT: Wesleyan University Press, 2002), 25.

35. Fernando Jr., "Dance the Pain Away," 80–84.

36. Johan Huizinga, *Homo Ludens: A Study of the Play-Element in Culture* (London: Routledge, 1998), 10–11.

37. Devereaux, "'What Chew Know about Down the Hill?,'" 319.

38. Mary Rizzo, "Love Letters to Philadelphia: Gendering an Urban Brand (Part I)," *History@Work*, National Council on Public History, June 20, 2012, https://ncph.org/history-at-work/love-letters-to-philadelphia/.

39. Steve Macek, *Urban Nightmares: The Media, the Right, and the Moral Panic over the City* (Minneapolis: University of Minnesota Press, 2006).

40. Al Shipley, "Sex in This Club: Gender and Sexuality in Baltimore Club Music," *Words.Beats.Life: The Global Journal of Hip Hop Culture* 4, no. 2 (January 2010): 42–47.

41. Lawrence Burney, "Baltimore's Creative Community Still Looks to Queer Icon Miss Tony for Inspiration," *Thump*, October 19, 2016, https://thump.vice.com/en_au/article/baltimores-creative-community-still-looks-to-queer-icon-miss-tony-for-inspiration.

42. "50 Objects," *Baltimore Sun*, May 12, 2013, 18.

43. Shipley, "Sex in This Club," 43.

44. DeRay Mckesson, "I Am Running for Mayor of Baltimore," February 3, 2016, https://medium.com/deray-for-mayor/i-am-running-for-mayor-of-baltimore-34b4e214d582#.2nco8k9jc.

45. Brandon Soderberg, "Joy, Riots, Resilience: The Life of Baltimore Club Legend Miss Tony and the Death of Freddie Gray," *Fact*, May 17, 2016, http://www.factmag.com/2016/05/17/miss-tony-freddie-gray-baltimore-club-joy-riots-resilience/.

46 . Todd Inoue, "Rod Lee, Putting Baltimore on the Map," *Washington Post*, July 31, 2005; and Jon Caramanica, "For 'The Wire,' Rap That's Pure Baltimore," *New York Times*, September 10, 2006.

47. Devereaux, "'What Chew Know about Down the Hill?,'" 327.

48. Mary Rizzo, "'For Us, by Us': Hip-Hop Fashion, Commodity Blackness

and the Culture of Emulation," in *Testimonial Advertising in the American Marketplace: Emulation, Identity, Community*, ed. Marlis Schweitzer and Marina Moskowitz (New York: Palgrave Macmillan, 2009), 207–30.

49. Fernando Jr., "Dance the Pain Away," 84.

50. Baltimore also appears in films as other cities as well. *Beauty Shop* (2005) was filmed in a Baltimore that was standing in for Atlanta, while the Baltimore shooting location of the TV comedy *Veep* actually represents DC. Terry Gilliam's dystopian *12 Monkeys* was filmed in Baltimore, while *He's Just Not That into You* (2009) was filmed there because the creators had never seen a romantic comedy in Baltimore before.

51. Devereaux, "'What Chew Know about Down the Hill?,'" 329–30.

52. Al Shipley, "Various Artists—*Wow, That's What I Call Gutter Music*," *Government Names* (blog), December 5, 2007, http://governmentnames.blogspot.com/2007/12/various-artists-wow-thats-what-i-call.html.

53. Tom Breihan, "Zidane Headbutt Caused by Baltimore Club Music," *Village Voice*, July 10, 2006, http://www.villagevoice.com/blogs/zidane-headbutt-caused-by-baltimore-club-music-6385588.

54. "Club Science," *Fader*, June 22, 2006, http://www.thefader.com/2006/06/22/club-science.

55. FBI, "Uniform Crime Report," https://web.archive.org/web/20080201090241/www.ci.baltimore.md.us/news/crime/crime.html.

56. Jamie Smith Hopkins, "Seeing a Hopeful Change," *Baltimore Sun*, March 22, 2005, 8A.

57. Sam Sessa, "Hon-estly Hon It's Just Fun," *Baltimore Sun*, June 13, 2008, A1.

58. Michael Schulman, "Who Loves Baltimore?," *New Yorker*, April 28, 2008.

59. Frank DeFord, "Bleeve It, Hon," *Smithsonian Magazine*, January 2007, 22.

60. Joanne P. Cavanaugh, "Kitsch and Tell," *Baltimore City Paper*, March 21, 2007.

61. Jacques Kelly and Annie Linskey, "Dixon Wants to Help Cafe Hon Owner Get the Flamingo Back Up," *Baltimore Sun*, October 22, 2009.

62. Benn Ray, "Anderson Automotive Walmart Testimony," BMore Local, March 20, 2013, http://bmorelocal.tumblr.com/post/45886191495/anderson-automotive-wal-mart-testimony-by-benn.

63. Brendan Coyne, Benny Ray, and Genny Dill, "Apt Response to Wal-Mart," *Baltimore Sun*, May 16, 2010.

64. Denise Whiting, "Wal-Mart Would Be Good for Hampden," *Baltimore Sun*, June 3, 2010.

65. Mary Rizzo, "The Café Hon: Working-Class White Femininity and Commodified Nostalgia in Postindustrial Baltimore," in *Dixie Emporium: Tourism,*

*Foodways, and Consumer Culture in the American South*, ed. Anthony J. Stanonis (Athens: University of Georgia Press, 2008), 264–86.

66. Jill Rosen, "Sorry, Hon, It's Trademarked: Café Owner Owns Right to Word," *Baltimore Sun*, December 9, 2010.

67. "Baltimoreans to Businesswoman: Not So Fast, Hon," *National Public Radio*, January 3, 2011, https://www.npr.org/2011/01/03/132620838/baltimoreans-to-businesswoman-not-so-fast-hon.

68. China Martens, "This Is Hampden, Not Café Hon Town," in "Hon: Past, Present and Future," special issue, *Smile, Hon, You're in Baltimore* (zine), 2011, 23.

69. Rafael Alvarez, "Robert Irsay in a Dress," *North Baltimore Patch*, December 31, 2010.

70. "Cafe Hon," *Kitchen Nightmares*, February 24, 2012.

71. "Help Change Baltimore's Official Slogan to "Welcome to Baltimore, HON!," https://www.change.org/p/baltimore-city-leadership-help-change-baltimore-s-official-slogan-to-welcome-to-baltimore-hon.

72. Brittney Johnson, "Baltimore HonFest," *Afro-American*, June 15, 2018.

## Epilogue

1. David Harvey, *Spaces of Hope* (Berkeley: University of California Press, 2000), 133.

2. Baynard Woods and Brandon Soderberg, "In Baltimore, Police Officers Are the Bad Guys with Guns," *New York Times*, May 14, 2019; and Justin Fenton, "Cops and Robbers," *Baltimore Sun*, June 12, 2019.

3. Devin Fergus, *Liberalism, Black Power, and the Making of American Politics, 1965–1980* (Athens: University of Georgia Press, 2009), 51.

# INDEX

Page numbers in *italics* refer to illustrations.